# Here Comes the Bogeyman

*Here Comes the Bogeyman* is an essential text focusing on critical, cultural and contemporary issues surrounding writing for children. Containing a critically creative and a creatively critical investigation of the cult and culture of the child and childhood in fiction and non-fictional writing, it also contains a wealth of ideas and critical advice to be shared with writers, students of children's writing and students of writing. With scores of published children's fiction books and films to his name, Andrew Melrose shares his extensive critical, teaching, writing and research experience to provide:

- a critical and creative investigation of writing and reading for children in the early, middle and pre-teen years;
- an accessible and critically important challenge to the latest international academic research and debates in the field of children's literature and creative writing;
- an evaluation of what it means to write for a generation of media-savvy children;
- encouragement for critics, writers and students to develop their own critical, creative and writing skills in a stimulating and supportive manner;
- guidance on writing non-fiction and poetry;
- creative writing craftwork ideas that could be used as seminar topics or as individual reflections.

This 'one-stop' critical and creative text will be an indispensable resource for critics, writers and students interested in the cult and culture of writing for children; on Creative Writing BA and MA programmes; Children's Literature BA and MA programmes; English BA and MA programmes; Teacher Training, PGCE students and for those studying at Doctoral and Post-Doctoral level who are interested in writing for children.

**Andrew Melrose** is Professor of Writing for Children at the University of Winchester, UK. He has also written *Write for Children* and *Monsters Under the Bed* available from Routledge.

# Here Comes the Bogeyman

Exploring contemporary issues in writing for children

Andrew Melrose

Routledge
Taylor & Francis Group

LONDON AND NEW YORK

First published 2012
by Routledge
2 Park Square, Milton Park, Abingdon, Oxon OX14 4RN

Simultaneously published in the USA and Canada
by Routledge
711 Third Avenue, New York, NY 10017

*Routledge is an imprint of the Taylor & Francis Group, an informa business*

*British Library Cataloguing in Publication Data*
A catalogue record for this book is available from the British Library

*Library of Congress Cataloging in Publication Data*
Melrose, Andrew, 1954–
Here comes the Bogeyman: exploring contemporary issues in writing for children /
Andrew Melrose.
p. cm.
Includes bibliographical references and index.
1. Children's literature – Authorship – Vocational guidance. 2. Children's literature –
Technique. 3. Children – Books and reading. 4. Creative writing. I. Title.
PN147.5.M43 2011
808.06'8 – dc23
2011021087

ISBN: 978-0-415-61752-9 (hbk)
ISBN: 978-0-415-61753-6 (pbk)
ISBN: 978-0-203-15687-2 (ebk)

Typeset in Bembo
by Taylor & Francis Books

MIX
Paper from
responsible sources
FSC® C004839
www.fsc.org

Printed and bound in Great Britain by
TJ International Ltd, Padstow, Cornwall

# Contents

*Acknowledgements*                                                          vi
*Introduction*                                                             vii

**Part 1**                                                                   **1**

1   Here comes the bogeyman …                                                3

2   A cultural, critical and creative context                                7

3   Bridging the gap between child reader and adult author                  27

4   The (im)possibility of writing for children …                          33

5   Elements of storytelling for children                                  42

6   Engaging with Icarus                                                    54

**Part 2**                                                                  **67**

7   Considering the bogeyman …                                             69

8   Story structure                                                        75

9   Early readers, middle years and pre-teens: not short stories but big stories
    told short                                                             95

10  Social realism, narrative non-fiction and *The Tiger Who Came to Tea*  109

11  Poetry for children                                                   120

    *Notes*                                                               123
    *Bibliography*                                                        129
    *Index*                                                               135

# Acknowledgements

Writing is a solitary job and yet a writer never writes alone; many people helped to make this book possible. Thank you to Alison Foyle who commissioned it and has been especially helpful throughout. Thanks too, to the University of Winchester for supporting the research through their Research and Knowledge Exchange fund and to colleagues in the Department of English, Creative Writing and American Studies for their encouragement and support – in particular Mick Jardine, Inga Bryden, Neil McCaw, Judy Waite, Jill Barnes, Leonie Lipton, Ian Roberts and Judith Heneghan who runs the MA: Writing for Children. Vanessa Harbour, University of Winchester and Jen Webb, University of Canberra allowed me to bounce ideas off them – and they always bounced back better than they left. And thanks too, to Karenanne Knight who illustrated the wonderful cover. My family, Diane, Abbi and Daniel, have been brilliant, they continue to give me space, time and love in their busy lives. Throughout the book I talk about allowing children to explore the radical and special *social space that is childhood* and it seems appropriate that it is dedicated to my mother and father, Margaret Melrose (1933 –) and Andrew Melrose (1929 –) who still give all their stories and much more …

# Introduction

'I am not being coy,' wrote Jack Zipes, 'children's literature does not exist' (Zipes 2002: 40). At face value, this quotation may seem a little odd, especially in a book of this nature, but it is far more complex than at first it appears. Zipes encapsulates a huge intellectual deliberation on the cult and culture that is a child and childhood. He is immediately waving the red flag of critical pessimism and it would be foolish to ignore it because this notion, and its wider significance, has been prevalent in child and children debates over the past 30 years or so. And to the many other critics involved in the surrounding deliberations, it is a statement that hardly holds any controversy whatsoever (although that is not to say there is consensus and agreement, the enquiry is ongoing). Furthermore, it doesn't just apply to 'children's literature' but to the wider discourse that is child-centred, and I will expand on this idea as I progress because it is extremely important to the entire critical understanding.

I have no choice but to summarise and question some of the critical debates here but, and perhaps I should write that in capitals, BUT, I should say right from the start that the critical world I am about to address is full of Snapes,[1] that is to say the critical discourse is grumpy as hell but with a heart of gold. But I will be looking to redress the gloom by trying to address a way forward, not as a critic but as a cultural practitioner engaged in the critical dialogue. So instead of looking at all the negatives, I will seek to reveal another way of seeing, for the writer at least, for I feel that it is time for critical thought to become a force for optimism right now, at the beginning of this new and shiny twenty-first century, which will produce much for children to enjoy and experience. That said, then, in the tradition of children's cultural products, doomsayers beware, this book comes with the kind of 'advisory sticker' you often see on children's books, DVDs, etc. It says, 'Don't Read This Book Unless You Want a Happy Ending'. Furthermore, while it may seem strange to open a book on writing for children to find it offering ideas on culture, communication, media, critical theories and the cult and culture of the child (which will be explained in greater depth as I proceed) there is a very good reason for this. What children read or watch is only part of a much larger tableau of cultural practices, which has children firmly fixed in its field of vision. There is a whole industry in the world dedicated to child-centred consumption; only the other day I was in the Early Learning Centre (in Brighton, UK) purchasing a present for an infant; in a Waterstone's bookshop purchasing a teenage vampire novel; browsing in a shop called Claire's Accessories for a present for a pre-teenager; driving past a huge out-of-town toy shop and baby accessories store while being bombarded with images of Easter wrapped up in chocolate eggs; Easter-bunnies (for sale) and other such commodity products all targeted at the young, before being confronted in my own living room with children's television. The cult and culture of the child is a highly developed industry and a lot of the critical material targeted at the practice of writing for children (in books, film and television) overlaps with this wider picture on cultural transmission and the complexities of the cultural field of production, which cannot be separated or critiqued in isolation from many of the other component parts (although not everyone agrees with me on this).[2]

But I have also used the phrase 'the cult of the child' in a slightly provocative way in order to try and highlight that the unusualness of the discourse surrounding the relevant issues can often look a little eccentric. For example, phrases such as the 'constructed child' and 'constructive child' surface as explanatory critical issues alongside the opening quotation from Zipes, which I used above. Indeed it would be prudent to get these out of the way before we proceed.

Without really thinking, we can throw the terms 'child, children and young people' out as homogenous terms that describe those people below the age of 18 (in the UK certainly). Yet homogenising is far from ideal for the terms themselves are subject to gender, socioeconomic status and many further subdivisions. Furthermore, modern day sociologists seem to insist that childhood is socially constructed rather than being fundamental to the state of being; whereas developing psychologists see childhood as defined in large part by the state of being a child and focus attention on the complex process of individual development. I will not be exploring this at great length but I am persuaded by ideas that suggest the cognitive development in children is experience-dependent, and that older children have more experiences than younger children. But I will add to this by saying adults have more experiences than all of them and this will become relevant to the ideas that will unfold throughout this book, where I will be picking up on the radical proposal that experience is gained through a process of joint activity, where attending, remembering and reasoning are things done between people. Most powerfully, they are done between experts and novices, teachers and learners (Crook 2008: 32)[3] and, I would contend, the experts and teachers are joined by writers, artists and creators of story narrative. Because important for me in the proposal is the idea of 'joint activity' between the experienced and the less so. Later on I will call it 'exploring the connections' and we will look at it in depth, because the exciting challenge in a book like this is to explore the connections in the joint activity, as fundamental to the underpinning of child-centred discourse. Indeed the term child-centred discourse will also come under scrutiny because it is more complex than simply throwing it out as a catch-all term.

Therefore I propose to unfold some of the *cultural*, *critical* and *creative* ideas that surround the underpinning ideas in the discourse so that once it is contextualised the ideas will not look as strange as they do now. The book is split into two distinct parts:

**Part 1** plots a path through the cultural and critical context surrounding ongoing debates in the (im)possibility of writing for children; in summarising the cultural and critical discourse and discussion that have ensued over the past 30 years or so, I look at ways of taking the arguments and debates forward and then conclude by aiming to reveal a *new way of seeing* from a creative perspective.

**Part 2** concentrates on the creative aspect of the (im)possibility of writing for children, with a view to negotiating critically creative and creatively critical strategies involved in the process. This means the creative methodology has been influenced by the critical investigation. It is a combination of both elements which makes this book particularly informative.

# Part I

# Chapter 1

# Here comes the bogeyman ...

Sentences end with full stops. Stories do not!

Harold Rosen[1]

I deliberated on the issues I am about to explore once before. At the turn of the millennium, in a wee book entitled *Write for Children* (Melrose 2002), I made a very small point with a big idea, connecting the suggestion that 'children's literature does not exist' (Zipes 2002: 40), and the 'impossibility' of children's literature (Rose 1984) with an idea on 'nurture' (Phillips 1995), which addressed a much larger, critical issue on writing for children and children's literature. I didn't really develop it into a huge treatise at the time because it seemed to speak for itself. Indeed, it made perfect sense to me and it still does.

Since then, however, and despite the book selling extremely well, I find it has been hitherto ignored except in some undergraduate essays and a scattering of postgraduate research, and this is partly the problem with academe and scholarship in any subject. Unless we are flag-waving from the ramparts; taking part in the discussions; attending the same conferences and engaging with others similarly engaged in all the right journals, etc., like one of Bourdieu's 'privileged interlocutors', simple ideas, which at first we may take for granted, get buried; or lost; or forgotten; or (and *quite* likely) ignored because it appeared to be a childish, that is to say underdeveloped, 'bogeyman' of an idea and of little importance (for the aforementioned reasons); or even (and *most* likely) it simply remained unread because of the terms of engagement: it was a book on *writing for* as opposed to the *critical study of*. To some extent, then, at the turn of the millennium the book was essentially addressing the poorer cousin of the poor cousin.

This is all fine by me and I have no problem with it, after all, *writing for children*[2] as an academic field of study is even younger than the *study of children's literature*.[3] But all the same there is also something quite enigmatic about the fact that such an idea could be useful but is languishing still; where an initial thought with problem-solving potential is put into the public domain but it remains unseen or unheard and lurking, ghost-like, in the shadows. We, or at least I, could be entitled to ask: how child centred is that idea? And: how adult is it to ignore a simple, child-like idea when in fact it *may* have good potential for development?

For me those two questions are very important to the idea of 'writing for children', and on the ideas of 'impossibility' and the idea of 'nurture' in this process, and in the critical issues on writing for children and children's literature and indeed to this entire book. Perhaps I should highlight them, embolden and italicise them, though I will trust you, my reader, to cling onto them for I will certainly repeat them later. Of course, this idea of 'trust in your reader' will also become very important because I am predominantly writing as a writer for children and not as a critic, albeit a writer with a critical view.

Therefore, it is also important to record this is not just a book on writing for children, but an opportunity to bring the disciplines of the writing and study of children's fiction, the cult and culture of child-related discourse and its component parts into a cultural, critical and creative context between the covers of a single book.

The important thing to record here is that it has more to do with cultural and communication ideas than literary studies. The cult of the 'child', 'children' and 'childhood', the culture of the 'child', 'children' and 'childhood' and the idea of cultural transmission and communication with children is much more complex than simply writing a book (say) and sending it out for them to read.

However, it is also crucial to acknowledge that this cosy marriage between writing *for* children and writing *on* writing for children is not without controversy. There will be other bogeymen to confront for it consists of a collection of small but critical reflections on what can best be described as fantastical critical culture that will accumulate to form a bigger, 'hybrid' set of critical and cultural ideas, with which not everyone in either the writing *for* or writing *on* camps will agree on. Although it is to be hoped there will be common ground.

For example, although I will not necessarily be promoting all of the critical ideas on 'hybridity' proposed by David Rudd (Hunt 2004: 35) there are issues of agreement between us. He does come close to what I am about to propose, albeit tangentially, without fully expressing it thoroughly. At some point in this book, then, these ideas will converge into a coherent whole, for it is one of those curious academic coincidences that bring them to a meeting point. We both, and independently, from different starting points – me on writing and he on criticism – invoke the similar ideas on translation and related issues[4] that deserve better scrutiny. I will develop these ideas further as I take this study into a wider theoretical discourse.

But by the simple nature of these things, there will be much cutting and pasting of ideas. For example I also (but do not always) agree with Nodelman (2008: 90) and McGillis (1997:130) whom I can paraphrase in saying my ultimate aim is not to 'try to shield children from the world they live in', rather to help you (my reader) to provide them with the 'tools to read this world carefully and critically'[5] – the secret is in making the connections, as I have also written elsewhere (Melrose 2010), and this will become much clearer as we progress. These connections come from a voyage, a journey, a quest to try and collate useful critically creative and creatively critical fragments into a coherent whole, so that others may be able to comprehend and make sense of them as they go about their own literary and cultural quests and critical journeys into the cult of childhood.

Thus, by coming, as it does, from that previously ignored engagement in the 'impossibility and nurture' idea, I will go back and re-engage with the available critical material in order to explain it in more depth before bringing it up to the point I see it at the start of this second decade of the new millennium. Critics such as Nodelman, Rudd, Hunt, Rose, Steedman, Kincaid, Lesnik-Oberstein, Nikolajeva, Zipes alongside critics who have much to offer in tangentially important ideas, such as Adam Phillips; Jean Baudrillard; Slavoj Žižek; Jacques Derrida; Michel Foucault; Homi Bhabha; Walter Benjamin; Mikhael Bakhtin; Sigmund Freud; Milan Kundera; Italo Calvino; Pierre Bourdieu and too many countless others to mention here will be revisited (and those listed are in a completely random order since ideas are incorporated from all but none privileged). What I will be doing is simply revealing the connections as I see them but one that may allow us to address what, for the time being, I call the *hidden child*[6] in writing for children. Throughout such studies, aspects of the child and childhood can get a little lost in the fug of critical discourse and this is not a good position for the writer and critical practitioner to be in.

But in doing so I will be steering a critically creative and creatively critical course, thinking as much about writing as critiquing and commenting as I go. The reasons will become obvious but as a colleague recently commented:

> It is the introduction of a much broader sense of knowledge into the reading process that offers the best potential for bridging the gap between functional interpretation and the more expansive forms of textual interpretation that are likely to further ... understanding and appreciation of how writing works and what being a writer means within the context of a wider culture.
>
> (McCaw 2011)

I endorse this idea completely because the whole idea of writing for children is all too often swamped by the idea that it is not a serious job. And I am not the only one who has been asked, when are you going to write a real book, or, when are you going to write a grown-up book? My response will come to the fore as this grown-up book will reveal. In some ways, however, this ongoing critical enquiry I am pulling together here begins a little like Bertrand Russell's dream. The mathematician, G.H. Hardy once reported:

> I can remember Bertrand Russell telling me of a horrible dream. He was in the top floor of the University Library, about A.D. 2100. A library assistant was going round the shelves carrying an enormous bucket, taking down books, glancing at them, restoring them to the shelves or dumping them into the bucket. At last he came to three large volumes which Russell could recognize as the last surviving copy of Principia Mathematica [written by Alfred North Whitehead and Bertrand Russell, 1910]. He [the library assistant] took down one of the volumes, turned over a few pages, seemed puzzled for a moment by the curious symbolism, closed the volume, balanced it in his hand and hesitated. ...
>
> (Hardy 1940)

This says a lot about the 'how' of choices, the randomness without really addressing the 'why'; the randomness is intriguing; what to include and leave out; what to keep and what to ditch; do we keep what we understand and discard what we don't, or do we keep re-reading the book to learn what we don't already know? It is all about furthering knowledge with a view to being able to choose from a position of knowing.

It is about making connections, about thinking around the unknown unknowns, the things we don't know we don't know in getting a broader sense of knowledge – how else is knowledge and experience understood and transferred? Of course it was another numbers genius, the physicist, Albert Einstein, who said: 'Not everything that can be counted counts, and not everything that counts can be counted.' Therefore, this issue of choice and of reasoned reflexive thought is essentially where the central idea for this book comes from. But when I was trying to frame this in a critical and cultural context of writing for children and children's literature, the question that sprung to mind was: can any of us do anything else?

My entire notion of knowledge in this field leads me not to attempt to provide a proven mathematical formula; a definitive idea or an empirical statement that says *this is the theory of writing for children and children's literature* although I will be referring to this idea of a 'theory', especially in relation to ideas by Peter Hunt and Maria Nikolajeva.[7] But my aim is to reflect on issues raised and nurture ideas and then to move thoughts and thinking forward on the possibilities and the possible connections.

Thus, ten years after I first thought of a basic premise of writing for children, and the fraught ideas of a culture, communication and media context in the cult and culture of childhood, and having seen the thought balanced precariously in the librarian's hesitant hand, it's probably time I wrote the idea out more fully in order to make it more accessible.

Though it should be noted that it did not take me ten years to write this book, I was thinking about it a lot but during much of that time I just couldn't find a pencil (how child-like is that).

# Chapter 2

# A cultural, critical and creative context

The tableau of ideas that surround the cult and culture that is a child and childhood is fraught with complexity. Write down the question, what is a child?: then try to answer it and you will see what I mean, for the answer may seem perfectly obvious. But when we expand on a basic dictionary description, or a broad brushstrokes summation, meaning begins to wobble and try as you might, you can never get it back into the mould you first thought of. But we cannot evade the complexity or indeed that somehow we can address the cultural products created for child consumption (like writing a book for them to read) without considering the fact that the child is 'an infinitely varied concept' (Hunt 2001: 6). And so what I propose to do in this chapter is to collate some of the ideas on the cult and culture of 'child' and 'childhood' before moving on to provide a more critical approach proposal.

Understanding how we write for children, why we write for children, what is written for children, how children are represented and what to consider when writing for children in a cultural, critical and creative context, in this advanced age of communication and media culture, is crucial to developing an acute understanding of what it is to be expected from writers of and writers on children's literature. But inherently, the writer, critic and children themselves are increasingly confronted by experts in those who write, make, edit, publish, review, select, advertise, buy, sell, teach, study, research, critique and otherwise involve themselves in deciding what cultural products should be directed at the child receptor. Some, like the aforementioned critic, has even said it is complicity in criminal behaviour:

> It is one of the worst kept secrets in the world that, within the past fifty years or so, we have reconfigured our children to act and to behave as commodities and agents of consumerism, and we continue to invent ways to incorporate them flawlessly into socio-economic systems that compromise their integrity and make them complicit in criminal behaviour such as mutual economic exploitation …
>
> (Zipes 2009: 27)

Of course, not everyone will agree, I certainly do not entirely, though I do know what he means – and already we can see how the ideas around the cult of the child and their collected identity under the moniker of 'children' begin to take shape in the field of critical discourse that surrounds the issues.

\*

As a Scotsman, the years 1706, 1707 and 1708 were embedded in my memory at a very early age because I had a Scottish Nationalist schoolteacher who taught us about the Treaty of Union; the Act of Union and the beginning of the Jacobite Rebellion when James Edward Stuart, son of the deposed James VII/II, made the first of three unsuccessful attempts to regain his throne. These dates and facts were thrown at me as a young lad aged around 11 and they have stayed with me ever since but I have never really found anything to do with them, hence their almost gratuitous mention here (before I leave it too late). Left to my own devices, I imagined the stories, James, 'the old pretender', being thwarted, his son, 'the young pretender' Bonnie Prince Charlie, coming back to revive the challenge. Romantic images of swashbuckling heroism, honour and valour were fertile ground for youthful imagination. Of course it took me a long time to realise that the end of the story saw the Jacobites slaughtered in battle at Culloden Moor, where they had arrived starving, exhausted, untrained and ill equipped. There was no romance in that knowledge or indeed the image – it was no fictionalised *Braveheart*[1] either. What I didn't know until recently was that, in the same year as the start of the Jacobite rebellion, 1708, the song come nursery rhyme, 'Boys and girls come out to play', was first published in the UK. And in tying this information together we can begin to see how history can be recorded in different ways through the process of storytelling:

> Boys and girls come out to play,
> The moon does shine as bright as day;
> Come with a hoop, and come with a call,
> Come with a good will or not at all.
> Loose your supper, and loose your sleep,
> Come to your playfellows in the street;
> Up the ladder and down the wall.
> A halfpenny loaf will serve us all.
> But when the loaf is gone, what will you do?
> Those who would eat must work – 'tis true.

The 'boys and girls' rhyme', for those interested in this kind of thing, essentially refers to the labour (and play) conditions at the end of the seventeenth century when most children had to work. The line, 'Those who would eat must work', gives a strong enough clue. But working time was dictated by daylight hours and thus, 'The moon does shine as bright as day … Loose your supper, and loose your sleep' says evening time is the time to play. And to some extent the song sets up an early recognition that children were different from their adult co-workers, who are not being rallied here. But this is not a history of the progress of child labour, because that is available elsewhere, but it is a reminder, a personal aide-mémoire, that in discussing the cult and culture of childhood in this new twenty-first century, I am referring to something that can only be defined in Western legal terms, which is that a child is a 'being' who we know does not come of age until they are 18 years of age in the UK where I am writing from. And yet, as Rudd reminds us, this 'being can be reduced to a psychological profile or even to its biological and anatomical features, but such depictions fail to capture the fact that children exist only within particular sociocultural contexts' (Rudd 2010: xiii).

It will be easy for me to write this book from a personal reflection and ideas I encounter in my own field of vision, at times this will invariably be the case. It will also be easy for me to write abstractly and in a detached manner on the issues being raised; this is a natural process in writing this kind of book, for there has to be some kind of way of addressing what constitutes the 'child' and delimiting the field. To some extent this will be a culturally homogenised child of Western culture, in the education system (mostly), textually literate (televisually and reading-wise) but nevertheless interesting and interested as young people. And this idea of them being young people, with voices and thoughts and ideas, will come through the book as I proceed because it is, as will be shown, critically problematic.

However, it would be remiss of me to write this book without drawing your attention to the fact that, according to UNICEF:

> An estimated 158 million children aged 5–14 are engaged in child labour – one in six children in the world. Millions of children are engaged in hazardous situations or conditions, such as working in mines, working with chemicals and pesticides in agriculture or working with dangerous machinery. They are everywhere but invisible, toiling as domestic servants in homes, labouring behind the walls of workshops, hidden from view in plantations.[2]

This is before we get onto other exploitation and problems such as violence, trafficking, prostitution, sexual abuse, the list goes on and on. The song, 'Boys and girls come out to play … ', published in 1708, should also serve as an aide-mémoire, we adults have much to consider when using the term 'child'. It is not hard to Google this kind of information, but that kind of easy access should not lead to our ambivalence and I urge you to remember this.

But one step at a time because while we can see how children exist within particular socio-cultural contexts, we do have to consider the question of power; and Danahaer et al.'s reading of Foucault is useful on this, viz:

> While categories such as 'childhood' were generally understood as being stable ('everybody knows what a child is'), in reality they were subject to transformation and revision as new forms of knowledge were developed … the 'truth' of childhood (and doubtless the same applies to categories such as adolescence and youth) can be understood as both stable and unproblematic, on the one hand ('the truth of childhood is the sum of those knowledges that take it as their object') and, more problematically, as a site of discursive and institutional 'battles' (and therefore lacking in final authorization, not the truth but a set of 'truths') … while we all think we know what a child or adolescent is, in fact these categories have histories … and are always in the process of being transformed.
>
> (Danahaer, Schirato and Webb 2000: 78)

Children and youth are becoming more and more defined by the 'cult' and 'culture' of childhood being created through commodification, advertised lifestyles, media and an unalienable cultural crisis wrapped up in the irrepressible rise of capitalism. But for a storyteller to be aware of this allows for a certain amount of resistance, which this book will propose (in time) although we need to look at it in more detail.

In her fascinating and useful explanation of *aetonormatvity* (Lat. *Aeto* – pertaining to age), Maria Nikolajeva reminds us that the 'child/adult imbalance is most tangibly manifested in the relationship between the ostensibly adult narrative voice and the child focalizing character' (2010: 8). Essentially, nowhere else are power structures as obvious as they are in the relationship between adults and children through home, health, education, educators, extended family, social and cultural exchanges, and in the culture adults produce for children, such as books, toys, television shows, etc., all of which are created by those in power for the powerless. In this sense, too, the idea of the 'expert' in this relationship does not make life any easier for any of us because the *only* qualification required to be such an expert is to be an adult.

The fact is that almost anyone who read (say) as a child (and probably some who didn't) will have an opinion on books suitable for children to read. The same goes for films and television targeted at a child audience – and I am conscious of Roland Barthes' 'Toys' in this context too (although I will come back to this later). I know I have such opinions on suitability, and you must have too, but it is true to say that the only thing that validates the opinion in most cases is the simple fact that those experts are indeed, and almost without exception, adult, which is equally problematic, and I think it's important that we explore this because the potential to question the adult in the adult/child relationship is desirable on many levels.

For example, in May 2010, *The Guardian*, a UK newspaper, an adult, grown-up broadsheet (as opposed to a tabloid), with a slightly left of centre politics, published two articles under the following headings:

> The best children's books: 8–12 year-olds[3]
> &
> Best children's books: 12-years-old and over[4]

As you can imagine, I was immediately intrigued and extremely interested to find out what these best children's books were. Although I was more interested in finding out what research had been undertaken to identify them. However, it soon became clear that in typical newsprint fashion, the trumpet-blowing hyperbole of the headlines was an exaggeration of the actual content contained in the articles.

What in fact transpired was that with a little library borrowing research, reference to bestseller lists and a lot of personal nostalgia, Lucy Mangan and Imogen Russell Williams had hand-picked their ' … *must reads* for 8–12 year-olds' and their ' … *top reads* for children aged 12 and over' (my italics) and it soon became clear that the headlines were championing little more than the personal, though well-meaning, choice of two journalists, who felt confident enough to say particular things about particular books, like, 'No, they're not great literature. But, like Enid Blyton, they give new readers quick and convincing proof that reading can be fun … ' or, 'a modern classic … ' and indeed, Lucy Mangan's personal choices in 'A book lover's guide to building a brilliant children's library', which ran once a week for 52 weeks, is equally contentious[5] if only for reasons of choice.

I am not singling these journalists out, or passing judgement on their list of choices. There is essentially nothing wrong with this kind of publishing in a national newspaper. We are all entitled to air an opinion and even write and publish a list – and indeed the more coverage children's books get the better, as far as I am concerned. The articles themselves are well meaning and address some important views I share, one of which is that literacy education should start at home and children need to be introduced to books and reading earlier than starting school and should continue to have access to them out of school.[6]

To be honest, the lists are good enough for what they are, though I wouldn't have included a lot of the books they did and how they could have missed others out defeats me. I confess I would also have omitted a lot of the older books for the more contemporary – in my opinion the myth of a literary canon should be fired (and I will address this later too). But it must be acknowledged that is just my opinion and a personal choice list isn't really much more than a subjective view – even if it is an educated one. And to her credit (though it wasn't really required) when the articles were collected online under the single heading 'The best children's books ever', Lucy Mangan did write her own disclaimer, saying they were precisely 'a combination of personal recommendations, enduring classics and currently popular borrowings from school and public libraries ... [as] suggestions and starting points only ... '[7] Of course, the same could be said for the book by another *Guardian* journalist, Julia Eccleshare, *1001 Children's Books You Must Read Before You Grow Up*. The title looks like it is addressing itself to children but the book is actually a best-buy guide for adults who need this kind of thing. Indeed, the title *1001 Children's Books* actually comes up a wee bit short and as before there are some I would remove and some I would include – but that's just the nature of these things.

What is crucial here is the underlying truism, which is that the articles and this book were not actually targeted directly at children at all, but the newspaper's interested adult readers who should happen upon them, and this gets right to the heart of a crucial issue in the writing for children/children's literature debate, which is: ' ... children's literature is not written *by* children; it is written *for* them, and indeed is almost always written by anyone but them ... ' I have deliberately opened and closed this pronouncement with ellipses because the problem with making a statement so boldly like this is that it has a long *history* that came before and never went away, and needs further extrapolation in cultural, critical and creative context, because it also addresses the *present*, which is ongoing, and its *future*, which is yet to come. As Perry Nodelman rightly suggests:

> Critics and reviewers [and I would add writers] not only have the job of trying to make sense of children's books, but also, and just as centrally, their opinions and choices tend to shape what texts have power and how those texts might be read; thus, what texts critics and reviewers consume and how they consume them profoundly affect the nature of what producers choose to produce.
>
> (Nodelman 2008: 134)

Crucial to this idea is that writing for children is a critically creative and creatively critical *adult, child-centred discourse* – and the concept of an *adult, child-centred discourse* is one I will come back to.

Nevertheless, this does not mean the discourse can be allowed to be hijacked with misplaced adult agendas for no good at all, hence the intervention of critics such as Jack Zipes. Bourdieu would highlight how adults cannot fail to take partial positions on their views on children's culture and it is accepted that we cannot escape those we disagree with, in my case it is censors whose own agendas remain questionable to me.[8] But crucially, too, there is a considerable and complex critical discourse underpinning the discipline that increasingly positions itself as a force for good. Children's literature is, as Maria Nikolajeva explains, 'deliberately created by those in power for the powerless' (Nikolajeva 2010: 8), and while interested critics cannot always rescue it from the forces of power, be that good, bad or otherwise (and whatever banner their power agenda flies), a huge effort is being made to continually address the many contentious and controversial issues that are ever present. For these reasons alone, it is appropriate that I begin to address some of them here, in context, in order to show that, for all of their complexity, the contentious and controversial do indeed exist under conditions of rigorous scrutiny.

\*

Way back in the early days, when these issues were beginning to surface and studies in children's literature as a cultural discourse was still a relatively new field (and let us not forget that the study itself is still in its relative infancy – although getting much stronger), John Rowe Townsend (1971: 10) said, 'the only practical definition of a children's book today – absurd as it sounds – is a book which appears on the children's list of a publisher.' Of course this idea could refer to many other things (almost everything) in the child-centred culture industry. My first reaction to it was, well I just don't believe that. Even if it was written in 1971, there has to be more to it than that. But at the time of reading, I was thinking as a writer not a critic and further research reveals that the idea simply refuses to go away. In 1993, for example, Michael Steig (1993: 36) laid claims that books were books and that 'children's literature and its various subcategories can be seen as artificially generated designations … ' that were intended to attract parents so they could buy them for children. Not quite the criminal venture outlined by Zipes, but not an endorsement of the cultural field.

It is actually difficult to argue against this idea in some terms. Child-centred culture, such as toys, films and books, is, without doubt, a constituent of products made by adults and targeted at adults as the purveyors in the child-centred market, adding to which, children do not usually buy their own books, etc., and despite (from my personal experience) having ideas and very good browsing skills (in some cases – though this is becoming a dying trait[9]) they are still more prone than adults to having most of their consumable cultural choice decisions hijacked by well-meaning adult others, like teachers, parents, librarians, journalists' lists and reviews and indeed book buyers in shops – and we cannot overlook the power of the book buyer in a seemingly diminishing market.[10] Having to rely on the politic of adult choice and opinions is as subjective as the opinions themselves though. Imagine, just for a moment, our entire life choices being dictated by the newspaper we buy. Goodness, what an Orwellian 'big brother'[11] idea that is. Imagine being a child growing up on *The Truman Show* (Weir 1998), because of course not all teachers, parents, librarians, journalists and so on are going to have the kind of educated values and advice children might desire or need – or not in some cases. Who to trust for advice: it is problematic for all different kinds of reasons.

For example, if we go back to the list recommended in *The Guardian* newspaper and discussed above, works by both C.S. Lewis and Philip Pullman were considered worth reading. But do we accept the recommendation blindly, or do we consider Nicholas Tucker's ideas regarding the *Chronicles of Narnia* when he says: 'C.S. Lewis' Christian doctrines of atonement and resurrection … sometimes push the plot into directions that seem cruel and illogical … '? (Tucker 1981: 100).

Or indeed the idea Julia Eccleshare hailed in the same newspaper, that Philip Pullman was a 'heretical fantasist' in writing the final part of the *His Dark Materials* trilogy, *The Amber Spyglass*,[12] before going on to reveal Pullman's own problems with the work of J.R.R. Tolkien and C.S. Lewis. 'Pullman's insistence on truth to human nature,' writes Eccleshare, 'lies behind his dismissal of the fantasy writers to whom he is often compared: J.R.R. Tolkien and C.S. Lewis.' Whereupon, Pullman is quoted as saying:

> I dislike them for different reasons. *The Lord of the Rings*, for all its scope, weight and structural integrity, is not a serious book because it doesn't say anything interesting or new or truthful about human beings. It tells an essentially trivial story. The goodies are always good and the baddies are always bad. C.S. Lewis comes from a different tradition: in the Narnia books he struggles with big ideas. I dislike the conclusions he comes to because he seems to recommend the worship of a god who is a fascist and a bully; who dislikes people of different colours; and who thinks of women as being less valuable in every way.
>
> And it is a god who hates life because he denies children life. In the final Narnia book he gives the children the end-of-term treat of being killed in a railway accident so they can go to heaven. It's a filthy thing to do. Susan is shut out from salvation because she is doing what every other child who has ever been born has done – she is beginning to sense the developing changes in her body and its effect on the opposite sex. For all those reasons I profoundly disagree with Lewis and with the conclusions he reaches.

There is no point in my unpicking the bones in this kind of debate here, for it is all around us and there is a lot invested in it. Pullman is the only writer out of the three mentioned above still alive (at my time of writing here, though long may it continue) and I am sure a (fantastic) dialogue between the three of them could have been fascinating. Nevertheless, having been chosen alongside Lewis on a list of 'best children's books' Pullman reveals that he doesn't necessarily feel comfortable in the company he has been asked to keep: and who can blame him!

While the fact that '[C.S. Lewis'] career as a misanthrope, misogynist, xenophobe, and classroom bully has been well and depressingly documented' (Goldthwaite 1996: 223) should matter little in considering his writing, Andrew Blake has clearly observed that his books reveal that '[all] too often even the most cynical or historically informed reader is brought up hard against the very limited boundaries of Lewis's world-view', and the subject of his books simply 'have nothing to do with contemporary widely travelled, hybrid, multicultural Britain, or indeed anywhere else' (Blake 2000: 53). So much for book recommendations on subjective lists, then! The problem is we cannot hold all such lists up to scrutiny, all of the time.

But there is more to consider in this adult 'best children's books' discourse. Pullman and I agree on the failings in Lewis' work though others will not. For example, a small internet survey of children's book sites in the US, which we can all carry out if we have internet access, will reveal some sites promoting the Christian foundation of Lewis' work; while other sites will be demonising Pullman's daemons and indeed J.K. Rowling's witches and wizards. To be honest, researching this stuff is like swimming in treacle (I always advise my students to avoid clichés like the plague – but alas … ). It is like trying to define political correctness with a reasoned discussion but it is so agenda-laden that it can become more like answering what is the offside rule in football question with answers on the *Theory of Moral Sentiments* (actually, thinking about that ... '[offside] seems to have been given us by nature for a defence, and for a defence only!').[13] Well, surely we are entitled to have an occasional joke when making a serious point. We should get the point; sometimes it's a discussion divided by a common language; a common view; a common ideology, philosophy or ideas on 'others' and 'otherness' – where neither communicates with the other – and I will address some of this later too, for there is another cultural issue we need to consider presently.

That Pullman has joined Rowling and Lewis in the territory of the 'bestseller' (and they are probably the top three best sellers in the modern world to date, alongside Enid Blyton) also has a bearing on the debates already discussed. On one hand we have writers and critics addressing the work of other writers, on the other hand we have the discourse of a book review opinion that is designed to help put the book (the product) on show to be purchased and to keep it selling. Thus returning us to Townsend, we cannot entirely dismiss his publisher book list as being the defining litmus test on what is and isn't children's literature, but it's a little more complex than Townsend suggests.

As Zipes has written (extensively), it is 'impossible to discuss children and children's literature today without situating them within the complex of the cultural field of production ... ' (2009: 1) where we cannot escape the capital enterprise that writing for children is. And with any cultural commodity industry, there is an underlying truism (though perhaps not a truth) that the best is identified and delivered by sales figures. Having already quoted him above, I don't propose to go back to a full investigation of Adam Smith and *The Wealth of Nations* here but on the economics of this he refers to the 'invisible hand' of the free market as a term to describe the self-regulating nature of the marketplace. Although, and worryingly for this critic (and true I believe), as the Nobel Prize winning economist, Joseph E. Stiglitz, has written: 'the reason that the invisible hand often seems invisible is that it is often not there ... free markets, by themselves, often do not lead to what is best.'[14] 'Give me a book I can sell and I will sell it for you,' as a literary agent once said to me, without mention of literary merit.

Indeed a great deal of the later work of Jack Zipes concentrates on this idea when he discusses the relationship between capitalism and popular culture and of what he called its 'Disneyfication' (and thereby its commodification), especially in relation to the fairy tale (and thereby the children's story). He is concerned to highlight how storytelling itself has become commodified and writes:

> The more we invest in children, the more we destroy their future. There is no way out of the paradox that we have created, unless we reconsider our investment ... Everything we do to, with, and for our children is influenced by capitalist market conditions and the hegemonic interests of corporate elites. In simple terms, we calculate what is best for our children by regarding them as investments and turning them into commodities ...
>
> (Zipes 2002: ix–x)

Heady words indeed, but what he is actually saying is, for example (and this is a small example), even Disney's film adaptations of *Winnie the Pooh* (say) targeted at children, are written as a simple device to 'hook children as consumers not because they believe their films have artistic merit and contribute to children's cultural development, but because they [Disney] wanted to control children's aesthetic interests and consumer tastes' (Zipes 1997: 91). To which Jean Baudrillard may have offered this in agreement: 'the commodity form is the first great medium of the modern world. But the message that the objects deliver through it is already extremely simplified, and it is always the same: their exchange value. Thus at bottom the message already no longer exists; it is the medium that imposes itself in its pure circulation' (Baudrillard, in Foster 1985: 131). Thus, even aside from the other issues we have to confront in the idea of the children's story, book, film, etc., as a cultural site of authentic storytelling and communication, we find it is already and always contaminated by the omnipresence of capitalist ideology.

I use the word 'contaminated' purposefully because contamination can be good and bad and it is a much larger issue than I can explain here, and although Jack Zipes (Zipes, 2002, 2009) does go into greater depth, this part of his work does have to be read with an open mind for the alternatives he proposes are not easily addressed in our advanced age of capital and consumerism. Indeed Fredric Jameson had already written: 'We have seen that there is a way in which postmodernism replicates or reproduces – reinforces – the logic of consumer capitalism; the more significant question is whether there is also a way in which it resists that logic' (Kaplan 1988: 29). Furthermore, I am also aware of Webb's (Webb et al. 2002: 92) interpretation of Michel Foucault on this when she reminds us that 'Free-market economics is not the same as liberalism – but it is one of the paths that liberalism has taken during ... [the last] century'. Of course, what is meant by liberalism is also fraught and hardly a stable concept. These issues are complex and difficult to engage with in any meaningful way here.[15] But ignoring the existence and persistence of the economics and the commodification of culture targeted at children is not an option either.

Apart from writing that the 'industry' of writing for children (say) is an energy fuelled by the forces of capitalist ideology (and we cannot now deny that such an industry exists), then we are further confronted by the idea that writers and writing for children are themselves also problematised. I will quote Zipes at length again in order to frame a central issue, though there are a number of others[16] I could and will use as we proceed. You will recognise the first sentence as the epigraph I used in the Introduction:

> I am not being coy – children's literature does not exist. If we take the genitive case litarally and seriously, and if we assume ownership and possession are involved when we say 'children's literature' or the literature of children, then there is no such thing as children's literature, or for that matter, children ... 'children' and 'childhood' are social constructs that have been determined by socioeconomic conditions and have different meanings for different cultures ...
>
> (Zipes 2002: 40)

This idea of children and childhood as social constructs is one that I mentioned earlier and I will refer to again because it cannot be easily dismissed either, and indeed is the subject of much work and I address it at length in the section following – hence, once again, the idea of the cult of the child. But add to it this fact that authors too (as cultural practitioners and purveyors) are involved in the discussion and we are still confronted with the problems of definition. You see, despite appearing on a best of children's books list, Philip Pullman doesn't call himself a writer for children on his website, where he writes:

> My only real claim to anyone's attention lies in my writing. I've published nearly twenty books, *mostly of the sort that are read by children*, though I'm happy to say that the natural audience for my work seems to be a mixed one – mixed in age, that is, though the more mixed in every other way as well, the better [my italic].[17]

Not terribly ambiguous but hedging his bets a little, and who can blame him for that-? the journey between white to black has a lot of grey in between, especially for a writer who writes in hope that someone will read it, and we all recognise that person too.

Therefore having some predetermined idea that there can be any fixed theory relating to things like children's literature is opened wide by ideas on whether such a thing as writing for children, children's literature and indeed children actually exist, other than as a social construct determined by socioeconomics and other agencies of power. Joseph Zornado (2006) argues that stories told to children reflect the ideologies of the dominant culture from whence they came. And yet we, as writers and critics, still seem to be clear about one thing: while a common-sense view of the definitions of what is adult and what is children's literature does exist, the debate as it stands is not going away. Although it is not (in my view) as simple as saying, as Steig does, that the difference is an artificial device, nor to say, as Nodelman (2008: 137) does in defining children's literature, is it a genre in its own right, albeit a confusing one, in writing for children, in the 'field of production' as literary 'child-centred' culture, there are many other things to consider.

*

It is only my own personal and anecdotal experience, but it seems to me that every parent should know or learn through time that there is an unwritten rule, which is that driving with children in a car means you must forgo any choice in the music that is played on the stereo. And beginning with this (less than empirical but sensible) statement does have some merits in a critically creative and creatively critical adult, child-centred discourse. Part of it relates to the fact that the rule is unwritten and not empirical but sensibly practical, which is where I find myself drawn when thinking about critical theory, theories, ideologies, philosophies and critical contexts. However creatively critical and critically creatively presented they make me cross-eyed in frustration (may as well admit you are not alone in this). But if you think the issues on child-centred culture outlined above resembled the ramblings of Walter Scott's famed Dr Dryasdust, the path through the critical forest is no less fraught.

But back to driving; there I was, motoring along on a recent family holiday trip to the French coast. The sun was shining, the sea was calm and beckoning, and the stereo was blaring as we sang along. It was bliss and in a brief moment of contemplative reverie, during the musical refrain between the bridge and the chorus, I suddenly realised there was a big connection in ideas being floated by Maria Nikolajeva, Peter Hunt, David Rudd, Jean Baudrillard and the pugnacious pop princess, Pixie Lott in 'Cry Me Out', which happened to be playing on our stereo at the time: as I indicated before, the secret route through the complexity is in making connections. This will take some explaining but bear with me because it begins with this question: what does it mean to be a reading child and to be reading as a child in the twenty-first century?

As recently as 2010, Maria Nikolajeva wrote:

> In 1984 Peter Hunt called for a children's literature specific theory (Hunt 1984: 192). The encouragement is still legitimate. During the last twenty to thirty years, international children's literature scholars have been applying various theoretical implements to books written marketed for and read by young people. Yet, while many marginalized literatures have successfully developed their theoretical fields – feminist theory, postcolonial theory, queer theory – children's literature has so far not elaborated a theory of its own.
>
> (Nikolajeva 2010: 1)

The issue seems simple enough when highlighted like this, indeed how hard can it be to address it? As I have written elsewhere:

> The reading life of a child is a short one, around ten years all in all before they are expected to grapple with Shakespeare, Dickens and the various examination led authors which take them out of childhood into the dark forest of the grown ups. How well does material written specifically for children lead them down the path of experience before they hit the trees? Are they entering the forest unprepared, inexperienced and bewildered or does their literature give them the confidence to go boldly?
>
> (Melrose 2002: iv)

It doesn't seem too difficult to define or theorise this metaphorical, rhetorical, episte-mological, ontologically real decade, which we have all experienced in our own lifetime. After all, while children are defined as a person at the stage between birth and puberty and not yet adult, it is a simple truism that we have all been children; it is our one stable distinction; it is one real thing we all share in common: at different stages of our lives we were all much younger than we are now. Taking this simple thought further, it might be underpinned by a simple understanding, which is this:

> … childhood is not the opposite of adulthood; it is not solved by adulthood; it is not preparation for adulthood, it is childhood and children (young people, young persons) are children (young people, young persons) not apprentice adults …

This may seem obvious but once again the critical ideas surrounding this are too complex to easily dismiss and indeed finding a place to begin the exegesis is not simple because it doesn't have a starting point, rather a series of threads snagged on the forest branches, caught up in the brambles and tied in knots – there are bogeymen at play. The idea also has a past, present and future and for that reason I have, once again, purposely left the ellipses open at the beginning and the end. Therefore having begun this deliberation with a very recent quotation from Nikolajeva on the idea of a specific theory it seems only right to go back to a pronouncement made only two years earlier by Nodelman, which she was definitely aware of. He wrote: 'I believe that the term *children's literature* creates confusion because children's literature *as a genre* is confusing' (my italics). Of which he went on to say:

The confusions make the genre seem impossible only with the assumption that the differing definitions must be mutually exclusive and that one must be right in ways that makes the others wrong, which makes them all mutually defeating. But what if the contradictions of the definitions suggest some part of the more complex truth? [ … ] What if children's literature as a genre represents the complex field of shifting position-takings of the field that engenders it?

(Nodelman 2008: 137)

First, what seems to be at stake here is the terminology that haunts all child-centred cultural ideas and needs to be unpicked. Nodelman's book cannot be easily dismissed; it has many interesting things to say and indeed is an extensive and controlled piece of scholarship by an expert in the field. However, the claim that he is 'defining children's literature' as a 'genre' is part of the terminology that needs to be addressed.

A 'genre' is defined as a category or sort of literary or artistic work; a 'field' is defined as an area of human activity – such as a division of knowledge interest (which we are currently engaged in if we consider this a book about writing for children and the study of children's literature). Thus the chicken and egg question is: are writers writing in a 'genre' being addressed by critics, in a 'field', or is our writing genre defined by the complex field of study of children's literature that our writing has engendered? Does the field feed the genre, or the genre the field, or are we all lumped together in the meadow? Although we still have to address the fraught, almost Wittgensteinian,[18] question: is there a meadow at all? And also to deal with the Jacques Derrida notion that 'a text cannot belong to no genre, it cannot be without … a genre. Every text participates in one or several genres, there is no genreless text … ' (Derrida 1982: 61). Confused? Yes well I was too and this is the problem with trying to marry philosophy, critical theory ideas and plain old common sense, so let me try to explain it.

When I was researching and wrote: ' … childhood is not the opposite of adulthood; it is not solved by adulthood; it is not preparation for adulthood, it is childhood and children (young people, young persons) are children … ' I came across Ursela Le Guin's expression that 'an adult is not a dead child, but a child who survived … '. Which feels even more optimistic and relevant because I was making a commonsensical observation and thinking of a caveat to my own understanding, which is ' … furthermore, neither is childhood a construction of adults or adulthood … '. The problem with academic and intellectual thought is that sometimes the commonsense idea gets slightly misplaced. Critically speaking, however, the bogeymen start to appear when I try to justify this with some kind of theoretical positioning, which is indeed inevitable – because that is the discourse we work in (and I address this later too).

This is especially so, for example, in light of Roderick McGillis' comments on an article by David Rudd, saying he, Rudd, 'Argues that children's literature studies are "messy and complex" precisely because of the "constructed" and "constructive" definitions of the child' (Rudd, ed. 2010: 25). I might have suggested it is because of the discourse and discursive ideas they use, but in following the debate they are mulling over I know what they both mean entirely. Although, while we do not pretend this academic discourse is easy, neither is it so difficult that we cannot understand it – for it works in the same way as many discourses on ideas do. There is always a reference point that can be located and when we do locate it the issue becomes so simple we wondered why they wrote it in such a difficult way in the first place. I will try but cannot always hope to succeed in avoiding this.

In the article referred to, Rudd is attempting to pull factions of the debating critics together into a hybrid set of ideas that draws on a 'Foucauldian notion of power as both repressive and productive ... ' in trying to 'steer a course between biological essentialism and a cultural determinism' (Hunt 2004: 29–43), by arguing that children *are* necessarily both constructive and constructed. I will explain this 'constructive and constructed' idea in greater depth as I proceed but for now the explanation can be simplified, as Rudd does, by saying, 'on the one hand ... there is a notion that there is an underlying "essential" child whose needs we can know, and on the other, the notion that the child is nothing but the product of adult discourse ... ' (Rudd in Hunt 2004: 29). It is important to hold onto this as a thought because it helps to highlight the fact that there is *not* a single theory of children's literature when such disagreement exists.

Going back to the specific theory idea, for example, it might be said there is no 'childism' as (say) in the same way as there is 'feminism' because, 'unlike other disempowered groups such as women, who can speak for themselves, or through the collective voice of feminism, children, in culture and history, have no such voice' (Lesnik-Oberstein 1994: 26), although while this idea of feminism too is fraught with problems, differences and even talk of a post-feminism, that is not to say we cannot summarise the debates and take some (common) sense from the voices which presented them. It's complex, I know, but this idea of the 'mute' child who cannot speak for itself and the aforementioned 'constructed' and 'constructive' definitions of the cult and culture of the child, childhood and child-centred culture is probably the best place to begin trying to pull the debates and sense together, as I will now try to do.

*

It has already been pointed out above that a central and convincing theoretical position taken by some critics on writing for children and children's literature is problematised by the idea that unlike those in more singular, subject and theoretical discourse positions, such as those represented by race, gender, sexuality and class, which can turn their oppressed or negative individuality into a positive collected one (under a banner like feminism, for example), the child's ability to inhabit a claim to collected identity is muted by its own silence. This, in the eyes of some critics, renders child identity, individually and collectively (by adult marketers, educators, legislators, etc., for example) helpless, to be constructed in the image articulated by an adult vision of childhood. And whether this construction is the capitalist conspiring exposed by Jack Zipes or the post-Freudian ideas of desire in the adult to create a child in its own vision of childhood, as revealed by Rose, the issues are not easily dismissed.

Now, I understand this is difficult to imagine even conceptually, sometimes, but I am following the arguments being made in the history of the theoretical context and it is important to know the case has been made. Understanding the critical underpinning and issues surrounding children's literature is crucial to an understanding of the subject, especially since I want to challenge it as I proceed. And I was thinking about this idea of the constructed child, the mute child, the 'Children, in culture and history [with] no voice ... ' (Lesnik-Oberstein 1994) and in pondering a way to explain it I remembered Richard Ellmann's biography of James Joyce.[19]

Ellmann tells several amusing anecdotes; among them is an account of Joyce and Gogarty strolling the shore on their usual search for money. One day they saw the poet (and their friend) W.B. Yeats' father, John Butler Yeats, walking on the strand and Gogarty, urged on by Joyce, said to him:

> 'Good morning, Mr. Yeats, would you be so good as to lend us two shillings?'
> The old man looked from one to the other and retorted, 'Certainly not. In the first place I have no money, and if I had it and lent it to you, you and your friend would spend it on drink.'
> Joyce responded, saying, 'We cannot speak about that which is not.'

It is Joyce's reply that is of interest to me here but I had to give the whole story to reveal its context. Why indeed should he confirm the suspicions of a man who was not going to indulge them in the first place? Yeats' retort, presuming he already knew the answer to his own hypothetical question, replicates the normativity of an adult/child exchange in many ways.

Following the critical exegesis, thus far, it would suggest that, as adults, we ask of children that which we have no right to receive answers to because the question is always rhetorical and the answer always already presumed, and thus always assumed that the child does not have an answer to give that we do not already know. But the key to this critique lies in Joyce's reply, 'We cannot speak about that which is not.' Sometimes writing about writing for children is seen to be just like that – can we speak about that which is not considered to be?

It does seem an absurdity to suggest it, despite the compelling arguments; and the 'constructed' and 'constructive' ideas don't go away. But perhaps the debate has been approached from the wrong angle here. So let me rephrase it in some way because as a writer I think it is important to the whole process of writing for children as an adult-written, child-centred discourse.

But having summarised the debates, thus far, we need to return once again to Jacqueline Rose, in her seminal and complex book on Peter Pan (1984). As I have said previously, her strong and thought-provoking, post-Freudian, psychoanalytical proposal is a different one from Townsend, Steig, Zipes *et al.* on children's literature as an artificial 'child' in full focus. Rose is the initial proposer of the 'impossibility' of children's literature, which I highlighted earlier. I feel it is probably better to split her ideas into three chunks. First:

> Children's fiction is impossible, not in the sense that it cannot be written (that would be nonsense), but in that it hangs on an impossibility, one which rarely speaks. This is the impossible relation between adult and child ...

(Rose 1984: 1)

Using her definition, when Rose or indeed any of us write the words 'children's fiction', or 'children's literature', we are constantly alerted to the notion that once again what we are actually referring to is fiction or literature written *for* children, not *by* them. Thus the possessive apostrophe in 'children's' is deliberately rendered problematic because the possession is not theirs, it has never actually been theirs and never will be owned by them. It is an adult concept that has been proffered to them; written for them; given to them (for many reasons, we know, such as literacy and even for the sheer magic of reading,[20] for example) on the basis that it is an adult's right to give it – and, it is to be hoped, not be squandered, in which case it 'could' be withheld, like Yeats' two shillings.

Therefore, on this premise it is immediately shown to be the site of a Foucauldian power and knowledge paradigm[21] that is hard to deny. Neither is it hard to deny Rose's Lacanian-informed psychoanalytical interpretation either but there is a lot more we could unravel first here.

In returning to the idea of the possessive apostrophe in *children's*, which renders it as literature written *for* children, not *by* them, we are offered an interesting, semantic, syntactic and (let's face it) rather pedantic, grammatical idea of the possessive apostrophe; it is indeed interesting in the context Rose offers it and any interrogation of the notion that the form could be children's literature in the possessive sense is immediately problematised as indicated. But, and this is crucial I think, surely it is possible to reconceive the apostrophe as rendering not the 'possessive' but the 'associative' – so that it refers not to literature owned by children, but literature connotatively and indeed denotatively part of the domain of children/childhood/the child state.[22] I appreciate any desire to avoid the ambiguity necessarily conjured up by the apostrophe, but think it is probably a clearer interpretation of the options to offer, as I have above, that in fact it is simply an *adult*, child-centred discourse – which, as I have already suggested, can be simplified as a 'child-centred discourse'. Unfortunately, however, because the debate exists we have to rehearse it here in order to take the 'child-centred' idea forward. Second:

> If children's fiction [and the writer for children] builds an image of the child inside the book, it [and the writer] does so in order to secure the child who is outside the book, the one who does not come so easily within its [the writer/adult's] grasp.
>
> (Rose 1984: 1)

This is where it becomes a little more complex, for surely the suggestion is that the image of the child and childhood is 'constructed' in the image of the writer of the book to become a cultural trope that stands for the defining ideas of childhood, such as innocence, virtuousness and purity, rendering them as sites of adult desire (as Rose explains) and open to corruptibility. What we really need to ask is can this (always) be so without denying it can (sometimes) be?

But this too is complex to leave as an open question, so let me tease it out. Central to this is the issue that critics are split in their ideas in actually defining the child and children, 'on the one hand … ' writes Rudd, 'there is an underlying "essential" child whose nature and needs we can know and, on the other, the notion that the child is nothing but the product of adult discourse (as some social constructionists argue)' (Rudd in Hunt 2004: 29–30), viz the aforementioned 'constructive' and 'constructed' definitions of 'child.'

What Rose is essentially saying is the (supposed) mute 'child' is a construct of the 'adult', where the adult writer (for example) 'secures the child' to an adult image or representation or reinforcement of childhood as innocence and that knowledge and maturation ultimately come from the 'experience' that is adulthood. And the idea that the child is 'mute' is reinforced by Lesnik-Oberstein, who I quoted above, and who writes that women in feminism can speak for themselves but children, 'in culture and history, have no such voice' (1994: 26). And yet there is something wholly unconvincing about all of this, for surely the point is that if 'children' are singled out as a special case in the realms of the disempowered then their identity is revealed as being in existence and therefore any further 'social construction' of their identity idea is, ultimately, a negotiation between the adult and the child, not a gift that the adult bestows or forces upon them. McGillis was provoked to write the following in way of a response Rose:

> What we call children's literature is an invention of adults who need to have something to write about, something to play with, something to help them construct a vision of the way things are and ought to be so that the present generation and more importantly, the next generation will behave according to standards those adults who write children's books and publish them feel comfortable with.
>
> (McGillis 1997: 202)

There is a strong hint of irony here and it highlights the problem with the 'no children, no books, only theory' idea, which comes from following the critical discourse rather than the representative literature.

But it's when we carry on to a third and important clip from Rose's thesis that we can begin to address a way of countering her argument and indeed repositioning the entire debate on the cult and culture of children and childhood. Rose says:

> Children's fiction is clearly about the relation [between adult and child], but it has remarkable characteristics of being about something which it hardly ever talks of. Children's fiction sets up a world in which the adult comes first (author, maker, giver) and the child comes after (reader, product, receiver), but where neither of them enter the space in between.
>
> (Rose 1984: 1)

Looking at Rose's idea, here, she implies that children's fiction rests on the simple idea that there is an equally simple child who is simply there to be addressed by an adult and that speaking to it might be even more simple. This seems innocuous enough, but nevertheless, we can surely reason that this still returns us to the idea that the identification of the child as a construction site (forgive the pun) immediately acknowledges the child as a social being and thereby a 'special being, subject to its own rules, distinct from other groups' (Rudd in Hunt 2004: 30). And that the claim that the child is mute within the social hierarchies of this adult, grown-up world of ours only serves to reinforce the idea that the child is a social being and any suggestion that it is muted by adult 'silencing' in order to 're-enforce' the adult colonisation of the subject of the child seems to me to be misguided by too many suppositions built on the idea that, to paraphrase the above quotation, 'neither of them enter the space in between'. This will take some time to explain, so please bear with me while I try to unpack it here.

*

In a theoretical exegesis on 'Orientialism', Edward Said helps us to understand this idea of 'colonisation' a little better because his Orientalism is a theoretical discourse about otherness and recognising the other, as Rudd says, 'The identification of someone as "Other" implies an unequal power relationship, where the one being "Othered" is perceived as inferior, or at best strangely exotic' (Rudd 2010: 221). It sets the colonial subject up as a binary opposite of the coloniser. In terms of the adult/child this might easily be explained in terms such as: experienced/inexperienced; active/passive; individuated/ unindividuated but surely we can rule this out too. It docs scem to have a convenient resonance and ties in well with Jacqueline Rose's idea but it makes me a little uncomfortable. I agree, as Jacques Derrida advises, that words such as 'child' only hold their meaning in contrast to other words, in the way, for example, male/female does. But, for example, child/adult is *not* a binary opposite. They are relational contrasts, one is the younger of the other, and can be better understood in Derrida's other use of the term, *différance*, which plays on the fact that the French word *différer* means both 'to defer' and 'to differ', which is a good way to address the constructed child idea.

A child as a living being differs from an adult through inexperience, which defers its maturity until he or she is ready to become adult. Thus, he or she is the constructive child and has a part to play in its own development as a person, as a cultural being and as a reader of the signs implicit in his or her own development. But we can take this even further. When Rose alludes to the writer who writes 'in order to secure the child who is outside the book ... ' she is less concerned to investigate what the child wants and needs, but what the adult desires, which is to secure the child to the adult view of what childhood is, and is open to adult suggestion and (unconscious) desire (Rose 1984). For the adult writer this idea is problematic because it is, of course, open to all kinds of abuse and not all of it conscious. The prospect of a persuasive, adult uncanniness[23] haunts all texts, not just those for children, but this is for the 'reader' to deal with and for some reason we seem to forget that is what children learn to do. Thus we need to go back and look at this idea of the child and the cult and culture of children and childhood. I lean on Foucault for a little leverage here, and to help me to express the idea that this can be looked at in another way. Foucault writes on Greek classical literature and not children's literature but for me the understanding is similar:

> Since there is an important and large literature about loving boys in Greek culture, some historians say, 'Well, that's proof that they loved boys'. But I say that proves that loving boys was a problem. Because if there were no problem, they would speak of this kind of love in the same terms as love between men and women. The problem was that they couldn't accept that a young boy who was supposed to become a free citizen could be dominated and used as an object for someone's pleasure ... they could not integrate this real practice in the framework of their social selves.
>
> (Foucault 1984: 344–45)

Equally, this implies that the engagement between the reading child and the adult writer is problematised by a view of one (the child) as spectator and the other (the adult) as seducer but only in the failure to recognise the 'problem'. And this is simpler than it looks. For example, it is perfectly simple to take these critical ideas on because all too often we rely on 'experts' telling us things when in fact we need a constant vigilance. For example, when someone I respect greatly like Maria Nikolajeva writes: 'One of the strongest conventions of the children's fiction is the absence of all the prominent aspects of human (i.e., adult) civilisation, including law, money and labour ... [and we cannot exclude sex here] Children, real as well as fictional, are supposed to grow up unaware of and unrestricted by these tokens of adulthood' (Nikolajeva 2002: 205). My reply would be: what a piece of nonsense that is. Even worse is Nina Bawden's tip to writers that

'You can, and should, leave out things that are beyond their [children's] comprehension' (Bawden 1974: 9).

I will address this in greater depth later but as you can see, this is not how I, as a writer, approach this critical reading (and do feel free to exclaim loudly when you think I am writing nonsense). But thinking around it, and as an example we have all surely witnessed, for who could have missed it, J.K. Rowling's *Harry Potter* septology[24] is full of tokens of adulthood and things beyond most people's comprehension. I never knew what a 'knut' was (money), or a 'muggle' (non-magical people), or 'Voldemort' (oops, he who shall not be named) but surely there was Hermione Grainger's S.P.E.W., The Society for the Promotion of Elfish Welfare, which dealt with the 'labour relations' of house elves. Indeed the entire series is full of issues on law, for example the Ministry of Magic; of money, Harry wins The Triwizard Tournament and uses the prize to fund Weazleys Wizard Weazes as a commercial enterprise; and labour brings in the boorish middle-class, Dombey-like company boss Vernon Dursley juxtaposed with the poor put-upon Bob Cratchit-like figure, Arthur Weasley. Then we have all the other odd stuff, like basilisks, boggarts, centaurs, dementors, thestrals, blast-ended skrewts, a whole manner of things supposedly beyond most children's comprehension, which actually take on meaning. In a lecture on Jung, Tom Davis asks this:

> What do children dream about? All sorts of things, but one odd thing. They have a tendency to dream, and play, about monsters. Wild animals. Fear of darkness. Falling from trees. Jungles. Fighting. Being eaten. And traditional children's stories reflect these dreams. Why? My children were brought up in Mosely, Birmingham (UK). No monsters, no jungles, no serious danger of being eaten by wild animals.
>
> (Boulter 2007: 50)[25]

Now I am aware in foregrounding *Harry Potter* I am only taking one author here, and there are hundreds to choose from; my teenage daughter can talk for hours on vampires including those from John Polidori and Bram Stoker and my son recently spoke to me about the contrasting writing styles between Oliver Bowden's *Assassin's Creed* and John Steinbeck's *Of Mice and Men* (which he is reading for his English GCSE), but they are the Potter generation and would continue to be if more books became available. Their attachment to the series contradicts Nikolajeva's and Bawden's statements, but this can't just be a straw poll taken in my household. Despite all its magical imagery, and it seems almost flippant to make this point, the popularity of the *Harry Potter* series (and indeed many children's books) is connected to a much more serious issue, which is that children understand more than they can articulate at all the stages of their life. The series (and I am only using it as an example here) is, as Peter Hunt has written, 'an eccentric blend of the comfortably predictable and the unsettlingly unexpected', of which he says, 'The critic's job can hardly be to point out the felicities, which seem to be abundantly obvious to the readers. Instead, it might be interesting to analyse the books … in order to inspect the minds of their readers' (Hunt 2001: 122–23). This is precisely my point and I will expand on the ideas around the 'comfortably predictable and the unsettlingly unexpected' as I proceed because I find the phrase and the idea behind it both fascinating and useful.

As I have already written (above) I am persuaded by ideas that suggest the cognitive development in children is experience-dependent, and that older children have more experiences than younger children. But I will add to this by saying adults have more experiences than all of them and this will become relevant to the ideas I will unfold, where I will be picking up on the radical proposal that experience is gained through a process of joint activity. And this becomes an all-important issue to some of my underlying ideas. This idea of 'joint activity' between the experienced and the less so is crucial to my understanding of the critical and creative process.

In the meantime, return again to James Joyce's quip, 'We cannot speak about that which is not'. This entire premise of the 'constructed' child rests on the idea that the child is, indeed, this site of innocence, a blank canvas awaiting the adult brush and paint to bring it into being by giving it words to speak. But this is simply not the case. Language is not merely given by an adult to a child, but gained by the child in many and multi-cultural ways,[26] and the reading child being addressed by the book can already understand more than she or he can articulate, especially as they become readers. This becomes a defining issue that I will repeat in isolation because it's very important to record it.

## Children understand more than they can articulate at all the stages of their life

Their articulation comes through dialogic[27] social and cultural negotiation and a journey through phonology, vocabulary, morphology and syntax, not as a list to tick off but as a dialogic part of growing up.

'The literature of childhood,' writes Natov (2006: 2), 'moves between innocence and experience, between initiation and reflection … ' and the '*connection* [my italic] between childhood and adulthood is essential to the potential coherence of consciousness'. But I emphasise 'connection' here because it's a loaded term that Rose seems to ignore and yet it is so important that I dedicate most of the next chapter to it. For our purposes here, then, the child can begin to be defined (for this writer at least – and I am writing as a writer and not a critic) by rejecting Rose's notion that the child is a ripe construction site for my literary development, and we could say that:

> … [a child] is *not* a text, not a narrative, master or otherwise, but that, as an absent cause [silent], it is inaccessible to us except in textual form, that our approach to it and to the Real itself necessarily passes through its prior textualization, its narrativization, in the political [and social] unconscious …
>
> (Jameson 1981: 35)

I have edited Fredric Jameson's idea for my own purpose but it fits well. This 'absent cause', the silent child, the muted, simply refers to silence as a hypothetical postulate, which is always expressed in ellipses … where the unsaid and unsayable does not mean the unknown (for the child's time being) because the language to express knowledge comes after, through ageing and experience (lived in and lived out) and is gained, minute by minute, second by second, both primarily and vicariously, in their ongoing development. Indeed it would be a mistake to assume that children are not engaged in adult discourse while developing, just as adults engage with children's. It is an ongoing dialogic experience of social engagement – and to steal Peter Hunt's phrase (which I am sure he will not mind) – they and we, children and adults alike, are constantly engaged in the 'comfortably predictable and the unsettlingly unexpected' on a day-to-day basis. All of us are; what a dull world it would be if we became too grown up to be surprised by the unexpected. But children are insiders in this process, not outsiders, and one of the central assumptions underpinning *their* experience is the significant overlap between non-fictional and fictionalised patterns of representation, precisely because these symbolic frameworks or discourses are in circulation through popular culture as well as real life situations and a fictionalised and non-fictional, experiential narrative combines to inform. Children frequently draw upon references to and images from fiction, film and television drama and the internet in combination with their real living experience in constructing *their* 'stories'.

When Rose refers to desire in her Freudian analysis of Peter Pan and the 'child' in the book, there is surely a need to also express its dependence on the 'increasing abstraction of experience' described by Walter Benjamin in 'The Storyteller'.[28] As a writer I am drawn to Foucault's idea on this, which is that 'it would probably not be worth the trouble of making books if they failed to teach the *author* something he hadn't known before ... ' (Foucault 1984: 339). Indeed, this is where we should go next in this book because it is all about making 'connections' as I will reveal. And this is predicated, though I am somewhat embarrassed to appropriate it here in an adaptation of Franz Fanon's famous phrase, 'The negro is not. Any more than the white man.'[29]

As a way of an explanation I could say, 'The child is not. Any more than the adult.' Questions to be addressed are these: are the terms, for exclusion, or inclusion under erasure, the same for the colonised as they are for the child – or sufficiently comparable for it to be a safe line of argument? And is it indeed safe to say: the child is not, any more than the adult? Because it is fraught with problems, and also it seems to me that we have to address these before we can even begin to address what it means to be a reading child in the twenty-first century, to understanding how children are represented, why we write for children, what is written for children and what to consider when writing for children in a creative, cultural and critical context, in this age of advanced communication and media.

The next chapter is about bridging the gap between child reader and adult author and this seems to be the obvious place to begin addressing the symbolic frameworks of this debate before moving to a new way of seeing and a new way of thinking about the cult and culture of the child and children.

# Chapter 3

# Bridging the gap between child reader and adult author

The child is not. Any more than the adult. It is an incomplete phrase (certainly not two sentences) made to make us think by supporting its own hypothesis in the silences that exist in the meaning, hitherto unsaid, unwritten and inarticulate because it is aimed at us imagining its articulation. Although and once again (see above) our thoughts on the issue are inaccessible to us except in textual form. And so a textual intervention on this begins with a child 'is' and an adult 'is' called into existence through its relation to the 'other' – if there was no child there would be no need for the term adult and vice versa, we would just be. But crucial to this co-existence is surely an attempt at understanding the other. Otherwise the child 'is not' remains, just as the adult 'is not' for while they are both designated 'other'[1] to each this needs to be recognised mutually, not with the adult as a dominant force, and for me this is something all writers need to be aware of. But what does it all mean? Returning to Rose's central idea that

> Children's fiction is clearly about the relation [between adult and child], but it has remarkable characteristics of being about something which it hardly ever talks of. Children's fiction sets up a world in which the adult comes first (author, maker, giver) and the child comes after (reader, product, receiver), *but where neither of them enter the space in between* [my italic].
>
> (Rose 1984: 1–2)

We are also confronted with the idea that

> There is, in one sense, no body of literature which rests so openly on an acknowledged difference, a rupture almost, between writer and addressee. Children's fiction sets up the child as an outsider to its own process, and then aims, unashamedly, to take the child *in* … Children's fiction draws in the child, it secures, places and frames the child.
>
> (Ibid.)

It seems to me that these ideas rely on certain assumptions that should not be taken as absolutes. For example, in support of her argument Rose repeats the idea that the writer can count *absolutely* on the willingness of children to enter into the book and *live* the story (Townsend 1971: 13), which supports her idea of the text being capable of 'soliciting' or 'seducing' the child 'taken in'. But like I have said before, we can disagree with this idea and it can simply be countered by saying the writer *cannot* count absolutely on the willingness of the children to enter the story and *live* the story. Further, neither can the writer expect the child who has entered the book to coalesce to the seduction. To suggest otherwise is to suggest the child has neither will nor desire of its own. In the 'acknowledged difference … between writer and addressee' (ibid.) we need to ask why must child-centred culture set up the child as 'outsider', rather than 'other' where neither can enter the space in-between? In fact I am not sure it does. While some texts may, and Rose's use of Peter Pan is exemplary here, can we really say the same for Pullman's use of Lyra, for example, who seems to negotiate 'the space between', allowing anyone who wishes to come together?

Thus, while I think that Lewis' assertion that 'a children's story which is only enjoyed by children is bad story' (Lewis 1966: 25) is a poor idea in the context he delivered it, I would suggest that the book, the film, the cultural product (if we must) that contains a story can be a negotiated site that fills the space in-between, it lurks in the gap between the adult and the child, where dialogue can take place between each other. Granted, this new site of negotiation, the children's book, is adult written, but I propose that it is not there to 'seduce' or 'solicit' the child but to engage with it. Although I don't envisage it as some utopian world of the storyteller, it is not an ahistorical space but an ideological position situated within concrete social experience. But if feminist criticism, post-colonial criticism, queer theory, etc., exist to remind us that indeed it can be a site for abuse, and feminism (for example) wouldn't exist otherwise if this were not true, surely we are in the same position when confronted by the child? Of course, understanding and empathy is never an absolute, it would be a nonsense to say we live in a post-feminism, post-postcolonial, post-queer-bashing century because they are still combating opposition. But being aware of the debate means it can be shown and therefore understood to be a site of ethical responsibility in facing oppression. For the writer for children in the twenty-first century the level of awareness is no less viable and indeed is necessary. And this takes us into new territory in this investigation.

Being aware of the debate is crucial, and being aware how differences can be negotiated is crucial here, but it does have its problems in a very real context. As Nikolajeva reminds us, 'As adults – writers as well as promoters of children's literature – we cannot unconditionally abolish adult normativity' (Nikolajeva 2010: 204). Yet we can think about how we negotiate the production of 'a social and aesthetic transformation of culture'[2] for children and indeed (re)negotiate the constitution of what is normative[3] although this is not straightforward.

I am not fully convinced about labelling the child as 'other', or about the analogue between children, women, gay community, people of colour, etc., it is just not that simple. I suspect that it is because I see children as occupying a radically different social space, and probably that is because theirs is contingent and genuinely temporary; in a way that is only ever shadowed in all the other demographic categories, they truly are in a process of becoming, not being, the woman, the black person, the gay, etc. Those other demographic categories are pretty much stuck with their markers. But a child is an identity under erasure; the child only has a few years before he or she is camouflaged as 'one of us'. And those marked groups are conspicuous on the basis of their morphology, made up of its interconnected or interdependent parts, while the child is marked more on the basis of their stage of socialisation and their neurological capacity alongside those interconnected or interdependent parts. Also the members of those groups have (wittingly or otherwise) entered the social contract, while the child has not yet reached that stage.[4]

As writers we need to be aware of the kind of cultural exclusion/inclusion this signals for it seems to me it is recognisable by looking at the idea of 'normative' in three ways (which I will expand on in greater length in the 'elements of storytelling' chapter – to follow) and it will help if I isolate them a little.

The *first* is the affirmation of the superiority of the adult over the child, which excludes the child from full participation in the discourse taking place in the space in-between. In thinking about it, it is a kind of denial of any free will as a 'do as I say' commandment, which seems a rather unlikely scenario in the twenty-first century.

The *second* is more likely, in allowing participation of the child but one where the adult dictates the normative rules without some kind of appreciation of what the child needs and wants. The reason being that mother, father, guardian, teacher, etc., knows better, which is itself problematised, as I have already discussed.

The *third* way (if indeed it is a way, I am only using the word as a means of expressing it) is about taking much more of a dialogic and vigilant approach to the idea of normative. The first and second ideas and attitudes are embedded in dominant adult ideology, institutions and practices, which have become normative in a hierarchical, symbolic framework of child-centred discourse, where the only qualification required of the expert is to be adult. But I would contend that us adults, and thereby producers of child-centred culture, do not need a new way of seeing or being but maintaining a state of constant vigilance in observing what is being done to and in the name of the child. Although rather than approaching this as a critic I encourage writers and practitioners to look at ways of addressing the social and aesthetic transformation of the culture of writing for children. And this can be done by writing in such a way that your reader will see an approach to ideas, issues and aesthetics that could radically alter their way of reading what the normative is.[5] In this way, writing for children could be a radical force for good.

I return to my adaptation of the Fanon quote, above. The idea that we can somehow accommodate the adult/child split as a conventional binary has already been addressed when I wrote child/adult is *not* a binary opposite. They are relational contrasts and can be better understood in Derrida's other use of the term, *différance*. In truth, the reversal and awareness with Fanon's negro and the coloniser can happen instantly at the moment of meeting and realisation, where Fanon goes on to say: 'O my body, make of me a man who questions' (Fanon 1986: 231).[6] But of course with the adult/child relationship, the child has the questions but has to wait until it can articulate its own position and in that sense there is a power balance problem. Not to mention other problems with neurological capacity (and growing up) and the variable nature of childhood across times and cultures. So the issue to be addressed is that the terms, for exclusion, or inclusion under erasure, are not the same for the colonised as they are for the child and vice versa – but they are sufficiently close, as a special case, for it to be a safe line of argument. It is complex I know and in order to open this out I will need to retract a little in order to show the ideas; it seems to me[7] that an early entry into ideas on post-colonial theory work very well as a means of starting the investigation – though without fully providing an answer, which I hope to do in time. So let's set up the ground first of all.

*

In the Fanon terms discussed above, and as I have adapted to, The child is not. Any more than the adult. Homi Bhabha writes of the caesura that separates the two statements by calling it the inter, the in-between space, viz:

> ... we should remember that it is the 'inter' – the cutting edge of translation and negotiation, the *inbetween* space – that carries the burden of the meaning of

culture … by exploring [as opposed to dominating] this Third Space, we may elude the politics of polarity [adult/child in our case] and emerge as the others of our selves.

(Bhabha 2004: 38)

I have inserted my own engagement with this in the brackets to help with the meaning, though I am not convinced by the last idea of emerging as the 'other of our selves' because of the special case of the adult/child discourse in the context I will be looking into, because we are not dealing with a master/servant dialectical idea, and I will address this issue, but what interests me first of all is the 'space *in-between*' and what I called the 'third way' above

Bhabha writes later that 'to exist is to be called into relation to an otherness' (ibid.: 44) and he quotes Jacqueline Rose (yes the same one) saying, 'It is the relation of this demand to the place of the object it claims that becomes the basis for identification' (ibid.[8]). Rose, as we have previously noted, essentially describes the 'place of the object' as provided by the adult as a means of domination but Bhabha does not. He says: 'it is the "inter"– … that carries the burden of the meaning of culture … ', which is negotiated by 'exploring' as opposed to 'dominating', and the difference between Rose and Bhabha is palpable in this.

Of course, this may just be wishful thinking on my part, but Bhabha's entire postcolonial theoretical position (for which he is renowned) pivots on this idea of exploration, hence my appropriation here. It does need more exploration and explanation but surely 'exploring' the radically different but real social space that exists between adult and child, who is contingent and genuinely temporary, where the adult, via a text, can visit the 'exploring' child rather than have the child come to the text to be dominated by it, is a real and radical prospect.

The post-Fanon, post-colonial's exploration case lies in the spirit of the colonial subject's 'right to translate' their own stories – as opposed to having their narrative imposed by a foreign other. Therein, it could say, lies identity. The problem in the child/adult situation is the mutability of the child in the face of adult discourse and indeed the problem that it cannot 'yet' narrate its own story, which is only just in formation. But it raises the following important question (and I would like you to refer back to the comments I made on the *Harry Potter* series earlier): if the reading child understands what is being written, does this not mean all the adult writer is doing is 'articulating' what the child already knows, while and at the same time helping the child to understand something it doesn't know by allowing the child to explore the radical, comfortably predictable and the unsettlingly unexpected special *social space that is childhood*? In this sense, the *Harry Potter* series as that 'eccentric blend of the comfortably predictable and the unsettlingly unexpected' comes to represent much more than just a description of Rowling's work. Indeed it becomes a talisman in describing child and adult literacy, knowledge, culture and ongoing experience.

If the location of culture is being met at the bridge, at the space *in-between*, is there not accord of sorts because surely it is also true that the adult author has no interest in writing unless the exercise, to paraphrase Foucault, 'failed to teach the *author* something he hadn't known before … ' (Foucault 1984: 339). But crucially too, while it is not the same space as that occupied by those other demographic categories, because the child truly is in a process of becoming, not being, the child, as the woman, the black person,

the gay in waiting, the oppressed minority, will in time come to enter a state of being permanently 'other' but can this really allow us to ignore the continual special case all children grow through and out of?

Of course, there are normative issues already defined in this idea and the problems they create overlap to a considerable degree, but to write without being aware of this is seriously questionable. It is impossible, I suspect, to propose a non-exclusionist normative definition of textual engagement in writing for children, but surely a normative structure that clarifies the intrinsic distinctiveness of child-centred storytelling can be proposed? I was fifteen films, ten picture books and ten novels into still learning this. I couldn't fail to learn, I am still learning as I write this and my relationship with writing for children continues to be challenged by this same idea – how could it not? It may be that I am the more experienced in the relationship but I would be a fool to suggest that writing teaches me nothing. Like Don Delillo, 'I write to find out what I know' and then some more.

Granted, the child is not, any more than the adult, but the space in-between remains as a metaphorical site where each 'other' has the right to negotiate and try to understand their own stories as well as the 'other's' stories. For a child, the problem is their narrative voice is not yet mature enough to articulate theirs. But just because there is not an instant response it does not mean they are not capable of thinking and knowing and indeed beginning to form the vocabulary, and it is more complex than we may think. As Jean Baudrillard says:

> A strategy of this kind is far from innocent. It is the strategy adopted by children. Whereas adults make children believe that they, the adults, are adults, children for their part *let* adults believe that they, the children, are children … They *are* children, but they do not believe it. They sail under the flag of childhood as under a flag of convenience … It is in this sense that the child is other to the adult …
>
> (Baudrillard 1990: 192)

In Rose's terms the child is 'secured' and forced to know itself through the mediation of the imaginary child in the book. But the writer of such a text fails to recognise that the child coming to the book doesn't recognise the bogeyman being presented as its doppelganger. The book is an adult written, 'child-centred discourse' that relies on children allowing themselves to be treated as such when in fact they just see themselves as people who do not, as yet, do adult stuff, which they may know about but as yet do not have the vocabulary to articulate. Although this is just as likely to be driving a car, cooking the dinner and being a school teacher or parent than the sexualised, post-Freudian reading, which Rose offers. Neither do I expect to secure and seduce the 'imagined' child at the border or indeed be met by a passive, compliant child whose willingness to enter the encounter renders it vulnerable to my own desire. Such an idea seems both a preposterous and unlikely strategy that denies the 'child' exists at all and indeed that the writer has no ethical understanding of the 'other' as an ongoing project of development. Therefore part of the maturing child voice is already preparing its opening argument and response – the job of the writer is to know this because such an understanding allows for the meeting at the bridge or the space in-between for mutual exploration. As Baudrillard also says:

> … [T]he secret of philosophy may not be to know oneself, nor to know where one is going, but rather to go where the other is going; not to dream oneself, but rather to dream what others dream; not to believe oneself, but rather to believe in those

who do believe: to give priority to all determinants from elsewhere. Whether they are legible or not, decipherable or not, is of no consequence – the main thing is to embrace the foreign form of any event, any object, any fortuitous being, because in any case you will never know who you are.

(Baudrillard 1990: 187–88)

The child is already trying to get to know you; the least you can do is reciprocate. This quotation comes from a chapter entitled 'The Declination of Wills'; declination means a polite refusal and to take it personally as I do. As a writer I politely refuse to be sucked into the space that persists between adult and child without first declaring that I do not expect contact to be mediated by my will alone. Writing is an art form and as such its engagement with words, culture and communication allows it to try and negotiate other cultural practices and normative ideas with a critical and creative vigilance – and it is in this sense that I consider writing for children to be a critically creative and creatively critical process that comes with a huge burden of responsibility.

I will expand on Baudrillard's exploration later as I move forward with the critical ideas, but I return to the point when we were driving to the French coast (remember this?). I was thinking about a theoretical idea when the pugnacious pop singer, Pixie Lott, sang, 'I got your emails/ You just don't get females/ now do you?'[9] I am an adult not a child; a man not a woman; white not black; not a colonial subject (although being a Scotsman might count); not in a repressed sexual minority etc., but I understand feminism, racism, post-colonial criticism, sexual and textual politics, queer theory, eco theory and so on. I cannot read like a child in the way proposed by a 'childist criticism' (for example) because as an adult I simply don't know how each 'child', who are all different, reads (Hunt 1991: 16) any more than I can read like a woman. But as Gayatri Spivak has already written: 'The position that only the subaltern can know the subaltern, only women can know women [only a child can know a child] and so on so … predicates the possibility of knowledge on identity … ' (Spivak 1988: 253–54), so why, we might ask, should we struggle so much with 'child-centred' discourse?

Of course we do not and will not all agree on everything on the subject, but do feminists, etc., agree with each other all of the time? I think not. The apostrophe in 'children's' denies the possessive participle but it does not and cannot exclude the associative. To deny that a child cannot meet at the space between adult-written, child-centred discourse and their own, often capricious, understanding of the world loses sight of the fact that children are other and themselves, not constructions of us and ourselves (or should that be me and myself, for I cannot speak for all men either?), but just like ourselves (as adults) are continually engaged in the discourse of experience, that 'eccentric blend of the comfortably predictable and the unsettlingly unexpected'. As Reynolds has written:

> With this in mind, children's literature can be equated with the 'monster child' that Jean-François Lyotard associated with creativity and the potential for change: 'The monster child is not the father of the man; it is what, in the midst of man, throws him off course [*son* décours]; it is the possibility or risk of being set adrift' …
>
> (Reynolds in Maybin and Watson 2009: 101)

What we can do as writers and cultural practitioners is help to make the 'connections' and this is where I will go next.

# Chapter 4

# The (im)possibility of writing for children ...

As David Rudd, and John Gordon before him, has shown, 'The boundary between imagination and reality, and the boundary between being a child and being an adult are border country, a passionate place in which to work' (Rudd, in Hunt 2004: 35; Gordon 1975: 35). Now this will take much more explanation than this short quotation gives (and I will move onto this soon). But let us make no mistake, at the meeting point, the border, the cusp of the bridge, the child is not a passive product of the adult on the other side. The writer is not crossing over to colonise the child subject but to engage, not through desire but to acknowledge that the child is a young person who is to be encouraged even helped to grow into a free citizen while and at the same time the adult continues to learn and experience too. And this takes us to the next stage of our thinking on the (im)possibility of writing for children. I should stress here that I am less taken with the idea of 'border' as opposed to a 'bridge', it is only an ideological difference, depending on how you read it, but I am with Primo Levi when he says: 'I always thought that [building] bridges is the best job there is ... because roads go over bridges, and without roads we'd still be savages. In short, bridges are the opposite of borders, and borders are where wars start' (Levi 1986), but this message will become clearer as we progress.

Returning to Rose's idea that neither child nor adult enter the space in between author and reader, it is obvious that I do not agree. I think I have addressed this at length but we have to take this forward and I will do so by referring to ideas that have hitherto been ignored in this field. But in moving on I would say that while the hybrid idea of addressing the 'constructed' and 'constructive' idea of the child in theoretical terms seems alive and an ideal explanation to the vexed questions raised by the critical discourses raised and previously discussed, it just doesn't work as a solution. Surely the constructed child 'is not', any more than the adult, so the question we should be addressing is what does happen when the bridge across the gap is recognised? Crucial to understanding this is that once again we have to disagree with critics, with Walter Benjamin, for example, when he suggests that when a child reader comes to a book they read it with limitless trust.[1] Well I just don't believe a child comes to anything with limitless trust, no more than the rest of us. I admit my scepticism and cynicism may have been sharpened over the years but despite the comfortably predictable aspects of my life, I am still cautious of the unexpected; who could not be? We have to return again to the idea that children occupy a radically different social space from the one hitherto investigated in this hybrid notion. Once again it is because theirs is contingent and genuinely temporary; in a way that is only ever shadowed in all the other demographic categories, they truly are in a process not being, but becoming one of us.

In a discussion of what he calls the 'hidden adult' in writing for children, Perry Nodelman says that he keeps arriving at the same conclusion, which is that the 'simplicity of texts of children's literature is only half the truth about them. They also possess a shadow, an unconscious – a more complex and more complete understanding of the world ... [which is] not childlike' (2008: 206). He uses Rudd's reading of the 'other', viz, 'Without recognition of what it is different from, differences cannot be sustained. Hence difference is always tainted by "the other", and must always be dependent upon it ... Children's literature is different, certainly, yet intimately bound to its parent literature, hence the slippage' (Rudd 1996: 8–17). And that 'slippage,' says Nodelman, 'allows the hidden adult ... ' (op. cit.) to remain present, which is to say that the 'not childlike' shadow in writing for children is the 'hidden adult', which is the central premise of his book with the same name.

To some extent this gets to the heart of the (im)possibility debate I will be trying to unfold. Because for me the 'adult' presence in an 'adult, child-centred' cultural product is ever present and in fact, far from being hidden, it is the elephant in the room. Everyone can see it and while as adults we may choose to ignore it (i.e., by not playing with children's toys, watching children's television or reading books written for children) its existence is no secret. In fact how could it be? Indeed surely it's a good thing that the 'simplicity of texts of children's literature is only half the truth about them'. But what does make me a little uncomfortable is the idea of this 'shadow' they possess, the unconscious, a more complex and more complete understanding of the world, which is not childlike. Because it seems to me that the word 'shadow' is used to imply something sinister, otherwise why use this word and its bogeyman qualification? Nodelman also suggests this shadow could possess an unsaid 'variety of forms of knowledge – sexual, cultural, historical – theoretically only available to and only understandable by adults' (Nodelman 2008: 206) so the shadow is considered to be adult just for that reason. But this too is problematic.

Going back to Nodelman's opening idea on the simplicity of texts, the problem lies in thinking how 'simplicity' in relation to texts can be defined, if at all, and indeed in using such terms may the text not also conceal the 'hidden child', lurking in a similar if not the same shadow? It seems to me that in investing a great deal of time looking for the (so-called) hidden adult issues in child-centred texts then surely too the child reader may be reading something I as an adult may not? Because the question remains, while my fantasies and socio-cultural experience may be more inclined to reflect my ageing years they do not and cannot pretend to be the same as those of someone much younger although they are equally relevant to them. We should look at this more closely because Nodelman is talking about 'not childlike' being 'inextricably tied up in binary habits of thinking' (Nodelman 2008: 206), which, as I have already revealed, make me uneasy because I think there is both a 'hidden' child and adult in the text that is negotiated through the text, and recognition of this is crucial.

Following on from the above, I still find Baudrillard's idea on the 'other' and 'otherness' useful although it is often a convenient hook to hang a theoretical coat on. But the issue here is that all too often the debate or critical discourse is simplified into a 'them' and 'us' that do not exist.

Let's visit the Baudrillard quotation again in shortened form:

> ... [T]he secret of philosophy may not be to know oneself, nor to know where one is going, but rather to go where the other is going ... Whether they are legible or

not, decipherable or not, is of no consequence – the main thing is to embrace the foreign form of any event, any object, any fortuitous being, because in any case you will never know who you are.

(Baudrillard 1990: 187–88)

In identifying with the 'other' as a binary idea, i.e., that a 'child' is simply 'other' to me as an 'adult', cannot be the end of the story because of course children are equally 'other' to each other, as are adults, viz: male-to-female, female-to-male, female-to-female and male-to-male – and that is just a start because we have race, sexuality, etc., to deal with too. And I am still drawn to this idea, which I repeat here:

> Whereas adults make children believe that they, the adults, are adults, children for their part *let* adults believe that they, the children, are children ... They *are* children, but they do not believe it. They sail under the flag of childhood as under a flag of convenience ... It is in this sense that the child is other to the adult ...
>
> (Baudrillard 1990: 192)

This also makes the idea that both adults and children caught up in the dialogic[2] web of discourse much more interesting. Indeed, Bakhtin might call it *heteroglossia* where the many layers and multiple voices of the author, the characters, the narrator, the genre and the reader combine in an energetic, inter-illuminating joust on the bridge.[3] If all along we consider that the adult is the coloniser and the child the colonised we lose sight of the fact that the child is complicit in the idea only to the extent that it pleases the adult for it to be so. For children do occupy a radically different social space and only have ten reading years (if that) before he or she is 'one of us', and a normative structure that clarifies the intrinsic distinctiveness of child-centred storytelling can be proposed. This also returns me to my earlier assertion then (and still in ellipses) that ... childhood is not the opposite of adulthood; it is not solved by adulthood; it is not preparation for adulthood, it is childhood and children (young people, young persons) are children (young people, young persons) not apprentice adults ... Nevertheless, there is something inherently persuasive about the 'flag of convenience' here, too. So let's wave it at the critics next.

Children should be seen and not heard, is a saying we have all encountered at some time in our lives. Indeed when I typed 'how to keep children quiet' into Google while I was writing this, I received 2,540,000 results in (0.16 seconds),[4] which isn't a bad tally at all but did anyone ever stop and ask why this phrase is often directed at children and yet (and at the same time) the idea of the 'quiet child' is met with suspicion? 'Must be up to something' is the oft-repeated, obvious supposition. This is because they are occupying social space that the adult knows little about because the child does not speak of it. And okay, I know this is immensely reductionist of me to even propose but it does help us to understand Baudrillard's idea above (without overcomplicating it). Because surely, while the writer for children is engaged in a 'child-centred' discourse, the child too is often engaged in the 'adult and child-centred' discourse, both and at the same time, thus the shadows Nodelman refers to are just that, shadows, the instantly recognisable forms of those out in the open, which, as every writer, especially of fiction, recognises, depends on the 'shadows of imagination [and] that willing suspension of disbelief for the moment'.[5]

This criss-crossing of adult-centred and child-centred discourse only serves to remind us that all discourse is about making connections. How can it not be the case that my experience does not filter into a text written by me for someone less so? In anthropological terms it would be called 'diffusion', where ultimately every culture borrows from other cultures and incorporates it into their own; equally children and adults are tangled up in the same language,[6] which is only differentiated by 'experience'. The fact that the adult does it noisily and the child quietly (at the adult's request) does not remove the burden of suspicion from the child and it should be remembered that the *différence* inherent in cultural knowledge *adds to* but does not *add up to* a dominant ideology. I should probably resist saying this but the adult in children's literature is less hidden than the child. This is because the adult is articulating for the child, while and at the same time the child who knows more than it can articulate is learning how to articulate its own story, while also learning something new. So we return to this idea that I have written about before because nothing in between has really challenged it (Melrose 2001: 39) and it relates to Rose saying (again): 'Children's fiction sets up a world in which the adult comes first (author, maker, giver) and the child comes after (reader, product, receiver), but where neither of them enter the space in between' (Rose 1984: 1–2), which takes me right back to the opening of this book.

I think this next issue is a huge, albeit ignored idea that we should be addressing in more detail than hitherto it has been. This 'space in between' is one of experience. The gap is between the child and the author or parent's experience, between the experience of authority and the child's inexperience. It is the writer's job to try and recognise the gap by providing a text allowing it to be bridged. How, though? Well knowing about it helps but let's think it through. Rightly, in my view, the children's psychoanalyst, Adam Phillips, observes:

> Children unavoidably treat their parents as though they were experts on life ... but children make demands on adults which adults don't know what to do with ... once they [children] learn to talk they create, and suffer, a certain unease about what they can do with words. Paradoxically, it is the adult's own currency – words – that reveals to them the limits of adult authority ... Adults can nurture children ... but they do not have the answers ... *what they can do is tell children stories about the connections* ...
>
> (Phillips 1995: 1–2)

For the writer, making the connections is the first job she or he has, and I share the wisdom of Milan Kundera here by repeating his idea that '[writing] is the art that created the fascinating imaginative realm where no one owns the truth and everyone has the right to be understood' (Kundera 2000: 159), and to take him a little further down this road, where 'Every novel says to the reader: Things are not as simple as you think ... ' (ibid.: 18). What we can do as writers is help with the *connections* because the child that comes to the book is already an intelligent person and it is the writer's job to know that. Thus, the connections are the sites of exploration already exposed by Bhabha in remembering: The child is not. Anymore than the adult.

Walter Benjamin wrote, 'Familiar though his name may be to us, the storyteller in his living immediacy is by no means a present force. He has already become something remote from us and something that is getting even more distant' (Benjamin 1973: 83).

His words are prophetic (since they were written in 1936) and to an extent I agree with them; this is only the emergent age of internet technology and already the parameters are expanding day by day. However, when Benjamin went on to say, ' ... the art of story-telling is coming to an end ... ' he entered a different debate and one I cannot agree with. There is a simplicity to this and once again it comes up against the idea that *children understand more than they can articulate at all the stages of their life.* Crucially, the role of storytelling and the designated site of storytelling in the twenty-first century, in writing for children (whether in books, television, electronic gaming, internet engagement – although Facebook™, etc., we will come to later), exist as a site for nurture and it is a space the writer and the child approach with caution – while knowing all the while that the child, being naturally less cautious, will not (it has to be hoped) be exposed to the inherent dangers. Now I know this is a contentious area for critics and there is a common view that 'Children's literature is literature that claims to be devoid of adult content that nevertheless lurks within' (Nodelman 2008: 341), but for writers, surely that idea is the big so what! This is the crucial area we have to address next because I contend that the 'adult' in child-centred culture is a force for good, as long as the 'hidden child' is not written out of the story, as I will now show.

\*

While the child already understands more than he or she can articulate, surely it can be said (again) that the reading experience is inherently no different from that which we all experience? We all of us come to a book, a text, a film, a website, etc., knowing what we already know, even if the writer of the content, issues, ideas, etc., can articulate it better than we could expect to, but at the same time we are all looking for something new, surely. This is certainly the case for me, whether I am reading my way through the huge library of English literature, or the Persian poet Rumi,[7] or the Italian writer Italo Calvino, or the Japanese writer Haruki Murakami in translation, or attending a biennale or a Picasso exhibition, or watching a Coen brothers' movie, I understand much but also and at the same time I am hoping to learn or receive something new. In fact 'hoping' is probably the wrong word, I unfailingly learn something new about the human condition, for that is what art does. It is about making connections with a critically creative and creatively critical engagement. It is the story of a self-conscious engagement with narrative, experimenting with form and processes that are still being shown to be connected to older stories and art forms, from whence they came as they are taken forward. As Jacques Derrida has said, the ' ... future, this beyond, is not another time, a day after history. It is *present* at the heart of experience. Present not as a total presence but as a *trace*.'[8]

It is in this sense then that the experience of the artist may help the child expand his or her field of vision through the vicarious experience of meeting at the space in-between. But so too with a child, for does the adult have nothing to gain or to learn from the less experienced? Indeed surely it is modernism acknowledging its historical antecedents in creating the new – the artistic narrative, the story, is surely one about connecting the experience of past times for a new audience. Out of the old comes the new, it is not an end of history or a death of the story and storyteller but new ways of colluding and adapting to ever-increasing demands of delivery, it is the exploration of life itself taking place in the space in-between. If I am engaged in child-centred art I would be a foolish artist to think I was the only person in the space would I not?

This issue of meeting at the point of knowing, knowledge and experience, to then go on to find out something new, or other, or different, or strange is not new, it is not some erstwhile twenty-first-century invention but the simple ongoing experience inherent in the act of engagement with culture and art, and indeed in the very act of reading. It is not a passive act but an act of participation in which artist and audience and the writer and reader are mediated by the cultural text. Walter Benjamin might have referred to this as the trading of experiences, the *Erfahrung*, where the shift between 'lived through' and 'narratable experience' is seen as a point of arbitration and negotiation, an exploration of ideas. For the writer, Dorothea Brande has a simple take on this: 'It is well to understand as early as possible in one's writing life that there is just one contribution which every one of us can make: we can give into the common pool of experience some comprehension of the world as it looks to each of us' (Brande 1934: 120).

In writing for children the writer comes up against issues the child will and will not be aware of due to the varying levels of experience, mostly (though not necessarily) dictated by years and ageing. In acknowledging the child as (an)other, though, the writer offers to nurture and share his own experience as a lived out experience for the child, so that the child too can begin to 'make the connections' between what he or she knows and knows not. There is an intimacy in this communication, which is personal and yet the 'death of the author'[9] never seemed more appropriate as a totem of necessity.

In order for the child to be able to reach into the space the author can do so as an absent presence, mediated by the book, the story, he or she has created. The author gives his authority over to the story he has created so that the child may engage in a world that has been re-represented so that 'experience' can be offered vicariously for the child to receive. This has been a tenet of stories and storytelling for centuries, has it not? Little Red's wolf; the danger of the gingerbread house; the biblical good Samaritan; Solomon having control over the winds and demons (jinns) in the Quran, the world is full of myths, fables and fairy tales; it is a cross-cultural, cross-national, cross-gender, etc., endeavour enabled by the storyteller who is bringing wisdom to light as a mediator of cultural life.

In this sense, the cultural product of writing for children, such as the novel, is central to the intimate relationship of nurture and experience in finding out the connections in the stories that make up our lives. Although, at the moment the child engages with the text, the adult writer (storyteller) is already standing aside, making her or himself absent in the knowledge that the child has not come to the text in ignorance but as a knowing person who is curious to know more about the connections.

Rose has stated that 'neither of them enter the space in-between' (Rose 1984) and yet the space in between is occupied. Not as a site of adult desire (although its possibility is not denied) but I repeat what I wrote around 7,000 words ago (lest you forgot): Bhabha writes that 'to exist is to be called into relation to an otherness … ' (2004: 44) and he quotes Rose saying: 'It is the relation of this demand to the place of the object it claims that becomes the basis for identification' (op. cit.[10]). The 'place of the object … is the "inter" … that carries the burden of meaning of culture', which is negotiated by 'exploring' as opposed to 'dominating' and the difference between Rose and Bhabha is palpable. The child is exploring the boundaries of its own knowledge by arriving at the mediated 'space in-between'.

I think it very important to say here that I am completely behind Peter Hunt's suggestion, way back in 1991, when he implies that as writers we should be heading for a position

that says, 'This text has certain potentials for interaction, certain possibilities of meaning' (Hunt 1991: 83), because therein lie the connections between what we know and have yet to learn. But as Hunt also says, we are now thinking here about the text and the reader.

That children are developing readers seems a sensible thing to say, but when we align it to the statistic that half of the UK workforce (around 16 million people) has the average reading age of a child of around 11–12 years old,[11] which is also the target range of the average tabloid newspaper in the UK, we should begin to realise the task at hand. As I have written elsewhere: 'it's a quite extraordinary view of both that population and the target readership of novels (i.e., readers) – especially when it's borne in mind that such newspapers are required to have sentences with only one verb, no subordinate clauses and usually only single, sensational qualifiers or modifiers such as "sensational"' (Melrose 2007: 112). With this idea in mind, though, I was thinking that as a statistic it looks pretty bad, but then I also thought, surely it can be concluded that actually the idea of being a 'developing reader' is almost universal. I am a university professor with a PhD in literary studies but I could never say I was no longer developing my reading skills. For me, personally, it's a life exercise in making the connections in the pursuit of knowledge that is always just around the next corner, over the next hill, across the next stream, under the next rainbow and ... well you get the picture. I write (and read) to find out what I know, and know not, and then some more I hope to know.

This confession from me only serves to confirm what Phillips has already written, which is that 'adults are not fully competent with their own instruments, but there is nobody else for the child to appeal to. Children go on asking, of course, but eventually they have to settle for the adult's exhausted impatience, and the *fictions of life*'(Phillips 1995). But it's when Phillips goes on to qualify this that it becomes useful to the writer for children. He says, children's questions, 'just like the answers, can be baffling', going on to add, in *The Interpretation of Dreams*, Freud wrote: 'nothing can be brought to an end, nothing is past or forgotten.' 'Curiosity is endless ... in a way that answers are not' (ibid.). I love that idea of endless curiosity, constantly seeking answers.

But this is where the writer has to step into the space between by providing a text that tells the reader who and what people are, what it is to live a life and what life can and is supposed to look like, what the writer does is to make 'connections between curiosity and nurture' (ibid.) through storytelling, where 'ideally childhood is a series of reciprocal accommodations (or "attunements" as they are now often referred to in an uneasy mixing of analogies)' (ibid.: 4). And it seems appropriate to say here (I am substituting 'analyst' in the original quotation for 'writer', why will be self evident):

> ... the [writer] is not only the one who is supposed to know; he is the one who knows that he is supposed to know, which is to know something of extraordinary consequence – to know, as every child does somewhere, the sense in which nobody knows the answers. Childhood innocence is not naive trust, it is incredulity (what the child has to repress is an ironic scepticism).
>
> (Ibid.: 2)

The (im)possibility of writing for children is preceded by the knowledge that children grow up by being listened to but the adult writer does not have all the answers to child questions, all they can do is tell children stories about the connections. And this sums up the debate for me, as I have already written:

The idea of nurture is a persuasive one. The so-called space between the child and the adult/writer is actually the place where the two collide, where the story exists, where experience and knowledge is nurtured and where real contact is made. Children do catch their parents/storytellers up (it is what growing up is all about – it is why the process is nurtured) and so in the meantime, on their catch up journey the storyteller can only ' … tell children stories about the connections'. So the issue becomes not 'why should we?' write for children but 'how?': to say 'story' articulates our existence, our essence, our very being as a thinking species, is a fact but it is no longer enough. It is necessary to understand it.

(Butt ed., 2007: 24)

The gap is already bridged as an extended part of dialogic experience and cultural exchange as an ongoing creatively critical and critically creative, ontological and episte-mological process of writing for reading and reading and writing where it has to be understood that ' … the full meaning of experience is not simply given in the reflexive immediacy of the lived moment but emerges from explicit retrospection where meaning is recovered and re-enacted … '.[12] It requires awareness not only of the adult's own currency, 'words', but also of the cultural context and of the world that is being constructed through the story. But the adult recognises something in the child too, it is not a one-way street of imposed power but a realisation that wrapped up in the imaginative idea of a child and childhood, we adults do not have all the stories.

In thinking about this here, I am reminded of Roland Barthes' chapter 'Toys' in the appropriately named book, *Mythologies* (Barthes 1972: 53–55), which I will address because it seems to me that he does have something indirect but interesting to say about reading, even if the chapter is about adult toys for children to play with.

Clearly, a book, a DVD, a film is not a toy, even if it has entered the lexicon of entertainment for cultural consumption. The problem with toys made for children, suggests Barthes (and we must remember this was written nearly 40 years ago), is that they are 'commonly … a microcosm of the adult world … as if … the child was … nothing but a small man'. And he goes on to say the 'child can only identify himself as owner, as user, never as creator; he does not invent the world, he uses it … '. But this is simply a wrong analysis. The toys he refers to may indeed be 'the alibi of a Nature which has at all times created soldiers, postmen and Vespas … and all the things an adult does not find unusual: war, bureaucracy, ugliness, Martians etc.' (ibid.: 53–54). But he com-pletely misses the point of play. Here is a very small biographical example that cannot be unique. I bought my children a computer so they could play games on it and (yes I admit it) to introduce them to a tool they will become more adept at using than I, in time. Having spent a goodly time unpacking it, assembling all the bits, plugging in all the wires, loading all the software, etc., I switched it on and went triumphantly to fetch them. Not now, they replied, they were sitting in the boxes, wearing eye patches and playing pirates. They had taken their own needs to the situation and turned it into their world. What was it Freud said?:

Should we not look for traces of imaginative activity as early as in childhood … ? Might we not say that every child at play behaves like a creative writer, in that he creates a world of his own, or, rather, rearranges the things of his world in a new way, which pleases him. It would be wrong to think he does not take life seriously

and he expends large amounts of emotion on it ... The creative writer does the same as a child at play. He creates a world of fantasy which he takes very seriously – that is, which he invests with large amounts of emotion – while separating it sharply from reality. *Language has preserved this relationship between children's play and poetic creation* (my italics).

(Freud 1990: 131–32)

Why should reading be considered any more passive when we are already addressing a creative being? We could, like Barthes' toys, present a text to children that encourages our adult way of thinking about how our society is ordered and organised but this does not mean we can expect compliance from our readers who bring their own transformative energies and their own ideas of their world to the text.

In accepting the above premise we need to take the idea further. According to Harper, 'Stories are our primary mode and means of exchange' (Butt ed., 2007: 152), and according to Bruno Bettelheim:

If we hope to live not just from moment to moment, but in true consciousness of our existence, then our greatest need and most difficult achievement is to find meaning in our lives ... [but] ... Contrary to the ancient myth, wisdom does not burst forth fully developed like Athena out of Zeus's head: it is built up, small step by small step from most irrational beginnings. Only in adulthood can an intelligent understanding of the meaning of one's existence in this world be gained from one's *experience* in it ... The child, as he develops, must learn step by step to understand himself better; with this he becomes more able to understand others ... In ways that are mutually satisfying and meaningful.

(Bettelheim 1976: 3)

And so once again we are confronted by the idea that stories are the means by which the connections of 'experience' are made – and equally, to read Bettelheim: 'In ways that are mutually satisfying and meaningful' (ibid.), because this takes us straight back to our understanding that the space in-between the writer and his child reader is negotiated by the 'exploring' 'mutually' and not one (the author) dominating the other – which brings us back to the Barthes' 'toys' idea above. Thus what I propose to do in the next chapter is take a journey through ideas on storytelling to reveal *what* the writer for children might offer in the negotiated space in-between. What I am *not* going to do is show the *how* to do it, because that will take place in Part 2 of this book, but I aim to reveal how I *see* it being possible.

It is in this sense, then, that the writer and the reader are involved in a shared project, where the writer must ask him or herself not, *am I a good storyteller*? But, *what kind of person do I want to* be? Because when you are faced with your reader, there will be many (especially critics) who will queue up to offer an answer to the first. Faced with the second question, however, as Phillips reveals, 'there may be terrors but there are no experts' (1995: op. cit.).

# Chapter 5

# Elements of storytelling for children

I return us to the highly persuasive but seriously understated idea that 'Adults can nurture children … but they do not have the answers … *what they can do is tell children stories about the connections* … ' (Phillips 1995: 1–2). As I have written elsewhere, and discussed above, storytelling is the key that opens the door to the connections that help us make sense of the world, from faith to fortune and everything in-between, as we grow in experience from children into adults, embracing spiritual, physical, irrational and intellectual uncertainty – it is the key to the future for the world's children and their children's children. Television, the internet, 24/7 media, etc., throws information at children at such a speed it is impossible to keep up with it. As Melvyn Burgess has reflected, there are few secrets we can keep from children these days: ' … in a world more embedded in fictions than ever, in the form not just of books but gaming, politics, film, TV, adverts, even education, kids are probably more able than their parents to appreciate the different ways *stories* are used [my italics]'.[1]

Thus, if we can keep them in the story loop, which is the site of both nurture and exploration, we can encourage them to think about the stories that will make up the connections in their lives; that define their existence; the rich intertextuality of their lives; the narrative that sustains their continuing sense of being in the communities in which we all of us co-exist, so that they may keep questioning the issues that threaten them: poverty, inequality, poor ethics, maltreatment, and so on. If we give up exploring the story, challenging the story, intervening in the narrative, defying closure in the tale, we allow the dictators, tyrants, despots and downright bad guys the last word – the world's children deserve better and writers for children should know this (Melrose 2010). As I have already said above, though it is worth repeating, Walter Benjamin might have referred to this as the trading of experiences, the *Erfahrung*, where the shift between 'lived through' and 'narratable experience' is seen as a point of arbitration and negotiation, an exploration of ideas.

It would be foolish to think children do not know much of this too, albeit in a less articulate way, and this has been a central argument in this entire book. Burgess concurs, as writers, storytellers, educators, parents, guardians, etc., we need to remember that children 'appreciate the different ways *stories* are used'. There is little point in writing for children in any capacity if you do not recognise who and what a child is, which is not the mute figure, proposed by other critics, but a very noisy person indeed who is getting smarter and noisier by the minute. Nevertheless their development and understanding of narrative, culture and the self is an ongoing mutual exploration undertaken by a mutual understanding that childhood is not the opposite of adulthood, is not solved by adulthood, is not preparation for adulthood, is not an apprenticeship for adulthood.

Where I find myself disagreeing with Walter Benjamin is his notion that the *Erfahrung* effect of storytelling, the ability to exchange experience, is lost to us because the story-teller is already distanced by the way twenty-first-century storytelling is disseminated, through books, TV, the internet, etc. Neither do I accept the homogenisation, deper-sonalisation and fragmentation threat either. This is because I agree with Jack Zipes when he says: 'genuine storytelling is not only subversive but magical in that it transforms the ordinary into the extraordinary and makes us appreciate and take notice of the little things in life that we would normally overlook' (Zipes 2002a: 135). But for me it's not just the 'little things' but all things that can be touched by a story context and I addressed this before with my colleague, Neil McCaw:

> … anxiety about the ideological implications of the narrative form is, I think, what lies behind the many (post)modern claims that the story is dead. There are no more good stories, apparently. We have lost the know-how necessary to tell a good tale. Rubbish. We may have become inhibited in our storytelling, or too anxious about the implications of our narratives, but that is not the same thing as there being nothing else to tell. Neither, as Christopher Booker would have us believe,[2] is it a case that there are no original stories left. The argument that all stories fit within one of a limited number of 'types' (rags to riches, quest, voyage and return, hero as monster, rebirth etc. etc.) is (to me, sorry) a depressingly reductive one. It's a bit like saying that modern football isn't exciting anymore because all the goals scored can be reduced to one of seven major types: the tap-in, the long-range shot, the header, the acrobatic goal, the own goal, the deflection, and the fluke. It smacks of the worst excesses of structuralism, which we have (thankfully) recovered from. It also smacks of a kind of fatalism that is the literary equivalent of Francis Fukuyama's *The End of History*. Yes I know that we are damn jolly clever these days, but does that HAVE to mean that we yawn at everything?
>
> (Melrose and McCaw in Butt ed., 2007: 21–22)

Once again, surely it's all about intervening to make connections! It is about separating scholarship from a twittering and wittering culture, where everyone has an immediate opinion and Wikipedia, the free encyclopedia, at the end of their fingers. Stories are there to be explored, critiqued and investigated. It is one of those rare private moments in culture and society that defines us as human, *homo fabula*, *homo historia*, we use stories to make the connections in our lives. And I fully endorse Philip Pullman's view of this when he says:

> As a passionate believer in the democracy of reading, I don't think it's the task of the author of a book to tell the reader what it means. The meaning of a story emerges in the meeting between the words on the page and the thoughts in the reader's mind. So when people ask me what I meant by this story, or what was the message I was trying to convey in that one, I have to explain that I'm not going to explain. Anyway, I'm not in the message business; I'm in the 'Once upon a time' business.[3]

'If you look at my face I am somebody, if you look at my back I am nobody; who am I?'[4] The dilemma of a riddle, such as this, is hardly a safe place to begin a chapter on storytelling. But surely this is the truth of it – the fact is stories are full of half truths,

oxymorons, paradoxes, inconsistencies, absurdity, contradictions, illogical ideas, strangeness, otherness, familiarity, intimacy, formality, informality, knowledge, wisdom, know how, erudition, culture, learning and, let's be honest, everything, even the downright daft. And yet even the daft is not without controlled meaning and meaningfulness, like in this exchange:

> ' "Angus Solomon," sighed Ms Lowry, "is that a penis you've drawn in your exercise book?"
>
> Angus jumped, startled, and remembered where he was. Ms Lowry was standing next to his desk, staring down at the page. Other kids were sniggering. Angus felt his mouth go dry and his heart speed up. For a second he thought about lying. He decided to. "No miss, it's a submarine."
>
> Ms Lowry nodded grimly. "I thought as much," she said ...'
>
> (Gleitzman 1998: 3)

Now we could be forgiven for thinking the meaning of this exchange is obvious, until, that is, we get the twist (and the information that Angus had decided to lie):

> ' "Now stop wasting time and draw a penis like I asked you to." She pointed to the one she'd drawn on the blackboard.
>
> That's not fair, thought Angus. I wasn't wasting time. He took a deep breath. "Excuse me, Miss," he said, "I wasn't wasting time. I was working on my pirate character for the school play. He lives in a submarine and ... "
>
> "Enough," interrupted Ms Lowry, "you know perfectly well play rehearsals aren't until tomorrow. Today we're doing human reproduction. I don't want to hear another word about pirates." '
>
> (Gleitzman 1998: 3)

At first glance, the mention of the word 'penis'[5] in the opening of a book written for children may be seen to be the shocking factor in the story. But for me it is the very real idea that Angus felt the need to lie and that the ellipses cutting off the end of his speech, ' "He lives in a submarine and ... " ' reveal much more about the difficulties I mentioned in the previous chapter, which is that ideally childhood is a series of reciprocal accommodations or attunements; for surely, while Ms Lowry has the power in this representative relationship, as a teacher speaking to a schoolboy, it is one that shows her meeting Angus head-to-head with a knowing appreciation.

As I revealed above, Nina Bawden suggested that when writing for children, 'You can, and should, leave out things that are beyond their comprehension' (Bawden 1974: 9). As I also commented it is a bit of nonsensical advice given in isolation in this context, but it does raise a fundamental question: what *is* beyond the comprehension of the child you are writing for? Bearing in mind I have made such a strong case above for both the adult and the child exploring the boundaries of their own knowledge by arriving at the mediated in-between space where exchange can take place, it is harder to pin down what is actually being explored. In a practical way I am extending this idea to suggest that it is life itself that is being explored. It may seem such a conceit to say this but for me this is the truth that underpins the processes of writing and reading and thereby thinking and living and being (which I will explore as this chapter proceeds).

If a writer has anything to give a reader it is the stories that carry the burden of the meaning of culture but the writer has to be aware of the reader at the other side of the equation and therefore their mutual engagement has to be one of ongoing exploration. Writing is essentially a tangle of words in which both the writer and reader try to find the lines of thought that help them to understand the world. And like Penelope's stitched story, keeping the suitors at bay, it is untangled and unpicked then rewritten constantly as the quest for meaning and knowledge accrues day by day (in the case of that story, for her boy Telemachus who spends the first four books of *The Odyssey* trying to gain knowledge of his father, Odysseus, whom he has never met). And then one day the learning child will become the giver of the ongoing narrative of experience.

Children understand more than they can articulate is a phrase I have already used, and it is a serious fallacy that their perceived lack of worldly experience makes them incapable of understanding that which is still beyond their field of experiential vision, or indeed their power of elocution. Indeed, young people are canny at segmenting commodities directed at them in all sorts of ways according to their cultural affiliations. Adding to which, they are so over-researched and consulted that many have developed clever strategies for dealing with it and indeed it is an ongoing battle of wills too.

This accounts for the *raison d'être* of web-based companies such as 'Dubit Research', which are based around this understanding, viz: 'Dubit has over ten years experience building relationships with young people and their parents, giving you unrivalled access to your key audiences. We are responsible, ethical, and we place the well-being of young people at the heart of all we do.'[6] In other words they research children so that child-centred products can be suitably targeted (and we come back to the cult of childhood). We ought to ask, what does this do to the child's sense of empowerment and indeed to the validity of the feedback in the virtual world? Because, in fact, a child should be able to come to a text, and here I mean a book, a film, a poem, a picture, etc., seeing how the familiarities of the world are represented and articulated, while, and at the same time, looking for and receiving something new. And this newness is something we can all relate to, surely, for none of us are beyond being surprised. Furthermore, I am not entirely convinced that researching the child as a consumer can really get to know the child.

For me this is modernism in action, narrative still being able to say something new, still denying the claims of pastiche and parody paraded by its postmodern imposters. And sometimes I see reading and writing's engagement with storytelling like this. We engage with the familiar, rearrange thoughts and ideas and then we hit a point of surprise and disbelief that we have to stop and (metaphorically) gaze at before we can react. It is the briefest point in the act of creative thought that comes before description, before language, which comes after the realisation and then becomes the story and the story of the story and stories, for they are all textual interventions on and representations of life thereafter.

Thus while children may view the world from a different viewpoint to their adult counterparts, as defined by age and experience, the astonishment and amazement at witnessing or hearing about the ongoing experience of sheer existence is the defining challenge at the meeting in the space in-between for both of them – and the adult has to be able to see this prospect in the child, who arrives in anticipation of not being patronised. On a purely practical level, I have to say that as a writer, Maurice Gleitzman's opening exchange in *Bumface*, '"Angus Solomon," sighed Ms Lowry, "is that a penis you've drawn in your exercise book?"' reveals a great insight into writing for children here. Like all good storytellers, he reveals that the element of 'surprise' remains the hook that leads the reader into the story and into reading on. To all intents and purposes, 'surprise' is the single, most essential ingredient in writing for children – and we will return to it in Part 2.

Articulating an idea of the ever-changing matter of the child and childhood through representation faces its own internal struggle with shifting consciousness, shifting culture, multiplicity and fragmentation. Furthermore, while it can be acknowledged that childhood is temporary for children and memory for adults, the memory is different from the real. My memory of childhood does not represent my own children's present, which will become their own memories in time – no two life stories can be the same and nostalgia too is a very unstable narrator (usually because nostalgia represents a return to a place that never existed). For this very reason we also have to dismiss Kimberley Reynolds' reading of Peter Hollindale's idea of calling for a 'childness literature'. Childness, which refers to both 'the adult's ability to remember childhood and recreate it fictionally for children, and children's sense of their developing selves' (Reynolds 2007: 192) doesn't really address writing for children in the way I think it should.

Roni Natov has also addressed this issue at length and writes, 'The literature of childhood moves between innocence and experience, between initiation and reflection. And, in establishing such a poetics, the child at the centre, presently and retrospectively, is, as Carolyn Steedman says, "the story waiting to be told" (Steedman 1995: 11)' (Natov 2006: 3). But speaking as a writer, this idea of 'retrospectively' as well as the 'ability to remember childhood and recreate it fictionally' troubles me because I cannot agree with it being a credible strategy for writing. I don't metaphorically go to meet the 'present' child to present a 'retrospective' view of childhood that once I had for real and now hold as memory, what would be the point? To me this is like asking a twenty-first-century child to read *The Old Curiosity Shop* by Charles Dickens so that Nell Trent can provide an objective idea of how they are going to progress through life – as if she was a fair representation at any time. Perhaps what we should say is 'childness literature' (if we have to use that term, which I won't again) is an ongoing process of mutual creative exploration because this seems to be eminently more relevant. The child does not need my musty old memories because in any case they will not recognise them as representing what they already know (the time-lag has been too great), and neither will they see them as being culturally relevant for the here and now, but more than that, they are looking for newness out of the ever same, not my rehashed stories – and indeed there are very few children reading Proust's *A la Recherche du temps perdu*. They are looking to make the connections and it is the writer's job to find a way to make this happen.

As Benjamin suggests, 'the important thing for the remembering author is not what he experienced, but the weaving of his memory, the Penelope work of recollection' (Benjamin 1973: 198), where the connections between fictional creativity and realism meet as a connecting story. And it is worth developing the Penelope metaphor because the remembering author is not just weaving the cape of memory, but also pulling it apart and then starting again, and again, and again. When the writer commits a story in the form of a text, the child doesn't come to see a hidden truth but that which was not there before, prior to their reading of it. In this sense too we can consider that what has to be acknowledged is the idea of the 'innocent child' no longer exists because it has been replaced by the 'knowing child' and this is a very important distinction

The book, the text, stands as the mediator (the Penelope cape) as an arrested moment of experience, of something new that will not stand still, for it will never be new again, but will always be starting over. Just as it did for the writer, so too will it for the reader. The arrested moment, the meeting between writer and reader, in that brief intercession is the point at which ongoing experience is confronted just as it is about to move on. Indeed, for the writer this is not just arrested time, the time of our writing, but the time at which we try to rationalise our internal struggles and strategies as well as those that exist outside to influence the historical moment of our writing, as reconstructed by our writing, in Jameson's words, its ideological subtext.[7]

As Hannah Arendt argued: 'The chief characteristic of the specifically human life ... is that it is always full of events that ultimately can be told as a story' (Arendt 1958: 72). I would extend this beyond 'events' to ideas and the Proustian idea of 'philosophic riches' that the story contains. Bertolt Brecht adds to this idea saying, 'Reality changes; in order to represent it, modes of representation must also change. Nothing comes from nothing; the new comes from the old, but that is why it is new' (Taylor 1977: 81).[8] And we are back to Barthes' toys; give children a cardboard box and watch them create something new from the old thing you had discarded – no words of articulation are necessary, they just get on with it, it is their narrative of the present. Isn't it curious how we can steer the critical thought through such channels and it still comes back to the one thing that is exploring the connections?

The desired outcome of the meeting between the child and the writer has to be a culturally relevant exploration (even in relating historical ideas) and to be looking in a more explicit and more sustained manner at the ideological, philosophical and political arenas of words and language. Pullman's *His Dark Materials* trilogy, revealing its eclectic and vibrant influences, from Milton and Blake, ancient Greek myths, Christian theology and popular cultural influences such as films, comics and radio, speaks louder on the issues of human identity, meaning and the exchange of ideas than some nostalgic old bore (i.e., me) talking about when 'I was a lad' (they were only the good old days when I am in nostalgic mode). And in so doing the reader will have a better understanding of language, reading and writing as they begin to confront the experience and knowledges available to their maturing minds, which the writer is hopefully nurturing so they may make the kind of connections required to sustain them rationally and emotionally for the rest of their lives – and indeed in the rational and irrational emotions inherent in the illogical, paradoxical, ironic and absurd oxymorons life presents.

But it's more than just that. Research, by Mark Taylor of Nuffield College, Oxford University,[9] analysed the responses of 17,200 people born in 1970 who gave details of their extra-curricular activities at age 16, and their jobs at age 33. The findings showed that 16-year-olds who read a book at least once a month were significantly more likely to be in a professional or managerial position at the age of 33 than those who did not read. For girls, there was a 39 per cent probability that they would be in a professional or managerial position at 33 if they read at 16, compared to a 25 per cent chance if they had not. Among boys, there was a 58 per cent chance of being in a good job at 33 if they had read as a teenager, compared to a 48 per cent chance if they had not. Taylor, who presented the findings at the British Sociological Association's annual conference in London, said: 'According to our results, there is something special about reading for pleasure – the positive associations of reading for pleasure aren't replicated in any other extra-curricular activity, regardless of our expectations.'

What this really tells us is that readers are more able to make the connections. Story, especially fiction, is immensely significant in terms of building a sense of identity, capacity and sense of self. But, and sometimes I feel like shouting this, as writers we need to be aware of this because the terms of what we write should be negotiated around such information. And I repeat (I am doing a lot of repeating in this book but needs must) the writer and the reader are involved in a shared project, where the writer must ask him or herself not, *am I a good storyteller*? But, *what kind of person do I want to* be? Because when you are faced with your reader, there will be many (especially critics) who will queue up to offer an answer to the first. Faced with the second question, however, as Phillips reveals, 'there may be terrors but there are no experts' (1995). But in light of the research revealed above, it also asks: what kind of person do you want your reader to be and to become?

Reynolds reminds us that G.K. Chesterton once observed, 'in everything that matters, the inside is much larger than the outside' and it is a good representative quotation of what a children's book could be, and I say should be. She goes on to add: 'it is the words and images of often physically small texts that turn out to be capable of filling the minds of generations of young readers with experiences, emotions, and the mental furniture and tools necessary for thinking about themselves and the world they inhabit ... ' (Reynolds 2007: 1), and I think this idea needs no further comment here.

Crucial to this, for the writer to take note of, is Eleanor Farjeon's advice, 'Cast out of yourself the notion that "children" are a sort of static group that can be written "for" en masse. Otherwise, you will be addressing an imaginary audience, and aiming at a bull's-eye in a non-existent target' (Farjeon 1935).[10] It was true then as it is now. Furthermore, the children of today are not the children of your own childhood and to suggest that somehow you capturing your own nostalgic images for display can arrest this notion is unachievable, the world has already moved on, the only choice you have is an ongoing exploration while recognising that the child is only just beginning to establish the relationship in its own mind. And as I commented on Barthes' toys, the children they were intended for are already rearranging the bits, the words, into a new story, not the story of the old but the new, which 'comes from the old'. Perhaps this next section will help to explain this better. To some extent it will be written in the abstract, almost as personal experience but as a writer I am trying to intellectually rationalise something quite crucial, and telling a story about storytelling seems to be the best way to do so.

\*

When I said (above) it is impossible, I suspect, to propose a non-exclusionist normative definition of textual engagement in writing for children, but surely a normative structure that clarifies the intrinsic distinctiveness of child-centred storytelling can be proposed? I was thinking out loud and also of a way of saying it better. And it occurred to me that I could revisit an old story, one which most will be familiar with in an effort to try and describe what I mean but mainly because I think it is crucial to the 'elements of storytelling for children' that we can grapple with and demonstrate the issues it presents.

Reynolds (2007: 100) has written, 'Growing up involves making choices and shaping an identity. As a general rule, choosing one path, whether this is educational, cultural or social, closes down options.' And this reminded me of a story that has been with me for a long time. It isn't really a children's story, though it could be, but it is about a child, with all the hallmarks of a children's story because it is about a boy with no mother, who flies away from his father. It does not have a classic children's story ending in the version I will quote, but as I will go on to show, this could be rectified.

The story is a well-known one in Greek mythology; Daedalus, whose name literally means 'cunning artificer', was the greatest artist, architect and artificer of the ancient world. He fell out of favour with King Minos of Crete, who imprisoned him and his son Icarus in the labyrinth he himself had designed. Longing to escape the island kingdom, Daedalus constructed wings for himself and his son out of feathers, wax and flaxen threads, they strapped them on and flew away towards the mainland. But Icarus ignored his father's instructions to hold the middle course and flew too close to the sun; the heat melted the wax that bound his wings, and Icarus fell to his death (in his father's version of the story).

Here is an extract (below) from Ovid's version of the story that I want us to think about, and in doing so I want to address the ideas I proposed (above) that there are three ways to consider the cultural exclusion/inclusion of the 'child' and his or her exploring the space in-between ideas proposed in the story (and it would do no harm to read the whole story if you have a mind to). Picking it up for now, Daedalus is constructing the wings:

> Row upon row of feathers he arranged …
> Into a gentle curve to imitate
> Wings of a real bird. His boy stood by,
> Young Icarus, who, blithely unaware
> He plays with his own peril, tries to catch
> Feathers that float upon the wandering breeze …
> … the craftsman poised himself
> On his twin wings and hovered in the air.
> Next he prepared his son. 'Take care,' he said,
> 'To fly a middle course, lest you sink
> Too low the waves may weight your feathers; if
> Too high, the heat may burn them. Fly half-way
> Between the two. And do not watch the stars,
> The Great Bear or the Wagoner or Orion
> With his drawn sword, to steer by. Set your course
> Where I shall lead.'

(Ovid 1986: 176–78)

Famously, then, Ovid tells us that Daedalus made traditional, normative decisions on his son's behalf. While making wings, the boy Icarus is 'blithely unaware … ' playing 'with his own peril … ' and he is immediately addressed to the idea I proposed earlier. Daedalus is the maker and Icarus the unquestioning receiver. By affirming the superiority of the adult over the child, the poem demonstrates, *first*, the normative exclusion of the child from full participation in the space in-between exploration. Icarus was no apprentice at the well, or Daddy's helper, as they both explored the prospect of flight. He was there as his father's son and about to do his father's bidding.

When he hovers over his son, while strapping wings onto him, Daedalus is, *second*, allowing participation but one where the father/adult/maker dictates the normative rules without any kind of engagement with Icarus' feelings on the matter. Icarus is still the mute child, unspeaking and uncomplaining, doing his father's bidding. As I have already said, such an idea is embedded in adult and parental normative behaviour. Nevertheless, with Ovid, writing 2,000 years ago, having his father figure, Daedalus, say, 'take care … to fly a middle course', we have a good storytelling example of the problem this advice creates.

Consider this, were you the Icarus child, what would you think at that point? What would any of us think about the restrictions being put on our ability to fly once we had seen the possibilities? I propose to use this idea of the Icarus story to try and rationalise this whole 'elements of storytelling idea' because it seems to me there is much to offer as a working example. As I see it, Icarus is an example of every child in this storytelling narrative, and in my understanding the poem suggests that had the space in-between the maker and his child been negotiated by the 'exploring' 'mutually' and not one dominating the other, the story could have had a more positive outcome. The 'inventor' Daedalus and the 'innocent' Icarus hold a larger lesson than the one commonly presented.

While this 2,000-year-old story indicates that a utopian, 'golden age' idea of 'real storytelling' proposed by Benjamin, Zipes et al., is a bit off kilter, and there was no television, internet, etc., to intervene then, the *Erfahrung* moment is surely available to Icarus. Nevertheless, this is where I think Zipes really gets it right. He says, genuine 'storytelling, and especially storytelling with and for children', apart from being subversive and magical, '*has a special mission* [my italics] – to expose the wisdom and folly of all storytelling' (Zipes 2002: 145). The story of Daedalus and Icarus is such a story, with wisdom and folly being its heartbeat, but this is not, I would contend, as obvious in the common interpretation normally presented. In fact, contrary to common interpretation, the story is non-normative and thereby subversive and magical, as I will go on to reveal.

In the meantime, Pierre Bourdieu reminds us:

> the literary or artistic field is a *field of forces*, but it is also a *field of struggles* tending to transform or converse this field of forces. The network of objective relations between positions subtends and orients the strategies which the occupants of the different positions implement in their struggles to defend or improve their positions (i.e. their position-takings), strategies which depend for their force and form on the position each agent occupies in the power relations (*rapports de force*) … The meaning of a work (artistic, literary, philosophical, etc.) changes automatically with each change in the field within which it is situated for the spectator or reader.
>
> (Bourdieu 1993: 30)

Jack Zipes has written on this issue in relation to the fairy tale but the idea carries onto the myth, such as the Icarus story. As Zipes says:

> If we accept Bourdieu's notion that a cultural field of production is a force field of conflicts in which various writers, artists, and groups of people contend for power, then it is easy to see how the fairy tale [and myth] has certainly been used in almost all cultural fields to articulate positions and to criticize societal contradictions that reveal disparities …
>
> (Zipes 2009:122)

What I am about to do, then, after a short detour through some ideas, is take the Icarus story for a walk in order to emphasise this point about making the connections, and reveal how storytelling is still a live and vibrant part of our cultural discourse. Although it should be noted, as Jen Webb and I have written elsewhere, 'In drawing attention to this story we were aware that we ran the risk of falling into using the story of Icarus as an achrony but it should be clear that we do not intend to laminate the present and the ancient worlds, but only to use elements of their brief stories to frame and investigate other questions that occur' (Melrose and Webb 2011).

\*

My father was a coal miner and in his 'facts of life' talk to my then 15-year-old self he advised I should ' … work on the surface'.[11] That proved harder than I expected and this story will outline why. For it is a story of soul mining, a story of storytelling and a story of art developing and exploring ideas; the process in which an ontological journey is undertaken through an endless epistemological enquiry in perceiving, guessing, speculating, wondering, experiencing, experimenting, missing, mistaking, proving, implying, inferring, reflecting, refracting, corroborating, collaborating, dreaming, silences as hypothetical postulates and the endless ellipses that just go on and on … while exploring the space that existed in-between him (as adult) and me (as child).

From a first impression, my father is a shy and cautious man. At least that is how he appeared to us on the surface. He worked underground, away from the glare of onlookers and family and friends, well out of any spotlight. He was a mine driver and an explosives expert, where day in and day out he would face the danger of blowing up the coal face and driving the tunnels forward and shoring up the pit props so they could lay the railway track for extracting the coal. Imagine it, every day, at the coal face, miles underground and miles away from the pit shaft, burrowing tunnels deeper and deeper into the darkness. That was a part of him I saw little of. The man I lived with was dog tired after every shift and content to sit at the table reading the newspaper.

But looking back, I realise now that I had read his story wrong. When I joined him at the space in-between our two lives I saw that the quiet man was a magician, a craftsman, an underground adventurer in a coal-faced labyrinthine world where he was white but his skin was black (to paraphrase Salif Keita[12]), locked in his paradoxes, a cultural oxymoron, conservative with a small 'c' on the surface but an underground radical, a Daedalus dad to his Icarus son, and that is where the creative intervention and critical intercession of storytelling comes in. My father's advice to 'work on the surface' was uncannily like the advice given to Icarus by his father. Once Daedalus had strapped Icarus' wings on he spoke, '"Take care," he said, "To fly a middle course … "'[13] The sentiment of it being, work on the surface, not too high, not too low, but take the safe road!

But this is why I have been thinking about these elements of storytelling and also thinking about art and exploring a shared stock of ideas on life. As the craftsman's son I was thinking about the flying and my own adult life because I have come to my first major crisis!

The crisis is this: am I still Icarus or did I grow into Daedalus when I wasn't looking? You see as I write this my own son is now the age I was then. How can I advise him to fly the middle course when I am not even sure this is the best advice I can give? I mean, of course I want him to be safe, to live a safe life and to remain safe for a very, very long time; but I am torn because I don't feel I have finished flying myself, not yet.

Yet I see the problem I have set for myself, *first* is the affirmation of my adult given superiority, which excludes my child from full participation in the space I recognise in-between.

Well, okay I may relent a little and we can take the *second* option: I may allow a little participation but one where I dictate the parenting, normative rules of engagement.

And then I realise this may not be what my child needs or wants and I have to find another way, the *third* way in which we can engage and explore. All I have to think about now is how to approach it.

Looking back at my creatively critical and critically creative life, I realise my *curriculum vitae* doesn't tell the story that I need to pass on. Indeed, just like my father, the *curriculum vitae* that lists the product of a life doesn't capture the story that has been and continues to be that life. Sure, I have produced a pile of paper, film scripts, book chapters, articles, poems, songs and so on, just like my father produced a mountain of coal, but how does that address itself to an Icarus son? And then it became clear to me.

Michel Foucault implied that reflecting on our own life as a work of art (not just the product of the struggle but the story itself) helps us to approach the problem of succession (adult to child and in my case father to son to son) with a view to a better understanding of the 'aesthetics [which] can be used as a metaphor for the self, and can provide a set of practices in and by which to take care of the self'.[14] Not 'aesthetics' in the literal sense of the word but as a kind of model of appreciation for the 'self' and 'other' as my son and I explore the space of years and experience between us. I am not yet ready to stop flying but my son too (like every child) is flapping his wings in anticipation.

In other words, in reflecting on my own life as a continuous work of art in progress I am better able to take responsibility for other(s) – children, my own son, readers, students, etc., to ensure continuing 'harmony in our engagement with the broader community' (ibid.) that is art in life and life in art. And this harmony has accord with a wider sense of community and indeed storytelling, especially if we take note of the psychologist Dorothy Rowe, who said: 'If you make happiness your sole goal then you are not going to get it – the goal should be an *interesting* life [my italics].'[15] Trouble is; how do I tell that story? For the story of a life, my life, any life, is itself a bit of a clutter.

Personally, I am not sure I can do it in the way Foucault suggests; I am not so sure my life as a living example of self as art is actually that interesting. Nevertheless, I can stop for a moment to show through intervention and intercession what it means. I can write my story as precisely that, a story that will meet the child at the space in-between to explore our different view of the world from our different viewpoints, to witness our astonishment and amazement about the ongoing experience of being. What a rare treat that is. Not a rehash of my musty old memories of a childhood that has little to say to the twenty-first century except as nostalgia and historical recollection, but as an ongoing process of mutual creative exploration. Where one old storyteller is growing out of his skin while passing on ideological, philosophical and political connections in words and language and stories just as another, younger storyteller is emerging to grow into his own, keeping the story of life alive. But the stories will, Penelope-like, keep changing, day by day, night by night, as we become attuned to their nuances and ideas.

Isn't that what writing for children is all about? Isn't that what we do as writers? I think Philip Pullman might be embarrassed for me to mention him in this way, so too Malorie Blackman, J.K. Rowling, Margaret Mahy, oh the list is endless, but it is what their stories say to their readers. And I experience this as an adult too, names such as

Kundera, Calvino, Murakami, DeLillo, Roth, Rushdie, McEwan, Slossa, Marquez, Chandler come flying at me from the shelves above the desk I am writing this on (though as you might have noticed, my filing system is a little random). As Pullman has said, previously:

> Stories are vital … There is more wisdom in a story than in volumes of philosophy, and there is a hunger for stories in all of us. Children know they need them, and go for them with a passion, but all of us adults need them too. All of us, that is, except those limp and jaded people who think they are too grown up to need them.[16]

Thus, I was able to stop for a moment to reflect on what I should be thinking of saying to this Icarus son of mine and indeed for the generation that is following mine, for he is every child and they will all be looking to fly. In the space in-between I should, indeed could, be repeating bel hooks by saying:

> A seductive atmosphere of pleasure and danger surrounds the writing process. As a writer, intellectual, and critical thinker, I feel swept away by the process of thinking through certain ideas as well as by their potential to incite and arouse the reader.
>
> (hooks 2000: 4)

Though I cannot lay claim to all of this in content, she does go a long way to saying what I think about the potential of writing. I would say, 'am not going to cast you off to find out on your own, I will help you with your wings and indeed accompany you for part of the journey but then you have to find your own course, be it high, low or straight down the middle, for all aspects of the journey are a creatively critical and a critically creative expedition from innocence to experience … and the ellipses represent all the things we have yet to explore', because the simple fact of exploration is crucial to child development but also to the inter-illumination the adult–child relationship engenders in us as social beings.

The idea of 'making the connections' isn't a new one that I have just thought about. It goes back as far as Socrates, 469–399 BCE, as far as we know, but as far as we don't know it has been going on forever. Think about it, early man, bees, hives, stings, honey; someone made all these connections once. And nowhere is this more relevant than when we are dealing with ideas and the idea of experience being incorporated into a narrative. Socrates in the instance I am thinking about was attempting to explain a complicated mathematical theory to an uneducated slave. He did so simply by prompting the slave, step by step, with things he already knew. But this idea of slippage in the dialectical master/slave binary is very much what I have been saying. It's not so much explaining or showing but helping others to connect to what they already know from other parts of life and then asking them to take the ideas forward into something they may or may not have thought about but are ready to explore. The children will then take what you have offered and incorporate it with their own thinking to take possession of the knowledge the mutual exploration imparts. And is this not a true Socratic journey. Socrates never claimed to be wise, only to understand the path a lover of wisdom must take in pursuing it. It is such a simple idea and I see no reason why a writer of children's fiction cannot be thinking about it. It is not a question of binaries, them and us, me and you, adults and children, but a mutual stroll down a Socratic path, making connections. But of course that is just the start so let me break this Icarus tale into some of its component parts, as I see them.

# Chapter 6

# Engaging with Icarus

We are all bound by caution, even in youthful folly we know not to stick our hands in the fire. The vicarious nature of such experience being passed on is something we are all grateful for, surely! Personally speaking, there are a lot of experiences I would rather hear about than actually encounter. 'Fear ... [according to Adam Phillips] is a state of mind in which the object of knowledge is the future, but it is, of course, a knowledge that can only be derived from the past' (1995: 53). For Freud, fear is the shock of the old, a symptom of knowledge, the warning sign of experience being delivered even vicariously in its 'lived out form' to borrow from Walter Benjamin. And yet, fear, as Freud also says, is both a recognition of pleasure (and/or pain) in the offing, and is a secret form of pleasure in itself. In fearing flying we fear life and so choose to steer the middle way, undoubtedly. But the pull to those 'secret forms of pleasure' exist still, as Icarus revealed to Daedalus. After all, we are bound by caution but also a desire to test both our fears and the edges of safety. I am sure we have all done something we know to be risky, stick our hands in the fire to see what would happen, hold a hand over the candle to see how long we could bear the heat; as children we jumped off roofs, as did my children, and I still go to strange places, continents, places I know little about to see what will happen next, and of course the risks through childhood into teenage life and beyond are part of what Nigel Krauth called our 'insatiable appetite to be human' (Krauth 2006: 190). In some ways, this will come into the ideas I will soon open, relating to making one's life a work of art and refusing to fly the middle course or work on the surface.

The pull to adventure, the temptation, is strong and 40 years ago I, the protected boy, the son of the underground adventurer, the Icarus child, wondered and fantasised and dreamed of what was out there, out here. If I dug down, under the surface, or raised myself above the surface, flying higher, what was there that I needed protecting from, what was there to be afraid off, what would become of me if I failed to steer the middle way, skimming a superficial, shallow path, barely leaving a trace of a shadow as I 'worked on the surface' and made my way through life? After all, Freud also said: 'Life is impoverished ... when the highest stake in the game of living, life itself, may not be risked.'[1] And then it begins to become clear to me that it's a storyteller's job to talk about 'where the wild things are' but also to show through the story that 'the game of living, life itself', is a risk.

The perceived wisdom of the Daedalus/Icarus story seems to suggest that Icarus was a foolish boy because he failed to heed his father's wise advice – or should that be his wise father's advice? As Ovid said, 'Icarus was much taken by the pleasure of his wings'.[2] But one of the most remarkable things about the story and its subsequent translations is the way it has been moralised in a finger-wagging exercise of innocence to experience. Icarus, we are told, takes so much pleasure in his wings that they become the object of his downfall and that his recklessness should serve as a warning to youth and its follies. But let me unfurl something I have been thinking about for a long time here.

The story of Icarus (in its many retellings) is often tabled as a normative tale, it is usually presented as a tale of folly; the folly of the boy who didn't listen to his father's advice; advice gleaned from experience long stored as memory. Icarus' folly, as if we needed reminding, was that he flew too close to the sun, from which a lesson can be learned. And the lesson is as much about not getting above your self as it is a warning against reckless behaviour. Yet this troubles me – especially if we are to establish the moral authority of the story itself – because I feel the story is more subversive and magical than this moral message it seems to have accumulated through the centuries.

If we think about it seriously, Daedalus was the survivor who witnessed his own son falling into the sea. But a very real question remains: was Daedalus a credible narrator of the event that led to the death of Icarus? Let's raise a couple of questions here. Daedalus, the known murderer of Talus, creator of the *laberinthe hic minotaurus*, the great conjurer who gifted flight to Icarus, only to put a restriction on it: can we believe a word he says?

Moreover, can we subscribe to the proposition of the implied message in Ovid's narrative, that we should all live a humbler life? And humbler than whom? Humbler than Daedalus is, I suspect, a mere hypothesis but let's consider it. When Icarus was flying he ignored the height warning and, reckless as he may have seemed, he was already experiencing a high his own father never would: thus, Icarus became the knowledgeable one.

Having previously relied on the vicarious experience being passed on by his father, Icarus was now the one who knew what it really felt like to be alive. Then when he went into freefall he was gaining a further, heady experience, something else his father never would: the freedom of it, the sheer exhilarating, reckless freedom.

Therefore it's easy to suggest that Daedalus may have murdered his son because he just couldn't stand being the inexperienced one – in flying so high Icarus had surpassed the experience of his father, just as Talus the apprentice had surpassed the master by becoming the better craftsman. It's something we have to live with – the trace of our own reputations being surpassed by those of our successors (children, our sons and students). Icarus now had more knowledge than his father – surely a cause for jealousy (perhaps). After all, Daedalus had already shown what he thought of such an action. After Talus had shown he was the better craftsman, Daedalus murdered him – jealous? No doubt and indeed Daedalus is implicated in a number of other deaths:

> Whoever did the deed, Daedalus was no innocent bystander in the death of Minos. Indeed, he is directly or indirectly responsible for the deaths of: his nephew Talus (murder), his sister Perdix (suicide), the Minotaur (trickery), Ariadne (various options, all associated with her flight from Crete with Theseus), Icarus (wing failure), and Minos (suffocated in a bath). One has to wonder too about the fate of his wife, Naucrate ... Under contemporary law, Daedalus would be not only a criminal, but also a terrorist.
>
> (Melrose and Webb 2011)

So the question is open, did Icarus fall, or was he pushed? And what of Icarus himself, we see him described by his father as: ' ... a wretched youth ... now a dire example ...

for those who aspire to be supremely great … '.[3] A wretched youth: is this all he was for Daedalus? Hardly the words of a grieving father, you can almost hear him saying, ' … that'll teach you', as Icarus fell and we need to be reminded that Daedalus a means 'cunning worker'. Or is there something else for us to consider? For where in the narrative of life, death and storytelling does Icarus take us?

Of course, it should also be said that in drawing attention to this uneven treatment of the characters, despite my earlier warning I am indeed laminating the present and the ancient worlds, but only to use elements of their brief stories to frame and investigate these other questions that occur. In fact, the very paucity of their narrative is productive of thought and, potentially, of insights that extend beyond their historical era. Michel Foucault writes about those 'brief lives', those people who enter the record only in the form of 'a few lines or a few pages, nameless misfortunes and adventures, gathered together in a handful of words … chanced upon in books and documents'[4] and we can see how their as yet unwritten and unsaid stories can exist.

But such is the role of 'story' and 'stories' as a part of living, if we do not embrace the 'special mission' Zipes refers to, engage in the space in-between that allows us to connect and think about them and the ideas they can engender we are not critically engaged – and surely critical engagement is crucial to life itself. So before I move on I would like to dwell on Daedalus the 'cunning worker' and a 'big issue' as a means of explanation. And I will do it in a way that is recognisable, by taking a real event as a parallel because this idea relies on Daedalus as writer/maker dominating the space rather than allowing his child Icarus and nephew Talus to mutually 'explore' the space as a site of knowledge and experience – and I hope this parallel will become both obvious and a fertile ground for thought.

\*

Before I move into this next section it is crucial I make the lines of agency and context clear. This is because I am about to tie the myth of Daedalus and Icarus to a true and terrible story and the blurring of myth, fiction and fact needs to be addressed if I am not simply to aestheticise some important ideas without regard for the consequences, of which I am well aware. What I will be referring to is what Benjamin calls *Erfahrung* and the idea of 'lived through' and 'narratable' experience. My aim is not to shock or indeed to minimise the importance of the story I am about to address, but to hold it up to scrutiny as a 'story'. So in taking a deep breath, I begin.

Francis Fukuyama famously wrote *The End of History and the Last Man*,[5] in which he argued that the progression of human history, as a struggle between ideologies, was at an end, with the world settling on liberal democracy. Even when I read this for the first time I thought it was, well to put it simply, wrong. Was this the end of what Peter Hunt called the 'eccentric blend of the comfortably predictable and the unsettlingly unexpected' that was life as we knew/know it? Okay, I know this is a little reductive but the truth is we didn't have to look far for a response. What we saw, live and in recorded television images in New York on the fateful day now called simply 9/11, was the role of the artist being absorbed into the narrative of terror. It was a sadistic act that cannot be denied. For all its horrible consequence, watching the attack on the World Trade Center unfold had a rare macabre impact, which, because of the media used to record and reproduce it, forced itself into the soul of mankind and changed the inner life of the culture being targeted. As an event it was almost the exact opposite of Neil Armstrong walking on the moon, but it was still ' ... one small step for man, one giant leap for mankind' when, as Slavoj Žižek has indicated, via the ultra-right-wing US journalist, George Will, the US awoke from its holiday from history.[6] I am not attempting to laminate this story for my own purposes here, I do not dismiss it or disparage it to make a point but as a story it relies on an Icarus effect.

High on adrenalin for the audacious act, which would be witnessed, not just by the unstable narrator but all over the world just as it happened, art and terror collided as our gaze followed the images being offered and our immediate reaction was one of *Dialektic im Stillstand* – dialectics at a standstill[7] (to paraphrase Walter Benjamin) – because that is the impact of such an event. Historical time becomes encapsulated in images that form an arrested moment of experience, of something new which will not stand still, for it will never be new again, but will always be starting over, repeated images, in what Tiedemann called a historical constellation. Time was no longer past time, but, rather, coagulated in the imagistic configuration of the now; in the immediacy of the actual event as it unfolded – modernism still saying something new, still denying the claims of its postmodern imposter. Fukuyama couldn't have been more wrong, at the point of surprise and disbelief we stop to gaze before we can react ... it is the briefest point of intervention and intercession that comes before description, before language, which comes after the realisation and then becomes the story and the story of the story and stories for they are all textual interventions, thereafter.

Now I agree this is a big plunge into the huge picture of ideological challenges to liberal democracy – even when trying to contextualise it into the broad picture that is a story of life in art and art in life. But for me it serves as something more – the Icarus story is a fable whose bigger job as story, 'used in almost all cultural fields to articulate positions and to criticize societal contradictions that reveal disparities' (Zipes 2009: 122), extends as a metaphor for much of what I have been trying to explain. Childhood is an ongoing negotiation of experience that often oscillates between conformity and rebellion, as the Icarus story reveals. Icarus was certainly conforming when he donned his wings before rebelling to explore his own identity. Nevertheless, the text that negotiates the space in-between adult normative and the child is precisely an exploration in identity, emotion and sexuality that needs to be negotiated with care. And the Daedalus figure has a huge part to play here (if indeed we can appropriate him to represent the story). Let's face it, the father in the Icarus story is a criminal and no role model at all. As Jen Webb and I have written elsewhere:

> Let us return to the story of Daedalus, Icarus and Talus. Both boys were in an intimate relationship with the man: relationships not only of family ties, but also professional relationships manifested through his role as their teacher ... Talus was transformed from apprentice to partridge, Icarus from child to trope; and both were transformed from life to death. *There is a long history of men – fathers, teachers – transforming boys from life to death, usually in the process of teaching them (something) in the context of an intimate relationship* [my italics]. Indeed, one of the enduring characteristics of terrorism is of the teacher, the older man, crafting and shaping and training the younger, who is characterised by a longing for meaning and identity: to make what will necessarily be his brief life achieve more than a fragment in the long record of history. Interestingly, a somewhat pathologising official definition of terrorists identifies

them as possessed of contradictory yearnings: 'the desire for depersonalisation' *and* 'the desire for intimacy' (see Thackrah 2004: 208).[8]

(Melrose and Webb 2011)

And indeed, the historical constellation of normativity that surrounds the story of the man who gave his boy wings and then cast him off with instructions on what to do next suggests the boy's risk-taking was the action of a child keen *not* to do as his father did. Thus the mythical element of the story becomes a better representation of a modern child and childhood than could be initially imagined in the tale of 'folly' it has been classified as. The inner story in the myth repeats and repeats in images and ideas, and we return once again to Benjamin's idea where he says:

> ... the important thing for the remembering author is not what he experienced, but the weaving of his memory, the Penelope work of recollection ... For an experienced event is finite – at any rate, confined to one sphere of experience; a remembered event is infinite, because it is only a key to everything else that has happened before it and after it.
>
> (Benjamin 1973: 198)

It's a curious thing to note how often creative people, artists and poets and all kinds of writers, come to invoke the possibilities of this Daedalus/Icarus theme as a rejection of conventionality, as a rejection of the middle way, where the father/son; adult/child power relationship is less of a negotiation, a site for exploration, and more of a battle ground of wills in which the adult inevitably wins.

   Joseph Zornado talks about this in some depth in his book *Inventing Childhood* (2006). He doesn't take the Daedalus/Icarus route, nor the 9/11 inference, but he does take the brief reign of terror that was Columbine High School and we can see how the similarities are echoed throughout. He says:

> I offer a way of seeing Columbine as well as countless other ordinary expressions of violence as a system of an adult culture long gone blind to the child ... it may come as monolithic story that defies current sensibilities of an age dedicated to fragmentation and postmodern multiplicity. Yet even the postmodern intellectual perspective remains caught up in an ideology of obfuscation that blinds even the brightest scholar to the most obvious truth: *there remains a master narrative to the story of childhood that continues to play out in and through the dominant culture, through the stories the culture tells about itself to itself and through the lived relations that result between adult and child* [my italics].
>
> (Zornado 2006: xiv)

In other words, in exploring the thrill of flight for foolish boys we have to explore the issues of knowledge and experience, not just provide the wings that become twisted in a finger-wagging, moralising tale of prejudice from adults, who have become blind to the consequences of passive effect, of not challenging what has become the normative. The 'inter', the place of connection between adult and childhood, the connecting space, has to be approached with the idea that the 'experienced event is finite – at any rate, confined to one sphere of experience; a remembered event is infinite, because it is only a key to everything else that has happened before it and after it'. The memory of the event and the 'changed' life thereafter lingers if writers, like Daedalus dads, the adult involved in the production of children's literature, do not realise that he or she is less hidden than the child in the story. The adult/writer/creator/inventor is articulating for the child, while and at the same time the child who knows more than it can articulate is learning how to articulate its own story, while also learning something new. The learning of the new has to be the story that says experience is key to everything else that has happened before it and after the moment it is noticed and that building on this experience as it is narrated, rather than lived through, relies on remembering the Penelope-like weaving of memory is also a constant exploration, pulling it apart and making it again, and again, and again, *exploring* the connections.

The moral is, storytelling is about giving children wings and acknowledging they will want to fly but both they and the adult creator need to understand the narrative must be explored mutually, not given as gospel. Once again, like Freud said: 'Life is [indeed] impoverished … when the highest stake in the game of living, life itself, may not be risked'.[9] Vicarious experience cannot be the only experience we encounter – and although 'produced' art helps with this, helps us to understand it, surely 'living' art is the great cajoler, our cultural inheritance and legacy, the meeting at the space in-between that carries the burden of meaning of culture. Not the blindness of the adult when faced with a child's needs but the ongoing and constant exploration, building it up and taking it down, looking at it afresh, building it up and then taking it down again.

Again, Zipes is right when he tries to redress this in his work on storytelling and 'authenticity', and although I am not convinced by his methodology in trying to redress capitalism's failings, I am consoled by his efforts while being able to say that not all child-centred culture is going the way he suggests. This is also a struggle writers are trying to address. So too Zornado who concludes pessimistically that 'There can be peace in accepting the insecure nature of life … ' even if he says the caveat is that 'Unfortunately, peace has little chance in a culture that routinely and ritualistically interprets its relations of power and violence as signs of its civilizing progress' (Zornado 2006: 220). But part of the way we can address such issues is to be aware of this. If we know the story, understand the discourse we are involved in, then perhaps, just perhaps, we can begin to think what the 'elements of storytelling for children' should and could be.

Perhaps we should return to Freud's idea at the beginning of his *Interpretation of Dreams: Acheronta movebo*: 'if you cannot change the explicit set of ideological rules you can try to change the underlying set of obscene unwritten rules' (Žižek 2002: 32). As Zipes said so well: 'storytelling, especially storytelling for children, has a special mission – to expose the wisdom and the folly of all storytelling' (Zipes 2009) and I used the chapters above to show this. But I will also extend this idea below because we need to extend and analyse the unsaid-ness of story, and the fine webs of connection between the stories, the Penelope-like weaving of the web that shape and structure our culture and hence our lives. As Benjamin states, the Latin word *textum* means web and as the spinner of the tale, you have a special mission.

\*

Thus the idea of textually intervening in the Icarus story, refashioning the ideas, thinking about it from Icarus' point of view and thinking about its non-normative qualities and potential subversiveness, helps me to understand how the elements of storytelling come together. As I write this, as the computer accepts the tapping of my fingers, which are fed by thoughts in my head to become a narrative, a text, a story on storytelling, I am listening to Karine Polwart singing! And I was (for you are now reading the past tense of the story of an event that has already taken place) listening to her song *Beo*,[10] which made me think about how this storytelling chapter should close. She sings:

> I'm going home and I'm going home soon
> Beo beo …
> To where a boy at the window
> is opening up his wings to the world
> I'm gonna be there
> when he takes to the air
> I'm gonna watch them unfurl
> Beo beo. …

In correspondence, I suggested to Karine Polwart that the lyrics of *Beo* resonated with the story of the boy Icarus and I asked if I could include them in this chapter. She replied to say she was 'Surprised and delighted! I love all the "unsaid" stuff and the many possible stories … '[11]

All the unsaid stuff, the many possible stories, the unsaid-ness of story, and the fine webs of connection between the stories that shape and structure our culture and hence our lives is the ongoing relationship between the writer and the reader, while constantly exploring the special responsibility of wisdom and folly. And in taking the example of me reading Karine Polwart's story here, I can begin to show how this extended analysis can demonstrate how exciting it can and should be for the child coming to a story.

The story of Icarus, for all its fame, is a very short one, around 40-odd lines in Ovid's *Metamorphoses*, little more than a single page in a 380 page poem (in my edition[12]), and yet we can immediately see how the many possible stories, unsaid and unwritten variations, remain alive to the possibility that one day they may be written.

For example, I imagined the *Beo* lyric as a textual intervention, where Polwart adopts the persona of Naucrate to speak. Icarus' mother is talking about her boy, who is about to fly – even though Naucrate never actually appears in Ovid's poem, and indeed never seems to speak anywhere. In this respect, and certainly as a woman in the Daedalus world narrative, she is pre-feminist and as silent as a child. And this kind of textual intervention is a valid form of storytelling in trying to reveal the issues being explored – stories rarely remain static, as the brothers Grimm can testify and as fairy tales have been readdressed through the centuries. This idea has been explored on the Icarus theme; there is the famous Pieter Bruegel painting, *Landscape with the Fall of Icarus*, c. 1558, and W. H. Auden's equally famous poem *Musée Des Beaux Artes* as a textual intervention on the story of Icarus, and indeed on Bruegel's painting, i.e., a story that lurks yet untold, unsaid and in the ellipses waiting for a voice to articulate it remains possible. We actually know very little about the boy who flew, how it felt to fly and so on (see Melrose and Webb 2011) and even less about his mother, so that the possibility of ongoing engagement with the story is limitless. As Jen Webb wrote in a textual intervention:

Icarus woke one morning and found his mother gone. Daedalus looked up from his workbench and found himself alone. Minos looked north across the sea to Athens.

Naucrate went out of their story; she went out of her child's life; she went out of history. And with her going, Crete trembled, and the story of now shifted on its ground, and took a different tack.

(Webb 2010: 35)

This intervention too leaves the potential development of the ongoing, unsaid-ness of story wide open, where 'the story of now shifted on its ground, and took a different tack'.

Also, here is another idea of something as yet not quite developed, and I am not sure I have enough space for it in this book because it seems to be conceptually huge. But let me air it; if we compare the way Naucrate was written out of the story of her son's great and enduring story of flight and falling, and compare it with Penelope's stitched story, constantly being untangled and unpicked then rewritten as the quest for meaning and knowledge accrues day by day for the boy Telemachus. The story goes that one day the learning child will become the *giver* of the ongoing narrative of experience (Telemachus) and the other will *be* the story he (Icarus) cannot add to except in our own exploration.

Of course, in some ways the *Beo* lyrics I quoted are simply my subjective reading of the song. But what is wrong with that? Reading a pre-written story is not a passive pastime; every reader brings pieces of themselves, their cultural, social and personal effects, to the text. The reader's approach to the text cannot be qualified by the author's story of the story. The story itself has to exist, unsupported. I. A. Richards in *How to Read a Page* (originally published in 1943) extended this sense of readerly context further in acknowledging the multiplicity of differently situated (and educated and informed) readers:

we may reasonably doubt whether there is one right and only right reading … different minds have found such different things in them that we would be very rash if we assumed that some one way of reading them which commends itself to us is the right one.

(Richards 1954: 11)

As can be seen, not only does the poem allow us to contextualise the theoretical positioning I propose, the nature of it as a mythical story reveals itself as fertile ground for mutual child and adult literary exploration. For as I have already demonstrated, the unsaid possibilities, the many possible stories and the ellipses that live inside any writer's work, demonstrates, for me at least, how stories and songs and ideas intertwine and link through the centuries and across the miles and landscapes and the inescapable cross-cultural topography of storytelling 'simply there like life itself … international, transhistorical, transcultural' (Barthes 1977: 79).

*

Throughout this chapter, then, I have been thinking about exploration, intervention and intercession, and the 'elements of storytelling' in the space in-between, and trying to show how it can be a device that allows the storyteller, in whatever medium, to engage, to help metaphorically to articulate Foucault's idea of crafting and creating while explaining and still living our own life as a work of art. And this has to be understood as a metaphor, life is too fast for daily, one-to-one tutorials but I am suggesting that the narrative of childhood does not have to be about a twenty-first-century adult culture that defines itself through power, violence and consumerism.

The cultural shift into the twenty-first century has taught us much, thus far. The historicity of the concept of the child and childhood in the pre-Enlightenment, adult-centred world, where no one actually saw children as the future, with a need of nurture, education and attention; where they just grew up in a mixed-up world of adults, children, beasts and all, has given way to the present, a more noticeably child-centred world, where whole sections of libraries, shops, consumer products and, most importantly, schools are dedicated to them, and where they (the child and children) are our most precious asset and the future. We have to ask how and why this idea of overwhelming power, violence and consumerism, outlined by Zornado, can continue to raise its head amongst the other child-centred injustices in a cruel world.

Thinking about it historically, we could return to Foucault's notion of sexuality in the Victorian period when we didn't speak of it, and in doing so it became pretty much all we spoke about. I feel this way about the silent child, the voices are there to be heard, they may not be as articulate as you or I but we have to help them to explore the story that is theirs. Their ellipses are so crowded with ideas and concepts and politics, and silences that are so noisy even the Babylonians would hear the story being nurtured, where the art of life can be dedicated to negotiating the discourse of ongoing and mutual exploration; where, to repeat Kundera's idea, that '[writing] is the art that created the fascinating imaginative realm where no one owns the truth and everyone has the right to be understood' (Kundera 2000: 159). To take this a little further down the road, where 'Every novel says to the reader: Things are not as simple as you think … ' (ibid.: 18), what we can do as writers is help with the connections, because the child that comes to the book is already an intelligent person and it is the writer's job to know that the writing is not about me-the-author, but about engaging with them-the-readers (or the read-to) in exploring the connections.

In making this connection we look to representations of it, in fiction and in real life, we could all make our own check list, here's mine, straight off the top of my head: Dumbledore and Harry Potter; Will and Lyra; Dante and Virgil (in the *Divine Comedy*). Indeed there is an interesting idea on Nelson Mandela and James Gregory. I have this almost romantic notion of Mandela and Gregory meeting as jailor and prisoner, where the prisoner was educating the jailor, which blurs the teacher/pupil adult/child connection because it should be blurred, the slippage between the connections is not a caesura but a constant rubbing against each other when meeting in the space in-between, exploring their differences and getting to know each as 'other'. Of course this in turn sends Jacqueline Rose's ideas on Peter Pan into a tailspin − but that is another issue for another time. In this engagement, where elements of story are negotiated by exploring a text given by a writer to a reader, I am encouraged by something Noam Chomsky has written:

> Meantime, the world in which we exist has other aims. But it will pass away, burn up by the fire of its own hot passions; and from its ashes will spring a new and younger world, full of fresh hope, with the light of morning in its eyes.
>
> (Chomsky 1971: 110)[13]

The art of storytelling has no universal rules because each true artist melts down and re-forges past aesthetics; like Icarus reborn, rising phoenix-like from the ashes and forever taking flight anew; where invention is the spontaneous generation of individual creativity, it is the moment when we defy gravity without actually raising ourselves off the ground! Life and art and other ideas do indeed go on and on, regenerating, as authors try to make sense of the world, and like Foucault, when I say author of course I mean creative agent – artist is a better descriptor – but by definition, the world in artistic representation is a very modern and modernist world.

For me there is no end of storytelling as Walter Benjamin suggested, neither is there an end to history or postmodern angst blocking its way. But what does exist is the knowledge that if the *first way* is the affirmation of the superiority of the adult over the child, which excludes the child from full participation in the discourse taking place in the space in-between, where the *second way* is more likely, in allowing participation of the child but one where the adult dictates the normative rules without some kind of appreciation of what the child needs and wants, then the *third way* (if indeed it is a way, I am only using the numerical as a means of expressing it) is about taking much more of a dialogic[14] and vigilant approach to the idea of normative. But it does come with a health warning! If flying defies gravity and makes us like gods, then remaking and re-representing the world comes with responsibility to mutually explore not to dictate, for therein lies tyranny.

Finally, didn't Aristophanes suggest the possibilities of human love in that the desire for unity with another is symbolic of the desire of unity with the essence of the good? For me this is about the connection made in the arrested moment, the moment of surprise and wonder and awe, the ever shifting but impermeable connection in the ongoing shift through lived through and narratable experience. As Wallace Stevens wrote in 'Notes Toward a Supreme Fiction':

> The poem refreshes life so that we share,
> For a moment, the first idea … It satisfies
> Belief in an immaculate beginning
> And sends us, winged by an unconscious will,
> To an immaculate end. We move between these points:
> From that ever-early candour to its late plural.
>
> (Stevens 1953: 87)

The moment of the idea that eventually moves from the 'ever-early candour' into its plurality, how like a poet to get it so right in so little space, although I am going to reduce it to one word (and you can find your own because it is something we can all do). For me, this translates into something I was thinking about calling the sixth sense (though I am not fixated with numbers I had no idea what else to call it). Not one of the five senses that we use to hear, see, smell, touch or taste but the sense that makes us feel, for what sense records joy or pain or anger or love and then there are the associates, desire, passion and so on, none of them a visual or a verbal expression but these are all the elements we explore in stories. I am not sure I can quite explain it here, and so abstractly, for how does one describe joy, or pain, or love, except as an adjunct to a story and I have already told the one about Icarus. Perhaps I can give it here as a shortcut and just ask you to think about it. Well here goes, for example, a shortcut could simply be writing 'oh' so it can be seen as a visual image on this page, or if you can imagine me uttering 'oh' so it can be heard as a response to a suggestion or a visual or a feeling, half heard as a whisper at the back of the Tate gallery showing Rothko's *Red On Maroon*

(1959). The utterance itself, 'oh', seems to deny the subject and reflects on the internal joy and its wider, yet private meaning for the viewer; where the immediate reaction is one without language, the arrested moment of a *dialektic im stillstand* – dialectics at a standstill – again – for there is no way to express what it is; no language, however precise in choice of words and expression, of the subtleties of thought and imagination can match the moment of realisation that 'oh' simply doesn't even get close to. And the examples we could explore go on and on and on, as the poet Rainer Maria Rilke wrote on the manuscript of his *Duino Elegies (1924)*:

> Happy are those who know:
> Behind all words, the unsayable stands;
> And from that source alone, the infinite
> Crosses over to gladness, and to us –
> Free of our bridges,
> Built with the stone of distinctions;
> So that always, within each delight,
> We gaze at what is purely single and joined.
>
> (cited in Webb 2009: 123)

Which Webb suggests teases out Rilke's 'sense of what can only be felt, can never be said, and what for him lies behind all representation – the "unsayable" that nonetheless is' (ibid.). Imagine, if you will, how Icarus must have felt when he first took flight:

> ... the boy
> Began to enjoy his thrilling flight and left
> His guide to roam the ranges of the heavens ...
>
> (Ovid 1986: 178)

'Oh', the sheer joy! Or what about Harry Potter when that broom took off in *The Philosopher's Stone*, and Harry flew for the first time:

> Harry ignored her. Blood was pounding in his ears. He mounted the broom and kicked hard against the ground and up, up he soared, air rushed through his hair and his robes whipped out behind him – and in a rush of fierce joy he realised he'd found something he could do without being taught – this was easy, this was *wonderful*. He pulled his broomstick up a little to take it even higher and heard screams and gasps of girls back on the ground and an admiring whoop from Ron.
>
> (Rowling 1997: 110)

'Oh', the 'rush of fierce joy'; or what about Lyra when she first handled the *alethiometer*:

> It lay heavily in her hands, the crystal face gleaming, the golden body exquisitely machined. It was very like a clock, or a compass, for there were hands pointing to places around the dial, but instead of the hours or the points of the compass there were several little pictures, each of them painted with extraordinary precision, as if on ivory with the finest and slenderest sable brush. She turned the dial around to look at them all. There was an anchor; an hourglass surmounted by a skull; a chameleon, a bull, a beehive ...
>
> (Pullman 1998: 73)

'Oh', such vague clarity; such transparent mystery. And think how the reader would react to reading these extracts too – one of millions written for that purpose. As I write this, it has been reported on the radio that today is the fiftieth anniversary of 12 April 1961, when, to the cry of 'Let's go!', Yuri Gagarin embarked on a voyage lasting 108 minutes in a tiny, two-metre-wide capsule and successfully completed a single orbit of Earth, before landing in a field in central Russia: 'oh'. And then I wonder, like W.H. Auden, about the ploughman who may have heard another flyer fall ...

> ... Have heard the splash, the forsaken cry,
> But for him it was not an important failure; the sun shone
> As it had to on the white legs disappearing into the green
> Water; and the expensive delicate ship that must have seen
> Something amazing, a boy falling out of the sky,
> Had somewhere to get to and sailed calmly on.[15]

'Oh', that amazing Icarus boy ignored, the ordinary smashing up against the extraordinary, and everything shaking just a little bit. As Auden suggests in his poem, the juxtaposition between the ordinary events and extraordinary ones collide and are worth recording as an arrested moment of experience, of something new that will not stand still, for it will never be new again, but will always be starting over.

It is precisely an Icarian idea, the constant tension between the known and the unknown, the knowable and the unknowable, where, as Kundera rightly suggests, ' ... a young person's freedom and an old person's freedom are separate continents ... ' (Kundera 2007: 141). The word 'oh' uttered or written can never fully express what we feel, and 'oh' is only an example of an exclamation of that which cannot be committed to language; choose your own exclamation – it's your feeling after all, but a story, wherever it is committed, in a poem, song, novel or film, helps us to explore the space in-between so the giver and the reader can explore the connections.[16]

And then last night, as I was trying to unwind from a day of writing, I was thinking about stories, casting a backward glance at Auden's poem I had just quoted from, when he wrote: ' ... and *the expensive delicate ship that must have seen/ Something amazing, a boy falling out of the sky* ... '. It is a storyteller's flight of fancy, nothing more, but Telemachus was given a boat and Icarus wings and the two, well ... let me conclude this section, then, by saying: I leave you with the ellipses and the stillness of silence to ponder and explore the *connections*, while I catch my breath ...

# Part 2

# Chapter 7

# Considering the bogeyman …

Thou shalt not is soon forgotten
  but Once upon a time lasts for ever.

Philip Pullman

Having spent Part 1 of this book dealing with the critical aspects of the cult and culture of the child and childhood and summing up the critical problems, while addressing a way through to an understanding of what we should be addressing when writing for children, we can now concentrate on ideas of writing itself. But I make no excuses for taking so long in getting to this section in the book. An understanding of the critical discourse and key ideas is an important part of writing and I urge you to take it seriously. There is a serious, academic dialogue ongoing on this issue and engagement with it is surely desirable. And indeed I do feel it is important that we explode some of the myths and try to understand what it is we are doing, how we are engaged and what is expected of us as writers. There is much to consider for the writer and for the reader and I have tried to make it as accessible as I can. Furthermore I will not be looking at every nut and bolt of writing. I did that in a previous book, *Write for Children* (2002), and a lot of the information in there holds strong. What I will be doing is building on the critical ideas to bring some of that previously available material into the twenty-first century.

Roni Natov has already written: 'In its broadest sense … the literature of childhood represents a challenge to the world … in its varied imagined landscapes [it] suggests an inclusive society in which children can find a safe and creative way to live' (Natov 2006: 262). An 'inclusive society', this is exactly what I have been saying for you. It is a very specific readership that you potential writers need to recognise, and I return once again to Adam Phillips, who said: 'Adults can nurture children … but they do not have the answers … what they can do is tell children stories about the connections … ' (Phillips 1995: 1–2). But also ask you to bear in mind that the writer and the reader are involved in a shared project, where the writer must ask him or herself not, am I a good storyteller? But, what kind of person do I want to be? Because when you are faced with your reader, there will be many (especially critics) who will queue up to offer an answer to the first and this part of the book is designed to help you to understand the processes of storytelling. Faced with the second question, however, as Phillips reveals, 'there may be terrors but there are no experts', and if you have read the book this far then you will know how important your job as a writer is. Your relationship with your reader is a mutual exploration of the connections that is life and it should be an exciting, exceptional and special relationship that you cannot take for granted.

I ended Part 1 by musing on a possible link with Telemachus and Icarus, and it pleases me to think along such lines and indeed to be writing them down. I like the element of surprise, the feeling of wonder that such a story could exist. Telemachus, the only boy in Greek mythology to grow from boyhood into manhood, and Icarus, reported missing by his criminal father. That was a late-night musing as I was winding down, but the new day also reminded me that James Joyce had arrived before to give us just this kind of thing in *Ulysses*, oh well! But that doesn't say the story is closed, like most stories it is just simmering, waiting for the chance to be revealed.

In the meantime this section of the book is going to be split into sections, for easy access. But you will note I am not going to address picture books at length here, nor indeed the very early reader. These will be dealt with in the sister book to this, *Monsters Under the Bed: Critically Investigating Early Years Writing*.

## Considering stories for children

In the previous section I closed with a chapter on the 'elements of storytelling for children' and the rationale behind it was to look at storytelling in the abstract. But there is little point in denying that this cannot be broken down in a more practical and functional manner; the most important of which is that story is everything. 'Any work of art must first tell a story' is attributed to Robert Frost and I have already indicated this.

> In reading this book, you have already decided to write for children and you are looking for guidance. You already think you have a story and you want to learn how to tell it well. Your reasons are immaterial. You will already have some idea of what kind of story you want to write. Whether it's mystery, thriller, fantasy, science fiction, historical or whatever, the story will be germinating inside of you. But one thing is for certain – it will always be a *story*.
>
> (Melrose 2002: 16–17)

Story is what makes us human, it is the way we convey the narrative of the events of our lives, dreams, memories, disappointments, fantasies and hopes. It is also the narrative of experience and the meeting place of engagement between the writer and the reader. But the way stories are transmitted are many and multiple and multifarious, from the evening news to an encounter on a street corner; from a telephone call to a line from a poem, stumbled upon on a tattered fragment of parchment or an internet website. And sometimes you can come across a story that is made for you, unbeknown to you, but is about you, even as a trace. For example, in 2002 I was walking with my son through Busch Gardens in Tampa Bay, Florida (we had a week of roller-coasting – but that's another story). Every now and then people would smile at me and give me the thumbs up and at first I thought, what a friendly bunch of people we have here. And then I noticed the park's policy on US servicemen and I realised what was going on. A narrative was being constructed around my t-shirt that had (to my embarrassment now) FDLB printed on it with a badge that said Fire Dept 343, Long Beach, City California. I had bought the t-shirt in a ten dollars sale just off the i4 freeway because I had forgotten to pack enough (as usual) and because I liked the colours. But elsewhere, this was a post 9/11 narrative being constructed through the representative motif on the shirt. It said something about me that wasn't true, that I was a fire fighter and of course more than that relating to bravery and everything that goes with that narrative; and this has stayed with me. It reminds me of the power of representation; the power of semiotics and the potential for the story in almost anything we can see. I didn't mean to offer that story of a fictional me in the park; it just hitched a ride (as they say in the US), turned up with me and then presented itself to a willing suspension of disbelief.

Story, it could be said, is the narrative of events but the sense of parallax in reading the events, images and narrative isn't always what we will agree on. In writing for children I would rather describe story as the narrative of wonder. If you have a wonderful story then it should be told, I truly believe that. But, and this is so obvious yet difficult to hammer home, if it is not wonderful why does it deserve to be told? The answer is not always obvious. It is easy enough to say a novel entitled *Watching Paint Dry* targeted at nine-year-old boys may not inspire great enthusiasm, as the title might suggest, but we hear many not-wonderful things about the world and harsh as it may sound we cannot immunise children from them either. So in defining what is wonderful or not isn't as clear as it could be.

Thus, in some ways the writer for children is the *riddler*, which is a duality; for riddle means a story with a veiled or hidden meaning but it is also the tool we use to separate the stones from the soil or in our case the good stories from the bad. But most importantly we do need to remember a very basic fact, which is that we need stories as a means of communicating the narrative of experience or indeed engaging with the exploration of what it is to be human – and I have already discussed the way in which adults and children can co-exist in this narrative.

A good story, said Robert McKee, is ' ... something worth telling that the rest of the world wants to hear' (McKee 1999: 20). But before I go on with this chapter there are a couple of things you should know about writing a good story for children. However simple the story is, it has to be stimulating and this is one of the first things you have to consider. In his 1996 Carnegie Medal acceptance speech, Philip Pullman has indicated:

> There are some themes, some subjects, too large for adult fiction; they can only be dealt with adequately in a children's book ... stories are vital. Stories never fail us because, as Isaac Bashevis Singer says, 'events never grow stale.' There's more wisdom in a story than in volumes of philosophy. And by a story I mean not only Little Red Riding Hood and Cinderella and Jack and the Beanstalk but also the great novels of the nineteenth century, *Jane Eyre*, *Middlemarch*, *Bleak House* and many others: novels where the story is at the centre of the writer's attention, where the plot actually matters ... We don't need lists of rights and wrongs, tables of do's and don'ts: we need books, time, and silence. Thou shalt not is soon forgotten, but Once upon a time lasts forever.
>
> (Pullman 1996)[1]

In mentioning the 'great novels of the nineteenth century' here, I think Pullman is over-egging the case (lots of them are great books in search of a good editor but that is a debate for another time). However, he does make a good point, which is that having decided to write for children the question you are facing is not: do you have anything to write? But: do you have a story to tell? An accomplished story for children must have the same fundamental ingredients as a story for adults. Think about the insatiable demand for soap operas, television dramas, serialised or series fiction from Dilly to Horrid Henry,

Harry to Lyra, Sherlock Holmes to Inspector Dalgliesh, running comedy shows (how many years can *Friends* run for goodness sake?) and of course the endless stream of movies and even football/tennis/rugby matches we allow to take hours of our time: our demand for stories is as simple as this – *we want to know what happens next* (and my use of sport is not excused, it is just a story in a different form of narrative – although Pelé's bicycle kick in *Escape to Victory* (1981), like much of his football skills, was surely poetry-in-motion).

As I indicated in Part 1, it is important to realise that the child doesn't come to a story to see a hidden truth *but that which was not there before*, prior to their reading of it. In other words, in their own developing story of experience they are looking to find out what comes next. The story you can tell stands as the mediator at an arrested moment of experience, of something new that will not stand still, for it will never be new for them again, but will always be starting over: just as it did for the writer, so too will it for the reader. The arrested moment, the meeting between writer and reader, in that brief intercession is the point at which ongoing experience is confronted. And as Pullman also said: 'All stories teach, whether the storyteller intends them to or not. They teach the world we create. They teach the morality we live by. They teach it much more effectively than moral precepts and instructions' (Pullman 1996). But crucial to this formulation is the idea that children like to read up, that is to say they like to read what is in store for them. An eleven-year-old is already anticipating the oncoming teenage years, reading to find out what is in store for them, anticipating the future as a kind of vicarious experience. And this is not uncommon, few of us would want to read about ourselves, we like to read about others and elsewhere and things we know not. This evening I will read *The Lost Books of the Odyssey*, by Zachary Mason (2010), because of my interest in how 'differently' he has approached a topic I already like.

The point I am making here is, let your audience read up, to reach up and aspire to understand the generation immediately above them. That way writing the experience of an elder can pass on and assist in the anticipation of the experience the reader might even face in their own future (dealing with issues, etc.). Children like to read about what they have not yet experienced.

Nevertheless, there are varying and conflicting ideas on this issue of reading age. If you are to allow your reader to read up this means knowing your target audience when writing for them. Others disagree on this, saying just write the story and it will find its reader. Well if this is the case it will probably not find its publisher and you need to consider this. There is a huge disparity in the reading abilities between the ages of 5 and 15, and indeed even within similar age groups too. Not every 15-year-old reader has the same reading abilities, this is patently the case, but writers do have to think about childhood development and reading capacity when writing. But don't just take my word for it; research it by looking at publisher's lists and indeed the shelves in bookshops. These are usually categorised by age in the same way that schooling is. My use of the word 'usually', though, is a loaded one. Robert Leeson, in an analogy between the writer and the storyteller, tells us that in the actual experience of storytelling 'you match story to audience, as far as you can' (Leeson 1985: 161). The caveat, 'as far as you can', reveals the indeterminate parameters it addresses because you can only reach an approximation and for that reason we need to look at a form of categorising.

I find that looking at school years is a good way to think about categorising in terms of the length of story you wish to write but also the level of the story in terms of

experience, knowledge and knowability – although there are exceptions that I will address. On a fiction shelf/list these are roughly:

Age 4–7:
short fiction – read to/read aloud/read alone books, picture
books – up to 800 words; series fiction – up to 6,000 words
and collected short stories – up to 1,500 words each.

Age 6–9:
longer fiction – read alone, short novels, 12,000–20,000
words(ish); series fiction and collected stories.

Age 8–11:
read alone – novels, 20,000–50,000 words(ish) and series fiction.

Age 10–12:
read alone – pre-teen novels, 30,000–70,000 words(ish) and series fiction.

Age 12–15:
young teen fiction, teenage fiction, 50,000 words upwards.

Most recently there has been a category attached to this that has the label YA, 'young adult', but this kind of grading is open to slippage.

My listing here is less restricting than Random House's, which categorises books as: 5–7; 7–9; 9–11; and 12+,[2] where for example a book such as *The Emerald Atlas: The Books of Beginning*, by John Stephens, is also accompanied by this information: Children's Fiction, 9–11 year olds, Publication date: 14/04/2011, 432 pages. This is remarkably similar to Hodder and other lists I have seen. There is little point in my supplying information for all of the age categories when as a writer you should be researching this for yourself. However, later on I will address some of the relevant issues directly. But I cannot stress strongly enough the issues here are all about understanding the child's experience and development. You are not being asked to reduce the impact of your story but you do have to address the way you write it by bearing in mind the reading abilities and developing experience of the child. You are being asked to know and nurture your audience! But more than that, you are being asked to write for someone who is less experienced than you are but who knows more than they can articulate at any given time.

However, it is also important to think through certain other ideas, such as the *Harry Potter* phenomenon and the impact that had on child reading. The series broke series rules, in a way, or should that be the mould? Unusually, the reading child was allowed to grow with Harry. Progressively through each of the seven books Harry, Hermione and Ron, *et al.*, were getting older. We first encounter Harry age nine and three-quarters in 1997. My children were two and four when the first of the series was produced, but when they did latch onto the books they were five and seven, and at the stage of reading up/being read to. However, by the time they were reading *Harry Potter and the Deathly Hallows* in 2007, when Harry became 17, they were aged 12 and 14 and still reading up. This reaching up, looking ahead at fictional heroes older than they were, is common-place.

Although it has to be added that for all of the triumphs in the series, of which I and my children think are many, Rowling doesn't really get 17-year-olds. My son reread the entire series last summer and suggested that by the last book he still thought of Harry as being about the same age as himself, 15.

As I wrote previously (above):

> The idea of nurture is a persuasive one. The so-called space between the child and the adult/writer is actually the place where the two collide, where the story exists, where experience and knowledge is nurtured and where real contact is made. Children do catch their parents/storytellers up (it is what growing up is all about – it is why the process is nurtured) and so in the meantime, on their catch up journey the storyteller can only ' ... tell children stories about the connections'. So the issue becomes not 'why should we?' write for children but 'how?': to say 'story' articulates our existence, our essence, our very being as a thinking species, is a fact but it is no longer enough. It is necessary to understand it.
>
> (Butt ed., 2007: 24)

To me this means the meeting between the child and the writer via the 'story' has to be a culturally relevant exploration but also one that acknowledges the level of experience in the child being addressed. The reading range and experiential cognisance between the newly literate and the early teenager is huge. But as I demonstrated with the *Harry Potter* idea, while reading up is a general rule, the maturing reader can choose to read down too. It is not unusual for young readers to go back to picture books they read as infants. When I asked my own daughter aged around nine why she had gone back to (re)reading Enid Blyton (after a year or so of leaving them behind) she replied: 'I am tired, I just want to read something easy'. Never forget, the pleasure principle in reading for enjoyment is also omnipresent. She was too tired to read something more challenging but the lure of the story was still there.

But it is important to remember too, this applies to all child-centred culture. The movement through the years from childhood into adulthood is not a long march down a straight and narrow road. On the way we, all of us, stumble, back track, get snagged in the bushes, read books, put down books to watch films, read comics, play games, watch repeats of *The Simpsons* or old Harry Potter movies, facebook friends, sitt chatting on MSN ... the whole idea of child-centred culture, communication and media is about differences and choices and preferences and as I write this there are young people rioting in UK streets, showing yet another use for social media: all of these things go to make up the stories of our lives.

# Chapter 8

# Story structure

Assuming you do have something to say, then, in its most basic form, a story can be broken down into six very basic elements: balance, disharmony, inciting incident, problem, resolution and outcome. Let me open this up by giving a simplified example.

## Balance

Little Red Riding Hood is quite happy playing at home, nothing too interesting is going on and so the story has little to say except to introduce us to her. That's not to say there is no psychological profile or a multidimensional character available, it is just that we have not yet had the opportunity to 'show' that rather than 'tell' it beforehand.

## Disharmony

Suddenly the mood in the house changes: Granny Red isn't feeling too well and Little Red has to take her some cockie leekie soup (well it is my version). 'Mind now,' said Mother Red, as she waved Little Red off, 'take the straight path, don't stray from the middle way.' And with that Little Red waddled off to see her Granny. During this we have begun to see Little Red as a character as her profile unfolds; we know she is a willing soup carrier (or not); we know that she has a family (well there are three women in it – and an absent father, which may or may not be relevant) and we know she is old enough to be trusted to walk to Granny's house, although her mother still gives her a safety warning with regards to her route. And it is easy to see how we could play around with much of this – as Angela Carter[1] has done with such stories, for example.

## Inciting incident

Things were going just fine on the journey, a grass snake slithered nearby but Little Red knew it was harmless; a squirrel eyed her curiously too and Little Red just smiled while she picked a wee bunch of bluebells that were growing wild by the path. But when both the snake and the squirrel took fright and disappeared back into the bushes, Little Red looked up and saw what she thought was a huge dog eyeing her from the trees. The air turned icy cold and her pastoral walk through the forest had taken on a darker hue. But common sense prevailed and she ran off, congratulating herself for being so brave and brainy in doing the right thing to escape. And this early success is a useful part of the ongoing story narrative because the 'what happens next' is being anticipated. After all why introduce the dog if he hasn't scarpered like the snake and the squirrel but has stayed in the story as a trace, as an absent presence? You just know he is going to come back.

## Problem

Arriving at Granny Red's cottage brings temporary relief, and armed with a pot of cockie leekie soup and a bunch of bluebells, Little Red opens the door and sees poor Granny Red lying in bed. 'Oh Granny Red,' she says, 'what big eyes you have … ', and you know the rest.

## Resolution

The story can be brought through to a conclusion but this is where the storyteller is locked in with the reader to explore the connections to be or being made. What kind of message do you wish to send out? Is Little Red reckless, vain, feckless, a feminist, a kung fu expert? The list goes on because the story is dependent on the message you are trying to impart, the story you are telling for the child reader to experience and the story where the child is exploring the issues being raised. I would cite Jack Zipes on this issue because it is much more serious than just chopping the wolf's head off. Zipes (2009: 121) writes: 'It is impossible for anyone, male or female, whether heterosexual, transvestite, andro-gynous, homosexual, lesbian, sadist, masochist, straight, black, yellow, white, tan, or rainbow, to write a serious artful fairytale, even comical or farcical, without taking into account the vast changes wrought by feminism in the last forty years.' And for feminism we can also read into racism, homophobia, etc.

## Outcome

The outcome, the effect, the conclusion, the reward, the purpose of the story unfolds as it comes to the end, the moral issues become plain(er) but what has to be remembered is that the tale itself is not forced into a modern retelling that distorts the underlying idea that it has something important to offer. Instead it is nudged into this, our twenty-first century to reveal a sophisticated and experiential depth hitherto unknown to the child receiver. Written simply, without need to pause on literariness, literary dexterity and overblown rhetoric, which would just hold the story up, it does not preclude the potential for sharing and exploration of the issues the story presents – or indeed, the need to know what happened next, which was the secret to the story's success. Crucial to this, however, is the knowledge that this very basic template is just that, basic. But knowing this is very important. You can play around with it a little after you have mastered it as a basic model. I have seen a lot of work from writers who want to write but just don't know how to sustain the storytelling. Just take the story above, for example: what is the point in her getting lost in the forest, finding a candy covered mountain and some friendly Martians on the way if none of these things add to the story – and in fact merely become a distraction? Playing with the basic form is a writer's privilege but knowing the basic rules helps us to understand the process much more easily. Picasso knew this from an early age. He didn't just arrive at cubism or his blue period but developed it from his early pencil and charcoal drawings of his mother's hands as he learned his craft of representation. Storytellers are no different, there is an art and craft to writing and representation, and knowing this is really important to any writer.

Traditionally, then, this simple story would be set out as follows as I revealed before (Melrose 2002):

Beginning
     Meet the main character(s) and introduce the problem
Middle
     Focus on the problem, which gets worse through the inciting incident
     – introduce a focus of resistance such as suspense/surprise/tension
End
     Resolve the problem, whichever way, and then get out as quickly as possible
     with the important knowledge that every children's story should end with the
     *promise of a new beginning.*

Crucial to this, though, is the understanding that this is just a very basic formulation. The ideas of balance, disharmony and the inciting incident can all happen almost immediately in opening the story. For example, if you open the story with a crisis, all this suggests is that prior to this there was balance that is not worth speaking about. Let's be honest, the story of me writing this, here and now, might be of vague interest, but do you really need to know what I had for breakfast before I sat down to write? It was an apple and a cup of Earl Grey tea if you must know but has that enhanced your sense of my story at all? So we can simply take up the thread of the story, assuming that the immediate crisis is what triggers the story to be told. For example: 'Icarus sneezed feathers everywhere …' is a pretty good opener because it begs investigation: 'Where did those feathers come from, and what is my father doing with them … ', and therein begins the story. The never mentioned balance is introduced to disharmony, and as Icarus goes to investigate we can expect an inciting incident, 'Are those really for me to fly … ?', whereupon the story carries on, as I already indicated in Part 1.

The basic difference between story and plot can be summarised in a few short sentences. A story is a sequence of events, in its most simple form it is usually told in a chronological order and a plot is a means by which the themes, ideas, emotions and dramatic tension and events are arranged. Let's return to an example we have thought of before (after Ovid).

Daedalus wants to escape King Minos and Crete
He fashions some wings for himself and his son, Icarus
Daedalus straps his wings on and then does the same for Icarus
The father and son fly off the island
Icarus flies too close to the sun, the sun melts the wax holding his wings and he falls
     into the sea.
Daedalus laments his loss.

As Nabokov might have said, 'This is the whole story and we might have left it at that had there not been profit and pleasure in the telling' (Nabokov 1936). The series events listed are nothing but the cue cards of the story, but plotting it for dramatic effect even takes place in the Ovid version, which in itself, and by nature of the epic poem tradition, is scant but nevertheless slightly more emotive than the list I have given. As we can see it is devoid of themes, ideas, emotions and dramatic tension, and it needs these. After all, the Icarus story is more than just 'Escape from the Island'. The important thing in any story is the arranged sequence of events and through the sequences we move through the list of possibilities, and where each consequence has a cause and effect.

We can see this idea of a series of events extending the basic tenure of the above charts to six stages of plot development, which can be listed as:

The opening:
   Daedalus decides to flee King Minos and the island of Crete.
The arrival of conflict:
   how to do it requires major ingenuity and engineering skills.
The early achievement:
   the ingenuity works, Daedalus makes wings that work, they can fly, yay.
The twist and change:
   Icarus flies too close to the sun.
The denouement:
   Icarus falls into the sea.
The final outcome:
   Daedalus laments his dead son, the foolish boy.

It is often suggested that a story for children should open with conflict, but however minor the opening has to introduce it. In my own mind, the trick is not to delay the introduction of the conflict too long. Also, this is not a rigid structure but as you can see along the way, from start to finish, there has to be *change*! And this returns us to the Pullman idea:

> you can't put the plot on hold while you cut artistic capers for the amusement of your sophisticated readers, because, thank God, your readers are not sophisticated. They've got more important things in mind than your dazzling skill with wordplay. They want to know what happens next.
>
> (Pullman 1996)

In the end something has to have changed from the beginning, things never go back to being exactly the same as they were. As we can see from this plot model, these six changes are identified as progressive and all of them lead to the mantra – *what happens next*. But don't just take my headings as gospel. Try out your own and see what works for you, also think of variations and ideas on sub-plots, think of introducing other characters, Icarus' mother, Naucrate, might have had something to say about all this if she hadn't been excluded from Ovid's version of the story. But what is very important in this short description of a story is the characters must be seen to change from the beginning, through the middle to the end. The cliché 'he never changes' simply does not hold true. We all change; real life is about changes and change. Your child reader is changing at every reading (if you get more than one) and changing while reading and reading about change, which is the essence of experience being explored. And as I wrote above, the fact is stories are full of half truths, oxymorons, paradoxes, inconsistencies, absurdity, contradictions, illogical ideas, strangeness, otherness, familiarity, intimacy, formality, informality, knowledge, wisdom, know how, erudition, culture, learning and, let's be honest, everything, even the downright daft, where nothing ever stays the same. As I write this the words of Sam Cooke's *A Change is Gonna Come* (1963) are echoing through my head and indeed that song about change is a story in its own right.

A story for children does more than offer a story, it offers a point of view of the world in which ideas can be explored, it has to promote change, to respond to change and create change, especially for the story's leading characters, through whom the story is told and with whom the child reader identifies. Indeed, in children's fiction, especially for younger children, each chapter should be a story in its own right, with its own beginning, middle and end as it progresses the story into the next stage. But more than that, it offers an insight into people, into how characters deal with situations, and while you need to tell a story, you also need a convincing character to carry it.

## Characters

In what can only be described as an authorial intervention, Milan Kundera's narrator in *The Unbearable Lightness of Being* (Kundera 1984) found himself staring back at his characters, back to when he first saw them as a shadow or a silhouette in the window, back to the point before they were taught how to speak, and I always liked this idea of stumbling across a ghosted idea of a character in story. It is characters that interest us most when we read fiction. The what happens next is almost always about the person in the story: the girl abducted by pirates; the boy who lived; the girl who decided to change the world; the rabbit who couldn't cross the road; the car who could talk like a man; the monster whose job it was to scare children and extract energy from their screams; the list is endless and ongoing and ever changing and so it should be.

It is characters we come to love, hate, laugh at and with, cry at and with, empathise with, sympathise with. They are attractive, amiable, abhorrent, enjoyable, odd, funny, curious, creepy, angelic, devilish, good, bad, evil, cute, happy, sad, indifferent, objectionable, domineering, subordinate, bullies, bullied, boys, girls, men, women, rabbits, frogs, teddy bears, dogs, black, Asian, Scottish (like me), fair, spotty, freckled, pretty, pretty useless, my little sister, brothers, athletic, silly, funny, snooty, political animals, monsters, machines, robots, fairies, mermaids … the list is endless and I have been through it before (Melrose 2002: 21). But, and this is very important, they are never weak unless they are to grow strong; never dull unless they are to become bright; never nasty unless they are to become good or be exposed and defeated! Okay, so this is a generalisation but once again it's about knowing this before you can tease out the changes. I think one of my current favourite children's literature characters is Professor Snape in the *Harry Potter* books. Think about it, seven books and over one million words of sustaining him as bad just to reveal it was a red herring and he was good after all. Such a great piece of sustained character development, even if some of us did latch onto the clues being dropped, like how come he was a member of the 'Order'. It was very good work.

In the Icarus story I related above we can see it is the characters Daedalus and Icarus who provide the entire premise for the piece, but there is no character development there that we can attach our own perception to. To rewrite the Ovid poem as a piece of fiction for children is easy but it needs radical input on character development. Even the smallest tics can give much away and I will give three potential examples using the idea of the three ways of grading 'normative', which I discussed in Part 1.

The *first* is the affirmation of the superiority of the adult over the child, which excludes the child from full participation in the discourse taking place in the space in-between. In thinking about it, it is a kind of denial of any free will as a 'do as I say' commandment that seems a rather unlikely scenario in the twenty-first century.

'Achoo!' the feathers had tickled his nose and Icarus sneezed them all over his father's workbench.

'What are you playing at, boy? Can't you see I am busy?' Daedalus ushered Icarus into a corner, 'You are always getting in my way when I am working. Why can't you do something useful like feeding the chickens?'

'I was only … ' Icarus stammered.

'Only what? Only getting in the way as usual! Just sit there in the corner until I am ready for you.'

What we learn from this exchange is that by establishing the superiority of the adult over the child, the *first* normative principle I alluded to reveals the exclusion of the child from full participation in the space in-between exploration. Icarus was no apprentice at the well, or Dad's little helper, as they both explored the prospect of flight. He was there as his father's son and about to do his father's bidding. In fact the dialogue I left out was probably something like 'Useless boy!'

The *second* is the more likely scenario, in allowing participation of the child but one where the adult dictates the normative rules without some kind of appreciation of what the child needs and wants. The reason being that mother, father, guardian, teacher, etc., knows better, which is itself problematised, as I have already discussed.

'Achoo!' the feathers had tickled his nose and Icarus sneezed them all over his father's workbench.

'Look what you have done, here; look at the mess you have made? Can't you see I am busy?' His father frowned.

'What are you making?' asked Icarus. 'Is it another beast like the Minotaur?'

'No, not a beast! A bird! I am going to make you into a bird, Icarus,' said Daedalus. 'What do you think of that?'

'Hmm, I'm not sure,' Icarus replied. 'Would I have to fly?'

'I should think so. We both will, you'll see. Once I have finished I will show you. Now run off and play, I will call you when I am ready for you.'

Here, Daedalus is shown to be allowing participation but one where the father/adult/ maker dictates the normative rules without any kind of explorative engagement with Icarus' feelings on the matter. Icarus is still the mute child, unspeaking and uncomplaining beyond vague questioning and being 'not sure', while doing his father's bidding. As I have already said, such an idea is embedded in adult and parental normative behaviour.

Just to remind ourselves, the *first* and *second* ideas and attitudes are embedded in dominant adult ideology, institutions and practices that have become normative in a hierarchical, symbolic framework of child-centred, the only qualification required of the expert is to be adult. The *third* way (if indeed it is a way, as I have already said) is about taking much more of a dialogic and vigilant approach to the idea of normative.

'Achoo!' The feathers had tickled his nose and Icarus sneezed them all over his father's workbench.

'Look what you have done, here, Ic. Look at the mess you have made? Can't you at least try to be tidy?' His father frowned. 'What are you making, anyway? Is it another beast like my Minotaur?'

Icarus laughed, 'No, not a beast, something much better! What do you think about a flying boy? Wouldn't that be great?'

'A boy who could fly? That I would like to see. Could it be possible?' asked Daedalus.

'Well I have done some drawings on a piece of parchment, see,' Icarus sat up, brushing his hair out of his eyes, and showed his father what he had been drawing.

Daedalus turned the paper upside down and back the right way up again. 'I can't tell if it's a bird or a boy,' he teased.

'I call it a birdboy,' replied Icarus, 'and it could be me if you will help me.'

'Well I will if I can,' replied his father. 'But why do you want to be a birdboy?'

'So we can get off this island and away from him!'

'Him being King Minos?'

Icarus gritted his teeth, 'Yes!'

Daedalus nodded silently, 'I think you should build a model first.' He handed him the parchment back and pointed to the feathers and wax and string Icarus had collected. 'You already have a good drawing and you have collected the right materials, so that would be the next best thing to do.'

'A model, huh?'

'That's what I would do, and if it works, well we could try and build it full size.'

'Really, you really mean that? That would be so … ' Icarus hesitated, 'It would be brilliant, oh I wish my mother could see what we are going to build.'

What this tells us is that had the space in-between the master-maker and his child been negotiated by the 'exploring' 'mutually' and not one dominating the other, then the story in Ovid's poem could have had a more positive outcome. It also foregrounds the child in the story as being the positive character who acknowledges he could use his father's help, but he has the imagination to carry the project beyond his own experience of life. Also, we can see father and son engage in the politics of the situation they are faced with, Minos and Crete and the idea that the boy is affected by his father's treatment under the tyrant king. What this reveals for a reader is a child and adult both confronting the experience and knowledges available, and for Icarus to reveal his maturing mind, which the writer is hopefully nurturing so children may make the kind of connections required to sustain them rationally and emotionally through a text that addresses other issues in their maturing lives – and indeed in the rational and irrational emotions inherent in the illogical, paradoxical, ironic and absurd oxymorons life presents. Icarus' reference to 'him' indicates the kind of inarticulate gesture we expect from an inexperienced youth who isn't quite sure of the language of politics he is confronted with but remember and remember and remember: *children understand more than they can articulate at all the stages of their life.* For Icarus read the reading child who is confronted with his or her own challenges day-to-day without necessarily having the means of articulation – yet! But it is an ongoing project of maturity and cognitive development.

And okay I am not trying to laminate real life with the life of a fiction here. But this type of exchange is representational and replicated in, for example, the Dumbledore/ Harry Potter relationship, so too in the Lyra Belacqua/Iorek Byrnison/Lee Scoresby relationship, and I firmly believe the effect is a radical and desirable rejection of the Rose position (see Part 1) and one about 'making the connections'. Of course, it is still fiction but a legitimate effort is being made in the representation. While we keep the focus on the child character we can see that he or she is not subordinate in the discourse but an integral part of it. But what does it tell us about the character, Icarus?

He is inquisitive
He is creative
He is interested in exploring
He thinks (perhaps that should be *knows*) a flying boy is real
He has a wistful longing for a missing mother
His father's pet name for him is Ic
His relationship with his father seems to be a good one
He wants to escape Crete
He does not like King Minos
He is not quite articulate enough to speak of the politics behind his wish to fly
He is determined
He is also likable, which isn't a bad start with around 200 words to play with.

Do your own exercise! Think about the character you want to write about then create a little narrative that includes who he or she is. Think about what defines him or her, where do they stand in relation to?:

The story world at large
The context of the story
What might be going on in his head
What might be going on in the head of others close to him
What might be real
What might be imagined
What might be possible and not
Where they might be going
What they might say
What others may say to him or her

This isn't a tick box, check list, just a bunch of suggestions in thinking about your character. But important to this too is the level of maturity shown by the child. Here I would put Icarus around 11 years old; old enough to think of life's possibilities without having his dreams dented by societal realities. I coach youth football and I can guarantee that every player aged 13 and under thought they were in training to be major football stars. As the years progressed and they matured (at different times) and thought about it more, they began to realise differently, but who was I to puncture that dream and ambition they all had in youth. If ever I was asked, 'And, do you think I could make it?' my answer was always, 'Yes, of course you can.' My job was to help them explore their own abilities and to be as good as they could be, to help them get to the very peak of their potential, which varied.[2]

   But I can also say through this anecdote that thinking about the age of your characters is very important to the readership. Some may disagree and there are instances where exceptions can reveal themselves. Pullman's Lyra Belacqua is one such character. Aged 11 years in the book she shows a maturity beyond her years. But consider why Harry

Potter arrived in our lives aged nine and three-quarters and asked readers to grow with him through seven books to the age of 17; or for example, why evidence exists to show Philip Pullman (1997) reduced Will Parry's age to 12 years, from his original idea of him being older in *The Subtle Knife*. The fact was that making Will 12 released the character from the potential sexual frisson and tension that could be read into him as a YA (Young Adult in publishing is a categorisation of children's literature).[3] But think this through, it would have been a complicated thing to have Will older because a central theme in the trilogy is the youth and innocence of the two children. So, Lyra too is a representational age of pre-pubescence until the end of the trilogy when it is suggested that she is getting ready to become adult.

Age determinism in writing for children is crucial to the idea of development. I have written Icarus (above) as 11 and I would expect my reader to be in the 9–11 age bracket, allowing for the fact that some younger children read better than others and some of the older children are less able readers and it is impossible to get anything more than an approximation on this. That is not to say older readers don't read down, it is just rarer for them to do so and Pullman's trilogy is one of the exceptions in that rule, although there is plenty more to keep the older reader interested.

## Voice and point of view (POV)

The difference between a narrative voice and a point of view is marked. It would be fair to say that if you read this book cover to cover you might have a narrative voice in your head in which you may think you can hear me speaking. A vaguely mild Scottish accent perhaps (east coast); a scholarly tone (though not fusty); not young but not (too) old either, but in truth my narrative voice gives very little away. What does keep it alive though, and this is true for every writer, is your belief in it as a reader and your reader's ear. You read the voice and hear what you want to hear because it is, to all intents and purposes, one of the things a reader brings to the text. You don't even know whether I am male or female, and there is no point in looking at the name on the front cover, I could be Mary Ann Evans[4] for all you know. But I cannot help the way I write, well that is not true, I write in different ways for different mediums, but when I sat down to write this book the tone it takes is very much related to the message I wanted to convey.

For example, if you read *Write for Children* (2002) it has a far more informal tone than this book. Also, this Part 2 is much less formal than Part 1. But the narrative voice I have used is not mine alone but one gained through experience of reading and listening and in trying to convey the message the book contains. For an academic text it is more informal than some but more formal than books on 'writing' for example because I have tried to tread a path in-between – oh yes, walking the middle way (I can fly elsewhere another day if I choose). And the reason for that is simple: I am trying to gauge my readership, you my reader. Of course I have absolutely no idea what you look like, sound like, dream about, and so on, but I have seen enough students of writing and critical, cultural and communication ideas to get some sense of who you are as a homogenised body.

Now this idea of homogenisation of storytelling is something I railed against when I said I do not accept the homogenisation, depersonalisation and fragmentation threat to storytelling, going on to add that this is because I agree with Jack Zipes when he says:

'genuine storytelling is not only subversive but magical in that it transforms the ordinary into the extraordinary and makes us appreciate and take notice of the little things in life that we would normally overlook' (Zipes 2002: 135), because it's not just the 'little things' but all things that can be touched by a story context, which interests me. But there is a limit to how far we can go with this. I have written songs and poems for one person and one person only, in which I have personalised it to such an extent that only makes true sense to them (although that does not discount the interpretive sense of it for the other who happens upon it). But for this reason I echo Amanda Boulter's idea that we are all 'individuals' in the writing and reading process, when she writes:

> Even in the teeth of theoretical tradition that has torn such humanist ideas to pieces I still want to claim that 'human life is not (essentially) a fiction, and that fictions are (essentially) about human lives'.[5] Theorists who argue that identity is constructed by political ideologies and unconscious repressions still have to recognise that each finite individual is uniquely positioned (historically, geographically, biologically, socially) in relation to those external or internal forces. And even if our identities are total fictions [which I doubt] as many theorists claim, then each one will be telling a subtly different story. There will always be individual differences – as well as species and social sameness – for that is what makes us human.
>
> (Boulter 2007: 59)

From what I have written in Part 1, there will be little surprise that I think we are all individuals trying to make the connections in our socialisation. As I have also revealed, I agree with Brande when she writes: 'It is well to understand as early as possible in one's writing life that there is just one contribution which every one of us can make: we can give into the common pool of experience some comprehension of the world as it looks to each of us' (Brande 1934: 120).

Amanda Boulter has some useful and often quite radical ideas on the issue of narrative voice and I do recommend her book, *Writing Fiction: creative and critical approaches*, for an extended thesis on this. But hopefully what I have made clear is that writing for children is about using a voice that will encourage the child to read on and I urge you to think about the way you address the text using the 'three normative' ideas I highlighted above. Children do not respond to the didactic, the dictatorial or the plain dull but to the nurturing tones of the storyteller who has transferred his or her skills onto the printed page so that they can make connections. They are both trying to find out what they know and know not and understand what they can find out – and as a personal aside, I have learned a great deal writing this book, not all of which will be agreed with or approved of or accepted – so write and tell me.

After you have decided on your story, easily one of the most important decisions you will ever make when you begin writing, then, concerns viewpoint.

Who is going to tell the story?
Through whose eyes are we told the story?
How is the story to be told?
Where does the narrator stand in relation to the other characters in the story?

What age do you see your character as being?
What level of experience in life do you expect your character to have?
How knowing is your character?
How lucid is your character?
Who is going to read the story?

This is so very important to all of the above and the reason is a simple one, which I have written of in Part 1 and as I will repeat below.

The child comes to a story in anticipation of seeing the familiar they recognise and can relate to but also something new they do not know, or may know of but as yet have not articulated. Once again, the child doesn't come to a story for a hidden truth but that which was not there before, prior to their reading of it as part of their experiential development. It is crucial that you address these issues and answer the questions in your own mind. Then once you have decided on the viewpoint you have to stick to it. Once children begin hearing or reading a story, they become absorbed by a central voice and it becomes familiar to them. At the beginning of his book on series fiction, Victor Watson wrote:

> My thanks are due to a boy in Year 6 at Stapleford Primary School, Cambridgeshire, who, while talking to me about series fiction several years ago, explained that starting a new novel was like going into a room full of strangers, but starting a book in a familiar series was like going into a room full of friends.
>
> (Watson 2000)

This sums up a great deal for me and it is the wisest of words for a writer. It is so important to get the narrative voice into such a good sense of the familiar so that the 'room full of strangers' are the potential new friends – but the consistency of the voice must be maintained even in a stand alone novel, though even more so in a series – and few could really complain about Rowling's and Pullman's efforts there but this is one of the very great things about twenty-first-century children's literature, the writing and publishing standards are extremely high.

Choosing your narrative voice is important then and it is essential to understand its power. This is especially so in writing for the early years, where changing that narrative voice only leads to confusion, although moving into teenage fiction gives some scope for multiple voices. Choose your viewpoint carefully and remember you are not choosing for yourself but for your child reader who comes to the story with high expectations and it would be a shame to let them down. Now we can move onto viewpoint, which always comes under two very clear headings, called *objective* and *subjective*.

## Objective viewpoint

The opportunity to use 'objective viewpoint', often referred to as 'second person', in most literature, never mind children's, is slight because it relies on a style of reporting, where the narrator stays outside the characters at all time by precluding subjective thinking – in fact all thinking is 'reported'. The most prominent examples are those narratives that address a reader with the bare facts of the story. Indeed most commonly we can see this in the epic poem, and I can go back to Ovid's Daedalus and Icarus to reveal this:

> Row upon row of feathers he arranged …
> Into a gentle curve to imitate
> Wings of a real bird. His boy stood by,
> Young Icarus, who, blithely unaware
> He plays with his own peril, tries to catch
> Feathers that float upon the wandering breeze …
> … the craftsman poised himself
> On his twin wings and hovered in the air.
> Next he prepared his son. 'Take care,' he said,
> 'To fly a middle course, lest you sink
> Too low the waves may weight your feathers; if
> Too high, the heat may burn them. Fly half-way
> Between the two. And do not watch the stars,
> The Great Bear or the Wagoner or Orion
> With his drawn sword, to steer by. Set your course
> Where I shall lead.'
>
> (Ovid 1986: 176–78)

The narrator is a fly on the wall character, located outside the narrative and reporting everything that is going on with a matter-of-factness: 'Next he prepared his son.' The narrator is keeping well outside of the emotional character at all time and we can only guess at the internal thoughts during the scene. We get no sense of what Daedalus or Icarus are thinking here and our sense of the story is 'reported' through the actions and words overheard. Thus, this means of writing fails to really explore the emotional depth of the characters. Nevertheless, it does have its uses, for example in picture books for the very young. Think about it this way: 'The boy's dad strapped wings onto his back … ' You can see the picture without it needing to be drawn here, the strapline just nudges the storyline through. In a picture book called *Kyoto*, I used a similar technique when I wrote:

> Then the boy pushed his sledge down the hill and jumped on board.
> Once again he shouted, 'Wee … eee … !' as he slid down the hill.
> The little bear slipped down onto her bottom.
> She too began to slide down the hill.
> Down and down and down they both slid, slipping and sliding.
> The boy couldn't see the little bear.
> And the little bear couldn't see the boy.
> Suddenly there was an almighty crash.
> The boy and the little bear had bumped into each other at the bottom of the hill.
> 'Oi!' said the boy. And he laughed.
> The little bear didn't say anything (because bears can't talk). She just jumped up and shook snow all over the boy.
> 'Oi!' laughed the boy again.
>
> (Melrose 2010)[6]

## Subjective viewpoint

This is the most common viewpoint in writing for children and the term subject speaks for itself because it allows the writer to write subjective thoughts and allows the reader to get inside their character's head. Usefully, too, it comes in three distinct guises.

## Omniscient subjective viewpoint

Sometimes called third person unlimited, popularised by the invention of the novel and used widely in the nineteenth century by those golden age, early novelists, George Eliot and Charles Dickens, it is very rarely used these days. I have no immediate knowledge of it in modern children's books at all. Indeed publishing conventions have all but erased it, so let's get it out of the way quickly. The problem it presents for the reader is that while it presents an omniscient view of the world, everyone's thoughts, feelings, conversations, actions and setting are available too. Every scene is scrutinised and the author tells us everything there is to know, but so do the characters as we can get into their heads. But it makes it difficult for a reader to empathise with any given character because the narrative is a collective mass of polyphonic voices all vying for attention, often including the author's omniscient view. For example, let's go back to Daedalus and Icarus:

> Row upon row of feathers lay arranged in neat piles on the workbench. Daedalus moulded them meticulously into a gentle curve to imitate the wings of a real bird. Perfect, just perfect, he thought, as he coated the tip of feather after feather with hot wax and squeezed them into place. 'There,' he muttered, thinking, these will do just nicely. I wonder what the boy is up to, 'Icarus, Icarus, come here, come and see … '
>
> Blimey, thought Icarus, what does he want now, 'Coming father,' he said reluctantly. Just then Icarus heard a shuffling noise coming from behind a pillar.
>
> Don't look this way, don't look … urged Queen Pasiphae, silently praying she would not be spotted. She didn't want anyone to see her spying on the artificer, Daedalus. He was up to something. She didn't know what and she was determined to find out.
>
> 'Icarus, now boy,' shouted his father. 'Why are you dilly-dallying?'
>
> Young Icarus was blithely unaware of what was going on. But still he hurried as quickly as he could. But when he turned the corner his mouth opened wide in silent astonishment. His father was hovering in the air at about table height. No one could have been more shocked than Icarus.
>
> No one more than the spying Queen Pasiphae, that is. So that is what he is up to, she thought. The trickster, just wait until I get him on his own … The queen held her silence and kept her thoughts to herself. She would talk to Daedalus in time.
>
> Hmm, what is the wily Queen up to? We can only guess.

While the result might be worth the effort and I have to confess there is an addictive pleasure in writing like this, the writer doesn't have to work nearly as hard, but ultimately, you can see what will happen when more and more subjective 'voices' come to clutter the story – I mean what is Queen Pasiphae up to, what does King Minos think of it all and Ariadne and Theseus, what will they be thinking?: goodness they are gathering a crowd. And of course Pasiphae hasn't quite kept her thoughts to herself as the all seeing, all knowing, all hearing narrator indicated. You can try this writing as an exercise if you like (and I have seen people do this for real and thinking it's fine), but the days of Sir Walter Scott's panoptic, all seeing, all knowing narrative voice has really had its day.

## First person

Enid Blyton never wrote for children in the first person because she thought they didn't like it. I have no idea where I read this but as far as I have been able to gain from research, it does seem to be the case (and if not can someone please tell me?). But children do, indeed, like reading first person narratives. The reason is simple, it is the first point of view we all identify with. Even if we begin learning to write with what is essentially an 'objective viewpoint', we tend to develop the subjective through the first person and the pronoun 'I'. Our first writing comes from our own personal point of view, we think in the personal; we address the world from a personal perspective when we are telling a story and when we are formulating our own stories we begin by involving ourselves so how would a child not be able to identify with it? I gave this example elsewhere but it works as a true to life demonstration of this. When my daughter was four she sat opposite me at the breakfast table and said:

> This morning, after I got up, I borrowed your car and drove down to the pier. Then I drove it into the sea and got chased by a crocodile. So I drove home again. And you didn't even know I was gone.[7]

It is told in the first person and indeed, structurally, it has perfect symmetry and understanding. Let me digress a little to show this before returning to first person and because we could do this exercise on all the stories we write. But it is really relevant to a couple of things, the first is the explanation of the first person point, that is clear, but the other is the symmetry of the story because even from a four-year-old child it conforms to a very good storytelling tradition.

This story was pure fantasy, of course. We could analyse and critique it by resorting to post-structuralism or psychoanalytical criticism, as our profession often expects of us. Certainly there are issues to consider in a Rose/Peter Pan post-Lacanian kind of way, where we might have considered issues such as her safe return home after the adventure: where the crocodile threat coupled with my not knowing she had gone out actually referred to a previously unsaid expression of how secure she felt at home. And then we could go on to quote a little Jacques Derrida for critical support: ' ... as always, coherence in contradiction expresses the force of desire ... '(1978: 279). But I would rather dwell on the story itself, especially from one so young, because it reveals the following precise elements of storytelling:

Balance
Disharmony
Inciting incident
Problem
&
Resolution

So let me break them down:

Balance
    Abbi's story begins at home
Disharmony
    She steals the car to start her adventure
(introducing) Inciting incident
    She drives to the pier, i.e., somewhere 'other', 'different' and 'unheimlich'
Problem
    She drives into the sea only to get chased by a crocodile
Resolution
    Just as things get too hairy, she escaped by driving home and then
    pretends she had never gone out, in the hope that I wouldn't notice – and
    then we have the promise of a new beginning, which was the start of a new day.

We can see the story is perfectly formed, even from someone so young, and as the storyteller matures her sense of metaphor and simile, adjective and adverb, tension, pace, narrative voice and so on will mature with her. The story is not without psychological underpinning, conflict and a 'what happened next idea'. Neither is it without a good sense of imagery. Nevertheless, we can see the story conforms to a recognised form:

Beginning:
    meet the main character(s) and introduce the problem.
Middle:
    focus on the problem, which gets worse and introduce the focus of resistance
    such as suspense/surprise/tension.
End:
    resolve the problem, whichever way, then get out as quickly as possible – and
    of course she has this wonderful denouement raising a storyteller's awareness of
    my need to be informed.

But the main thing it has is 'surprise'; at each twist and turn the element of surprise keeps us reading and thinking and wondering what happens next. Abbi's story, then, from driving to the pier (we live in Brighton, UK), getting chased by the crocodile, then returning home before she is missed, is complete in every sense; and of course we can forgive her the crocodile in salt water, she was only four. But back to the first person, it can have a more sophisticated and mature feeling for the subjective and I can show this too by going back to the eleven-year-old Icarus.

Feeling hungry after you have just eaten isn't the best way to start the day. I know that all too well. And the king doesn't like me going anywhere near the kitchen before lunch. I wonder if my father has a snack stored in his workshop?
    'Ah, Icarus, there you are. I was just going to call you.'
    In the name of Dionysus, what is he doing? I must be drunk, how can he be …
'Father, how can you be flying?'
    'I am wearing my new wings. What do you think? Pretty good huh?'
    I watched my father, the great Daedalus, twirl in mid air. In mid air, I couldn't even say it out loud. Looking past him, I could see another set of feathers moulded carefully into a gentle curve to imitate another pair of bird wings. 'Are … are those for me?' I asked, pointing at the worktop.

'Of course, come on, come and try them on. I'll help you.'

Oh my god, Zeus, is he serious? 'Are you serious, you mean I can have wings and fly too?'

'If you want to?'

'Want to? I'll say I want to. Yes, father, yes I do … ' Oh my god, Zeus. I am going to learn to fly. This has to be the best day of my life. I wish my mother was here to see this.

Because the narrator addresses the reader directly, using the prefix 'I', the reader is drawn into a textual collusion with the narrator. Unlike hearing the story being told the process is internalised and the narrative is inclusive. This is especially the case when we are dealing with older fiction, where issues are dealt with as straight questions straight from the internal thoughts of the protagonist – i.e. putting onto paper those thoughts we never share or hear shared. But it works for younger fiction too, and my old friend Tony Bradman's wonderful *Dilly the Dinosaur* series is written in the first person. The narrative is given through the eyes of Dilly's sister, Dorla. And while it is a quite brilliant example of good, subtle, first person narrative, for the younger reader, the empathy of the 'sister' in that family unit is ever present.

## Third person limited

This along with first person is the most common point of view used in children's and indeed most fiction. It is a very effectual approach and probably the simplest to negotiate. Basically what happens is the entire story is written from the perspective of the main character. Children especially like this approach because it allows them to progress from the first pronoun 'I' to thinking more of others in the story narrative. The technique allows them to empathise completely with the character you have created for them (presuming, of course, the character deserves their empathy) and perfect examples are those I have used throughout this book in Harry Potter and Lyra Belacqua. But let's look at Icarus again:

The moon sat high in the midnight blue sky. Icarus was amazed at how bright it was. The silhouette of a lone falcon hovered on the breeze and the moon picked it out perfectly. And he was thinking, I wonder what it would be like to fly.

Just then Icarus heard a shuffling noise behind him and he ducked out of sight. The last thing he needed was his father telling him off. He had crossed Ariadne earlier and that was bad enough.

He had just managed to duck behind the wisteria that hung over the balcony when he spotted the dark moonshadow of another bird settle on the mosaic patio in front of him.

'God, Zeus,' he said to himself. And he was thinking, a heron must have landed on the balcony overhead. He will be after the fish in Minos' pond. Icarus stepped forward for a better look.

To his utter amazement, there was no heron, there was no bird, only a man with wings hovering over the balcony like some great flying mirage. 'Father,' said Icarus, anxiously. 'Father, is that you? Can that really be you?'

Icarus watched the smile cross Daedalus' face as their eyes met. 'Icarus, my boy. I was keeping this secret until after I had completed my first test flight. But now you see me, what do you think?'

> Icarus was almost too astonished to speak. 'What do I think? I … I think it's amazing … truly, truly amazing.'

What we read is the scene being played out through Icarus. It can be restricting because we can only convey Daedalus through the eyes of his son or through dialogue but as you can see, it is extremely effective. In a refinement of this technique we can informalise it even more to excellent effect so that it's only a whisper away from first person.

> Icarus didn't mind the stillness and the silence of the night. The moon was weaving its mystery of magic and he felt at ease. And for once, they were at peace with each other too. Mum and Dad, he had heard them squabbling so often he was getting used to it. But tonight Dad had been too busy inventing something to be grumpy with them.

It could be argued that this is a mixing of a third and first person viewpoint, but it has a persuasive quality to it, and for the child reader the informal 'mum and dad' brings the narrator closer. It is only a variant on the omniscient technique but the intimacy is implicit and immediate. It takes us much closer to the main character without having to rely on the restrictive and often self-important inflection of *me*, *myself*, *I* when using the first person.

Hopefully, then, you have managed to make some sense of viewpoint. The crucial point is make it clear. Choose your viewpoint carefully, then make it strong and make it interesting. To paraphrase what I have written in Part 1, your reading child has already come to the story with some ideas of their own even if his silence is a hypothetical postulate full of thoughts and thinking, which is always expressed in ellipses … where the unsaid and unsayable does not mean the unknown (for the child's time being) because the language, the point of view, the narrative voice you use to express knowledge comes after, through ageing and experience (lived in and lived out) and is gained, minute by minute, second by second, both primarily and vicariously, in the child's ongoing development. Indeed it would be a mistake to assume that your child reader is not engaged in adult discourse while developing, just as adults engage with children's. It is an ongoing dialogic experience of social engagement – and to steal Peter Hunt's phrase again (which I am sure he will not mind) they and we, children and adults alike, are constantly engaged in the 'comfortably predictable and the unsettlingly unexpected' on a day-to-day basis.

## Surprise

Crucial to writing for children is the element of 'surprise' in all of this. It should ooze out of the pages, and in the hands of skilled writers it does. All of us are continually in search of the textual surprise, in books and films and songs and poems. What a dull world it would be if we became too grown up to be surprised by the unexpected. But children are insiders in this process, not outsiders, and one of the central assumptions underpinning *their* experience is the significant overlap between non-fictional and fictionalised patterns of representation, precisely because these symbolic frameworks or discourses are in circulation through popular culture as well as real life situations, and a fictionalised and non-fictional, experiential narrative combines to inform. Children frequently draw upon references to and images from fiction, film and television drama and the internet in combination with their real living experience in constructing *their* 'stories'. Please bear this in mind when writing for them – in whatever capacity. The greatest element in any form of representation is surprise, it is what makes a good story great.

## Dialogue

You may have noticed that what I have established above is the very fact that a lot of writing for children is undertaken through the use of dialogue and this is as it should be. We live in a noisy world of verbal words; from friends, strangers, parents, teachers, radio, television, and so on, it is a polymorphous cacophony, a verbal Lernian Hydra, with each head jabbering away. But isn't it one of the great curiosities of living that we still manage to make sense out of words that come at us from all different angles? Boulter (2007: 68–69) calls this a Bakhtinian sense of dialogic dialogue when she discusses the three ways it is addressed in fiction. To summarise, briefly, the first is that the writer's words 'serve two speakers at the same time and express simultaneously two different intentions: the direct intention of the character who is speaking, and the refracted intention of the author', where the voice of the novel is to be found in the managed medley of its 'voices'. And important in this information is the idea that dialogue is not just novelistic chit-chat. It has to have a purpose in driving the story forward. And be assured, meandering around in a lyrical haze of purple prose will only put your child reader off.

The second way Boulter identifies is the dialogue that takes place between the characters, representing their different points of view and values (and each character will have the same differences we all have). Two children age eleven are not going to be cloned into thinking, feeling and being the same, unless that is material to the plot of course (say both of us here). 'For Bakhtin,' writes Boulter, 'these voices represent the soul of fictional writing' and it is an excellent description. Intrusive narrators and authorial intervention are considered to be at best a nineteenth-century anachronism and otherwise an idiosyncrasy these days. The dialogic dialogues are a way of allowing the writer to represent self-consciously aware characters as being able to speak for themselves. And this is immensely important in children's fiction, as you might have gathered by now. Allowing the child to 'speak' in a text is extremely important. Granted it is still your 'adult imported ideas' but remember what I said before about the writer and the reader 'exploring the options'. Because this brings us to the third form of dialogism, which is the dialogue between the writer and the reader, and I have discussed the implications of this at great length in Part 1.

Important to this idea of dialogue between writer and reader is something I have mentioned before. To some extent I am imagining you reading this, which we all do when we write. But you are a fiction to me, only an imaginary friend (it is to be hoped), but some of the stuff I wrote in Part 1 isn't going to endear me to everyone so even as I type I can see a mixture of faces staring back at me. In truth, part of me is looking at a fairground mirror of myself and trying to imagine what would it be like to read me sitting here, but as my colleague Amanda Boulter has said, 'it's perhaps one of the ironies of writing that we write in solitude in order to communicate with a host of strangers.' The important thing to remember is the imagined person at the other end of the chain begins with you writing. I as the 'real author' am writing to you as an 'implied reader' and you the 'real reader' are only engaging with me as the 'implied author'. You are the reader I imagine and I am the writer you imagine and along the way we may never meet (sadly). Writing for children is no different, you have to be able to imagine your reader. But crucial to this is the fact that your reader is also imagining you, so it is a reciprocal exploration of the text.

Before I move on I want to address another issue for you as a writer to consider. I showed some dialogue between Daedalus and Icarus (above):

> 'God, Zeus,' he said to himself. And he was thinking, a heron must have landed on the balcony overhead. He will be after the fish in Minos' pond. Icarus stepped forward for a better look.
>
> To his utter amazement, there was no heron, there was no bird, only a man with wings hovering over the balcony like some great flying mirage. 'Father,' said Icarus, anxiously. 'Father, is that you? Can that really be you?'
>
> Icarus watched the smile cross Daedalus' face as their eyes met. 'Icarus, my boy. I was keeping this secret until after I had completed my first test flight. But now you see me, what do you think?'
>
> Icarus was almost too astonished to speak. 'What do I think? I … I think it's amazing … truly, truly amazing.'

The dialogue between two people is generally more intimate than, say, when there are more involved. But the options are restricted. A talks to B and B talks to A, back and forth. As you can see the dialogue exchange possibilities are restricted.

Introducing another voice doesn't just make a threesome, it introduces the factor three to the equation and gives six options. See the diagram, below.

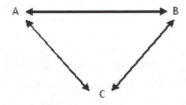

As you can see with this alternative, A can speak to B and C, B can speak to A and C and C to A and B. Thus the potential to open the dialogue out and widen the subject matter, give facts, etc., is easier to manage. But it allows us to play with tension and play characters off against each other. Now looking at the 'normative' ideas I discussed earlier, we can see how the narrative can manipulate the characters very simply.

'God, Zeus,' he said to himself. And he was thinking; a heron must have landed on the balcony overhead. He will be after the fish in Minos' pond. Icarus stepped forward for a better look.

To his utter amazement, there was no heron, there was no bird, only a man with wings hovering over the balcony like some great flying mirage. 'Father,' said Icarus, anxiously. 'Father, is that you? Can that really be you?'

Icarus watched the smile cross Daedalus' face as their eyes met. 'Icarus, my boy. I was keeping this secret until after I had completed my first test flight. But now you see me, what do you think?'

Icarus was almost too astonished to speak. 'What do I think? I ... I think it's amazing ... truly, truly amazing.'

Neither of them had seen Pasiphae approach. 'Bravo, bravo, now the trickster can fly. Can you see what is to happen, Icarus? Your father will fly off and leave us.'

Icarus looked stunned. 'My father would never do that, would you, father?'

'No?' asked the Queen, 'are you sure?'

'Don't listen to her, Icarus. Do I not teach you everything I know?' said Daedalus.

'Just like he showed Talus,' added the Queen.

'Hush, woman, do not speak about that which is not,' Daedalus snapped grimly.

Icarus looked from one to the other. Adult games were full of riddles and he wasn't sure what to think. There had been rumours about Talus.

As we can see the dialogue is best kept brief and each word weighted to moving the scene and the story forward. Elizabeth Bowen offers some excellent advice on this (cf. Boulter 2007: 155).

1. dialogue should be brief;
2. it should add to the reader's present knowledge;
3. it should eliminate the routine exchanges of ordinary conversation;
4. it should convey a sense of spontaneity but eliminate the repetitiveness of real talk;
5. it should keep the story moving forward;
6. it should be revelatory of the speaker's character, both directly and indirectly it should show the relationships among people.

Look at this checklist in relation to the small snatch of story dialogue I supplied and look for the links. Of course the line, 'do not speak about that which is not' echoes the Joyce quotation I used in Part 1, and we can see how Bakhtin's idea of dialogism also works in this contrived exercise, one which Bakhtin says will happen anyway – which is true for I confess the line I used popped straight into my head in writing this. But in the words of Frey, 'dialogue should be in conflict, indirect, clever, and colourful' (Frey 1987: 114).

# Chapter 9

# Early readers, middle years and pre-teens
## Not short stories but big stories told short

I wrote earlier that I wouldn't be addressing picture books because they are a specialty in their own right. A combination of pictorial and word narratives, there just isn't the space to do them justice here and a sister book to this, entitled *Monsters Under the Bed: critically investigating writing for early years* will address the issues more fully. But what I can say is that the picture book and early reader/read-to book has a space of its very own in the nurturing process of childhood. For the developing toddler these books are like television for early years but with a difference. With television a toddler can be plonked in front of it, allowing us adults to get on with other stuff. Any parent will know about that. But a book is a different prospect, which immediately brings together the visual and verbal as a combined experience. Much research on early readers and picture books concentrates on the critical aspects of cognitive experience and into differences and comparisons on reading the picture and reading the words. Indeed Nikolajeva and Scott (2006: 1) introduced their book on picture books by saying:

> The unique character of picturebooks as an artform is based on the combination of two levels of communication, the visual one and the verbal. Making use of semiotic terminology we can say that picturebooks communicate by means of two separate sets of signs, the iconic and the conventional.

And of course they are right in identifying these two important levels of communication. But they have actually missed the third and most important and unique component in the communication combination in which the picture book and the early read-to/reader are part. It is the one of shared experience, the relationship between the reader and the child as mediated by the book. It is as close as we can get to a critical and literary hug and to miss this point is to miss the function of the book and the potential it has in the nurturing process. Imagine if you will, that shared and nurtured experience. It is a very physical encounter, a sensory event where touch, sound, sight, story, warmth, security, affection and love are brought together in the shared experience of a story that is mediated by the book. As I have written before, 'This is nurture in action; this is experience in the making; this is about making the connections. I am even tempted to comment that never again in our lifetime will the relationship between adult and child ever get better than this – although this is not my field of expertise' (Melrose 2002: 93). In a reciprocal, shared experience the book becomes the mediator, as this simple diagram, which I have also revealed before, shows.

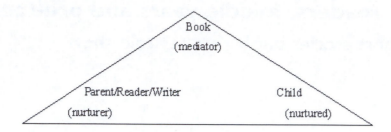

As mediator in an experience shared by both adult and child the book is a huge and important psychological and sociological tool. Rather than thinking of this as a diagram, think about it as an actual experience, think about it being a reader/parent (for example) on a sofa with an arm around the child while both of them engage with the book, one reading and the other looking at the pictures and listening to the words. The real unique character of picture books as an artform is based on the combination of three levels of communication, not two: the visual, the verbal and the physical as nurture. I would go further to say that with the best will in the world, the best story with the best illustration is nothing without the third component in the formative years. But get all three working together and the early 'exploration of the connections' is off to the best possible start.

Thus, rather than constantly looking at ideas on cognitive development and reading and literacy we surely need to try and understand how we can get involved in the process of nurture and this is a completely different matter. Remembering what Phillips said about nurture (above), about making the story connections throughout the experience is so much more relevant to us here. As I have already said above, though it is worth repeating again, Walter Benjamin might have referred to this as the trading of experiences, the *Erfahrung*, where the shift between 'lived through' and 'narratable experience' is seen as a point of arbitration and negotiation, an exploration of ideas and I have to agree.

While children may view the world from a different viewpoint to their adult counterparts, as defined by age and experience, the astonishment and amazement at witnessing or hearing about the ongoing experience of sheer existence is the defining challenge at the meeting in the space in-between for both of them – and the adult has to be able to see this prospect in the child, who arrives on the proverbial knee to see the space in-between them being mediated by the wonder of storytelling. The book, the text, the story stands as the mediator, as an arrested moment in experiencing something new that will not stand still, for it will never be new again, but will always be, Penelope-like, starting over. Just as it did for the writer, so too will it for the reader. The arrested moment, the meeting between writer and reader, in that brief intercession is the point at which ongoing experience is confronted just as it is about to move on.

Indeed, for the writer and reader for children this is not just arrested time, the time of our writing and reading, but the time at which we try to rationalise our internal struggles and strategies as well as those that exist outside to influence the historical moment of our writing, as reconstructed by our writing, in Jameson's words, its ideological subtext so that it can be shared by the reader and the child (in a read-to format).[1] I apologise if you have read this before but sometimes we have to thump the table to get home what seems to be obvious but is missing from so much critical material on the (im)possibility of writing for children – otherwise the child in the discourse remains hidden and mute and sidelined. Especially for early years' children, you are writing to help provide the story that allows them to explore that nurture moment.

One of the crucial things to remember in writing this early years fiction is that most early readers, and definitely all picture books, are written in real time. And the reason for this is simple – young children live in real time and reflection of something that happened the day, week, month before is a cognitive development. Thus, these books are designed to catch the moment of reading and flashback doesn't work. The best example I have seen of flashback 'not' working is in a book called *A Kitten Called Moonlight*.[2] It is a book that fails to address any of the issues I have addressed above and rarely have I seen such a poor choice of words, pictures, point of view and an okay idea gone bad all gathered together in one text. But this is generally rare and great effort goes into the production of such books.

Crucially too is the language used in such texts. Simile, metaphor, ellipses, flashback and an over-indulgence in qualifiers, purple prose, explanation and extrapolation should be avoided. For example, think about a picture book as 12 double spreads full of pictures and words that make an animated story. When I worked in animation film-making we would make one in 20 film cells made in the UK by a top animator, and the 19 joining the story together would be drawn/painted by younger animators. What you have in a picture book is the one in 20 cells where the narrative pulls the story along page to page. And it is important to remember that every page should be a surprise but continually aware of 'what happens next' to promote page turning. Important too is to remember that the story doesn't end at the end. It ends just before the end, so that the last word can be given to 'the promise of a new beginning'. For example:

Penultimate pages [picture description – Dan is standing at the foot of a big tree looking up]:

> It was no use. Dan just couldn't reach his pet dog.
> Digger was still stuck up the tree.
> Then all of a sudden a gust of wind blew through the branches.
> The tree swayed. The leaves quivered. Digger wobbled once; twice and then woosh … ! Digger flew through the air.
> 'Yay!' shouted Dan. 'I caught him. I caught him. I really did!'

Last pages [picture description – Dan and Digger are tucked up in bed and Dad is reading them a story]:

> 'Goodnight, Dan. Goodnight, Digger,' said Dad.
> 'Goodnight, Dad,' said Dan. He hugged his pet dog. 'And Digger says goodnight too. Tomorrow we are going down to the river. It will be safer than the trees.'

It isn't too hard to see what is going on here, is it? Dan rescues his stuffed toy that had been stuck in the tree. They get home in time for tea, tucked up in bed and ready for the next adventure tomorrow. Simple, safe and child focused – note it was Dan who caught Digger, too. The language is simple and so too the plot and structure of the story.

Early read-to, early readers are not much different from picture books except the pictures tend to be line drawings – see Tony Bradman's *Dilly the Dinosaur* as a perfect example of this. Basically, the story is the same structure as I indicated above, nice and simple but crucially, too, it has to be a good page turner. Don't dwell on your wonderful prose, if it doesn't take the story forward it should not be there – simple! Children need a reason to turn the pages and you need to provide it. Third person limited or first person viewpoints are the best to use too. The Dilly stories have a wonderful narrative voice – they are told in first person by Dilly's little sister, Dorla. And it is a narrative device that works very well where the naughty boy (dinosaur – Dilly) is observed by his little sister (dinosaur – Dorla) in domestic dramas. Read them, do the research, it is well worth it but always remember this advice – these are not short stories but big stories told short and they are as sophisticated as any story can be.

The story I gave above is such a domestic drama and to move this out of picture books into early read-to short stories we have to open the description out a little, as I can now show:

Dan stared up at the huge tree. It was no use. He couldn't reach his pet dog. It was already getting late. Dad will be looking for me, he thought.

Digger was still stuck up the tree. He looked very sad and Dan was sad too.

'I can't sleep without Digger,' he said to himself.

Throwing Digger up in the air had seemed like fun at first. Now it wasn't so funny.

Then all of a sudden a gust of wind blew through the branches. Dan was nearly blown off his feet.

The tree swayed. The leaves quivered. Digger wobbled once; twice and then the wind died down.

'Oh dear,' said Dan. 'I thought he would have dropped down then.'

WOOOSH … ! The wind blew again. Even stronger this time and Digger flew high into the air. Higher and higher he soared. Then he began to fall. Down and down and down he fell …

'Yay!' shouted Dan. 'I caught him. I caught him. I really did!'

Later that evening, Dan and Digger were tucked up in bed. Dad had just finished reading Dan's new story book to them.

'I meant to ask if you had a good day,' said Dad.

'Oh yes,' replied Dan. But he didn't tell him about their adventure. All he said was, 'Tomorrow we are going down to the river. That will be safer than the trees.'

Dad looked a little bit puzzled when he said, 'Well goodnight, Dan. And goodnight, Digger, sleep tight!'

'Goodnight, Dad,' said Dan. He hugged his pet dog. 'And Digger says goodnight too.'

You will see we have the slightest hint of a flashback here: 'Throwing Digger up in the air had seemed like fun at first. Now it wasn't so funny.' But that is about as close as it gets. What I have done is extend the drama, heightened it a little and given slightly more text on the visuals that will no longer be available, just to tease out the scene. Also Dan both 'speaks' and 'thinks' in the story. What this does for the read-to/early reader child is reveal that internal thought is not theirs alone. Once they see others can think too they begin to realise their place in the world is not just monitored by the adult voice – and of course Dan keeps his and Digger's little adventure secret from Dad, which the child reader had been able to share.

## Middle years

If I had to reduce this section to a single buzz phrase it would be 'keep them reading'! Literacy is an international problem that is initially addressed in the six to nine years age band when children learn to read. But the major problem is keeping the learning reader on board once they can read. The biggest drop-out rate takes place between the ages of eight and 11 years, which is actually really sad because in my estimation this is where some of the best stories reside. As a parent too it was a great time to observe the development of the thinking child. I know personal anecdotes have little function in an academic treatise but as a real writer/parent/teacher/adult seeing a real reader/child absorbed in the wonder of the story is heartening. And to be honest, if you really want to be a children's writer then you have to witness this. Go on, offer some time, an hour a week, to a school reading project where you can help the less able to read better. I did this for years at my local infant school and found it immensely rewarding but also immensely informative. I found the children could identify the words, and they were willing to read them. What they didn't seem to get, and once again this is just personal anecdote, was the story. They didn't seem to know how story worked and I found that profoundly sad. Had they been exposed to books earlier that function would have been more obvious, which also goes to show that story understanding starts before school and at home.

Another heart-rending thing I encountered was in helping a boy called Josh. I gave him a book I had written and said he could keep it.

> 'Does that mean I can take it home?' he asked.
>
> 'Yes,' I replied, 'it's yours to keep.'
>
> Josh turned the book over in his hands and said, 'I've never had my own book before.'
>
> I asked him if he would like me to sign it for him. 'Oh no,' he said, 'you are not allowed to write on books. I have been told that by my teacher. Writing on it would mean it wasn't new anymore.'

As I have written above at length, articulating an idea of the ever-changing child and childhood through representation faces its own internal struggle with shifting consciousness, shifting culture, multiplicity and fragmentation. Furthermore, while it can be acknowledged that childhood is temporary for children and memory for adults, the memory is different from the real. My memory of childhood does not represent my own children's present that will become their own memories in time – no two life stories can be the same and nostalgia too is a very unstable narrator. The adult's ability to remember childhood and recreate it fictionally for children doesn't really address writing for children in the way I think it should. Natov has addressed this issue at length when she discusses the 'poetics of childhood' and writes: 'The literature of childhood moves between innocence and experience, between initiation and reflection. And, in establishing such a poetics, the child at the centre, presently and retrospectively, is, as Carolyn Steedman says, "the story waiting to be told".' But where I disagree with Natov and

Steedman is in the ideas they promote on the 'imagined child' and the 'place of child-hood in the imaginative life of adults' (Natov 2006: 3). This is because as a concept it does not recognise the child except as an abstract figure. As Natov also writes:

> It is apt and not uncommon to characterize adulthood as severed, to one degree or another, from childhood memory, and therefore, from the imagination – for a nat-ural sense of wonder and originality of thought. Behind the fractured adult a child hides, estranged from his or her own history, deprived of the psychological and cultural richness of memory that is, as the British educator Peter Abbs claimed, our 'biological inheritance, part of what it means to be human'.
>
> (Natov 2006: 2)

I know I have been banging on about this but this is not about childhood or children but adults and the hiding child is this font of 'imagination ... a natural sense of wonder and originality of thought'. For the writer then, his or her job is to explore the possibi-lities and connections. Not to engage in the nostalgic attempt to recreate their own life stories through the reader. This is because the reader is already engaging with their own life as their own stories are taking shape. As I wrote above, I as the 'real author' am writing to you as an 'implied reader' and you the 'real reader' are only engaging with me as the 'implied author'. But take a look at Josh, he was nine years old, white, well cared for and his mother seemed a nice woman. But he didn't understand books let alone stories so it's no use thinking every child in a specific age group is sitting out there waiting on your story. And while J.K. Rowling may have her critics, you will never get me offering anything but praise for the entire Harry Potter phenomenon, for introducing books and storytelling to a hitherto lost generation, where a parental attitude to books had become ambivalent in this our televisual culture.

In writing, you should not be attempting to try and recreate your childhood self, trying to understand the person at the other end of the writing process who, in turn, is trying to understand what you have represented in writing for them. But what we, the writer and the reader, are both doing is exploring the space in-between, by using the text as a bridge into the world of ideas and thought and cognition. Both come to see what we know and recognise but to explore that which we know not. If a writer has anything to give to a reader like Josh, it is the wonder of stories that carry the burden of the meaning of culture but the writer has to be aware of the reader at the other side of the equation and therefore their mutual engagement has to be one of ongoing exploration. It can be repeated, then, that the adult in children's literature is less hidden than the child. This is because the adult is articulating for the child, while and at the same time the child who knows more than it can articulate is learning how to articulate its own story, while also learning something new.

Children's fiction has changed a great deal since I was a boy and indeed since I last wrote about writing for children, back in 2002 (although much of that book *Write for Children* still holds up). The fact is that day-by-day, week-by-week, month-by-month and year-by-year story in culture is ever shifting and writers and practitioners should be looking at ways of addressing the social and aesthetic transformation of the culture of writing for children. And this can be done by writing in such a way that your reader will see an approach to ideas, issues and aesthetics that encourages them to explore their own sense of self. In this way, writing for children should be a radical force for good because it is about interaction and social engagement not an overreliance on nostalgia and an adult normativity that says 'do as I say' – with the message being, write *for* children not *at* them.

The middle years' reader usually comes in two 'packaged' groups, which are:

Age 6–9:
longer fiction – read alone, short novels, 12,000–20,000 words(ish);
series fiction and collected stories.

Age 8–11:
read alone – novels, 20,000–50,000 words(ish) and series fiction.

This information is not a secret, look at publishers' websites and you will see these details are bandied about quite freely. But think about it socially and culturally too. What we have here are children essentially graded by school age. Having moved from the infants they are now primary school, age 6–9, and junior school, age 8–11. This is not a scientific fact and neither is it carved in stone; it is a loose arrangement so that publishers can help booksellers to target a market-led demographic. But this demographic should not hinder either your subject matter or storytelling process. You just need to be aware of the recognisable, average benchmarks.

Of course some children will read up and will look for more challenging work and others will read down, being less able. This is problematic for a couple of reasons that you are probably aware of. The first is the child reading up will undoubtedly encounter material that is experientially complex and a little beyond their focus because that which they do know is less obvious in the text too. For example, if a ten-year-old girl is reading about relationships she is doing so from a pre-puberty position. In fiction of her own age, her heroine will already be older than her (12 years old say) anticipating her own fictional puberty, but if the reader is reading an older heroine (15 years old say) the life experience and the sheer physical gap between the 12-year-old and the 15-year-old is quite tangible. Similarly the older child reading down is likely to be able to read the material for younger children but will find it likely the story content and context is too simplistic.

You will never get a piece to target every reader here and a happy medium is about all that can be expected. But just to give you an example of the problems we face. My son reread the entire Harry Potter series when he was 15 because he had begun with it being read to him and then reading it on his own. He felt he had missed much because he was always reading ahead of his own ability to quite absorb the story. But my daughter and I both read Philip Pullman's *His Dark Materials* trilogy at the same time, she at age 14 and me, well, much older, and when we discussed the books she commented, 'I think you were reading a different book to me.' So the reading experience is not something we can really anticipate except through researching what we are to write and then trying to pitch it as well as we can. This is not to say I approve of putting 'age' stickers on books, no one should be stigmatised in this way. It is hard enough getting some children to read without having to advertise their reading age range is lower than their actual age and so on. But it is quite nonsense to say that the very good novel, *Game Girls* by Judy Waite, is appropriate for nine-year-old girls. The author Celia Rees said:

When I'm writing I don't have a certain ideal reader in mind. Partly because I want to be read by either gender with the same amount of enjoyment. Though I have to be conscious of age, because that will determine the language I use, my sentence structures and the complexity of my narrative. There is no point in writing in an elliptical manner for 8–9 year olds, because they won't be able to read it or won't want to read it. With my new six part *H.A.U.N.T.S.* series – aimed at 8–12 year olds – I've had to be disciplined and to simplify the way I write.

(Celia Rees in Carter 1999: 202)

She doesn't have a 'certain ideal reader in mind' but she does have a precise demographic in mind. She wants to write for boys and girls but she knows what age grouping too. But this boys and girls issue too is important. I have said 'girls' above, in the context of the waite, book I mentioned, but this is something else we need to consider. Boys and girls generally (there are exceptions) read different books with different topics. Harry Potter is a notable exception but it is no accident that Joanne Rowling writes as J.K, the suggestion being that the publishers were worried (with good reason) that boys wouldn't read a book written by a woman. And a general rule on this is that while boys and girls will read a book where the central character is a boy, it is unusual for boys to read about a girl hero. Pullman's Lyra is a notable exception too, but you do have to consider how the Rowling series would look if the hero was Hermione Potter and the bookish boy was Harry Grainger. When you are writing fiction it is as well to consider what Fred Inglis has argued:

it is simply ignorant not to admit that children's novelists have developed a set of conventions for their work. Such development is a natural extension of the elaborate and implicit system of rules, orthodoxies, improvisations, customs, forms and adjustments that characterise the way any adult tells stories or simply talks at length to children.

(Inglis 1981: 101)

What does become important to every age and gender group is that they crave fiction. All kinds of fiction and it is there where the boundaries of knowledge can be explored. Indeed it is the place where fantasy and fact collide in experiential collusion. But consider this in story terms. The architecture of the Guggenheim Museum in Bilbao is fascinating and wonderful all at the same time. But what is interesting to a child, the building or the creepy goings on inside? And yet we can see how setting a story in such a building, absorbing the textual maze of twentieth-century art, paintings and sculptures juxtaposed with installations and electronic forms of artistic work, weaves a way around ideas as well as good guys and bad guys. Isn't this essentially what Pullman does with his Blake and Milton and the eclectic mix of cultural clashing diffusion, where ultimately every culture borrows from other cultures and incorporates it into their own? Equally children and adults are tangled up in the same language games, which is only differentiated by 'experience'.

At the top of this section I show you a typical fiction age split. This is just a guideline to help you understand target age groups. There are two ways to address this, one is to write your story and see where it fits, and the other is to target your writing. But I find it is still better to try and imagine the 'implied reader' so that they too can hopefully come to a text knowing it has been written for them. Some of this book is critically intense but that says more about my not patronising you than trying to show off my critical dexterity. The same goes for writing; try to lead your reader into a world they know but one that also contains that which they know not.

I am not going to give an explanation of options here because there appears to be little point when you must write what you write. It is up to you to research your own field. Although the following story categories do seem to be popular for all ages in the middle years:

Mystery
Adventure
Animals
Detective
Ghosts
Science Fiction
Horror
School
Thriller
School exchange
Travel
Friendship
Magic
Flying
Fantasy
Time travel
Myths and legends
History
Humour
Sport
Magical creatures
Domestic drama
Issues-led drama.

Make your own list, it's your story and of course a good piece of fiction is often a combination of these. Harry Potter gives us, hmm, let's see, actually, all of the above, not to mention love, dancing (or not) and full frontal snogging – did I miss any? How about drugs, what is Felix Felicis after all? Also called 'liquid luck', it is a magical potion introduced by Professor Slughorn in *Harry Potter and the Half Blood Prince*, which makes the drinker 'lucky' for a period of time, depending on how much is taken, and during which time everything they attempt will be successful. It is meant to be used sparingly, however, and taken in excess it causes giddiness, recklessness and dangerous overconfidence. Still, a little smidgeon won't hurt, will it?

I have already told you much about writing fiction in the previous chapters. What you need to know here is there are no boundaries, although if you want to write an extremely polemical piece be prepared to have it scrutinised and debated for that very reason. It is difficult to escape the fact that Julia Eccleshare hailed Philip Pullman as a 'heretical fantasist' in writing the final part of the *Dark Materials* trilogy.[3] But the crucial thing to remember once again is these stories have to be good. There is a huge amount of good fiction out there. Don't be fooled into thinking that all the best stuff has been written or all the best stuff is the old stuff – like the Narnia books (and you know what I think of the underpinning ideology being presented by them). There is a huge amount of good writing going on year on year and to be part of that takes a huge effort. In the past I called this being critically creative and creatively critical as part of a creative vigilance. Write *for* children can be replaced with write *well for* children.

## Writing for the pre-teen years

Age 10–12:
read alone – pre-teen novels, 30,000–70,000 words(ish) and series fiction.

Age 12–15:
young teen fiction, teenage fiction, 50,000 words upwards.

When I was advised by my children to 'chillax' recently, I knew that writing it here would be the first and probably the last time I ever used that hybridised, teen speak word, for the same reasons that 'cool', 'lush' and such other teen-speak words are not part of my vocabulary. Although 'cool' is definitely one that has followed me around. But what is clear is that we are beginning to get into pre-teen and teen territory, which is a different world to any we can ever expect to know. You know how I feel about nostalgia as a poor starting point for storytelling but the one thing I remember most about this time can be summed up in two words: 'confusion' and 'curiosity'.

In the child reading decade of age five to 15 (which I discussed right at the beginning) the last five years are immensely interesting for the storyteller. This is because the mature reader is emerging from the pupa as a fully fledged butterfly, which will flit from flower to flower in the garden of stories, chewing up the words for meaning and answers and hopes and dreams and more and more knowledge of what is to 'be' and what it is to 'be'. As you can see I have split the ten to 15 age grouping up a little. The reasons are all too obvious. This age grouping travels the width and breadth of childhood. They can see puberty and teenage life approaching, arriving and then leading them down the approach runway for takeoff and flying into adulthood. And let's not be coy, while they are still under 16 and not off age they do have adulthood in their sights (NB., while 18 is the legal coming of age in the UK, 16 and 17 allows leeway to prepare the way). And true to form, there is little they will not have heard of and perhaps even witnessed firsthand. But it is a huge age of vicarious experience, where their confusion and curiosity is tested to the limit of their knowledge.

Through stories, there is much a writer can do to help them explore the world they will be encountering and will be about to encounter as they get even older. Thus, the complexity of plot and language needs to be such that it can speak to the reader who is grasping for a hold on that which they do not yet know. They seek the comfort of the familiar in the story but their natural confusion and curiosity desires more than they have ever been able to comprehend. The stories need to step beyond the wonder of innocence to address the knowing child who needs and wants to know so much more. And while I gave a list of desirable writing topics, above, to this we could begin to add:

Girls and boys
Growing up

Abuse
Bullying
Sex, drugs and rock and roll
Texting
Smoking
Facebook
Illness
Computers
Race
War
Gaming
Music
Goths
Same-sex romance
Slimming
Fashion
Parents
Motorcyles
Junk food
Hedonism
Scoring goals (metaphorically as well as actually)
Sport
Refugees
Dancing
Conservation
Narcissism
Asylum seekers
Global warming
Slavery
Thieving
Sex trade
Organ transplants
Love
Prostitution
Self harm
Trauma
Vampires
Vicarious sexuality
Confessions
Loss
Ghosts, ghouls and broken rules …

Go on, add your own but remember they are all wrapped up in the aforementioned whether it be fantasy or ficto-realism, *Twilight* or *Junk*. Also, get to know what the different ages need in terms of experience, subject matter, gender difference, racial and cultural diversity. Splitting the ages as I have suggested helps us to identify the varying levels of maturity in which to begin to address the demographic.

Age 10–12:
read alone – pre-teen novels, 30,000–70,000 words(ish) and series fiction.

In this age range you are already looking at the reader who is top of the 'junior school'. King and Queen bees of the school, top of their year and teenagers in the making. They respond to positive and strong storylines that allow them to anticipate what lies ahead – which is the high school, teenagers and a world more grown up than they. And these are the gauntlet years where they challenge you to explore the newness to come. For they already think they know a great deal (which they do) but are as yet not quite able to articulate the next stage that looms bright.

What is crucial to writing for this age group is an understanding of genre. The child reader is already deciding for themselves and you need to research this. But it is important to realise that a good story, exploring important issues, can be written in many different genres because there is a difference between genre and subject. Also the child reader is beginning to exercise their own choice and purchasing power. Adult influence on their reading is still in place, after all who pays for it? But what has to be acknowledged is that children of this age are beginning to question adult choice in favour of their own. And the choice is huge but so too are the issues that can be read and presented. Michael Morpurgo's magical realism story, *The Sleeping Sword*, takes Bun Bendle on a magical trip through love and friendship; Zizou Corder's political *Lionboy* trilogy deals with political oppression, villains, circuses and Charlie Ashanti who can speak cat; Roald Dahl's *Matilda* deals with honey-coated charm and magic in the face of bullying; Jacqueline Wilson's *Tracy Beaker* is an imaginative child in care with adult declared 'behavioural problems'; and my own personal favourite, Louis Sachar's *Holes*, with the wonderful palindromic Stanley Yelnats whose life is as back to front as his name. And then there is David Almond, Margaret Mahy, J.K. Rowling, Bernard Ashley, Garth Nix, Paul Stewart and Chris Riddell; as I said in Part 1, lists are subjective and endless; this kind of list goes on and on, each story with something to say to an exploring child without being tied to some formulaic idea of what story should be. Doomsayers beware, this is fertile ground for storytelling and there is much to read and research.

Age 12–15;
young teen fiction, teenage fiction, 50,000 words upwards.

In thinking about the term early teens, we need to be reminded that the term teenager is loaded with cultural resonances that are little older than the turn of the twentieth century. In the absence of clear definitions, the term teenager can (and often is) applied variously to suit the needs of interested parties (marketers, educators, legislators, etc.). But titles such as teenager are problematised by the idea that unlike more singular subject and theoretical positions, such as race, gender, sexuality and class, they are given a collective heading with no means of speaking with a collective voice. Furthermore, their exposure to information through technology makes the job of the writer an ever-shifting experiential field of vision. What has to be acknowledged is that any idea of the 'innocent child' you may have still harboured, despite me trying to burst that bubble, definitely no longer exists in this age grouping because it has been replaced by the 'knowing child', and this is a very important distinction that you must take into consideration. Their access to information far outstrips anything that has ever been encountered before, as Lee, Conroy and Hii suggest:

> The acceleration of technology has helped define a new breed of consumers – 'net generation' or 'cyber-teens', terms used to describe adolescents of this generation who are computer savvy and techno-literate, and whose abilities often exceed those of their parents and teachers.[4]

But the word 'consumer' is a loaded one here because they consume in the capitalist sense but also borrow, steal and play with the conventions, gathering knowledge and information on the way. Want a copy of the new Steve Earle CD before it's in the shops? Well I would and I know that the person who can get it for me is 40 years younger than I, and I wouldn't have to pay, if I were so inclined. I am never surprised by the amount of technological material that floats around schools as the teenagers themselves keep their knowledge just beyond the protection placed on the material. But it is how this information is used and accommodated when we come to realise that childhood, as a legally defined term, is not much older than the last century, along with the knowledge that this age group are now conscious of the age they are at. My own father started working at age 14, in 1948. Fourteen and already a man, on the morning of his first shift his mother gave him two sandwiches and two cigarettes. He had never smoked before but it's what coal miners did, so he did too.

It is the stage at which children (if they can still be called this) are trying to make greater sense of their own and other people's personalities. As Nicholas Tucker writes:

> At whatever level of complexity, however, stories for the eleven to fourteen age group usually reflect their audience's increasing pre-occupation with the need to acquire a consistent sense of identity … readers are now chiefly interested in more adult-seeming behaviour.
>
> (Tucker 1981: 145–46)

And, to this end, they are beginning to understand the world in more abstract terms, where metaphor and metonym, relationship and simile take on a new resonance, along with adult realities.

Shirley Brice Heath (2011: xi) suggests that all of us are looking for stories that 'ring true'. But this truth remains fluid, imbedded in cultural difference and yet 'each new generation heads [to the point of truth] in their readings as they reach young adulthood and move through the lifespan.' For the early teenager this means a voyage through all kinds of experience, which the book can offer vicariously as a supplement to their own 'lived in experience'. They 'seek the privacy of self-reflection, psychological insight, thrill of the mystery, or seductive power of narrative that stimulates inner dialogue'. And the joy of the vicarious experience is in allowing the reader to predict what would happen in a new situation that has never personally been experienced. It allows them to take that 'risk' safely.[5]

Vicarious experience is a constant in storytelling. Armstrong highlights the importance and development of storytelling by suggesting that 'A novel, like a myth, teaches us to see the world differently; it shows us how to look into our own hearts and to see our world from a perspective that goes beyond our own self-interest'(2005: 149). While Jack Zipes, using the example of *Little Red Riding Hood*,[6] has demonstrated that '[t]he social function of the story [and the wolf] was to show how dangerous it could be for children to talk to strangers in the woods or to let strangers enter the house'(1993: 19). Whether oral or printed, story contains something useful such as contemporary mores and morals in the form of some practical advice, a proverb or maxim, subject, of course, to cultural shifts that reflect the moment at which it is composed. According to Walter Benjamin the storyteller provides counsel for his readers;[7] however, I don't have his sense of the death of the storyteller just because the means of delivery have changed. As Brecht said some time ago, and as I have already reported, 'Reality changes; in order to represent it, modes of representation must also change. Nothing comes from nothing; the new comes from the old, but that is why it is new' (Taylor 1977: 81).[8]

That is also why I feel the vibrancy of the writing for children, targeted at this age group, is teeming with potential and meaning and erudition worthy of serious exploration, which every writer should be aware of and there are many ways to address the importance of knowledge for this growing and knowledgeable reading group. But what interests me a great deal is the idea of story as transmitter. Important issues do not have to be couched in didactic, dry-as-dust and musty books, they can be embedded in vibrant and energetic stories written in many genres.

Pullman addresses many important issues in *His Dark Materials* 'fantasy' trilogy, including Lyra and Will coming of age as well as encountering a transforming spiritual experience; Anna Perera's fantastically real *Guantanamo Boy* takes 15-year-old Khalid from his home in Rochdale to the notorious US Guantánamo Bay detention camp; Melvin Burgess addresses drug culture head on in *Junk*; Jacqueline Wilson gave us a 'dustbin baby'; *The Lastling*, by Phillip Gross, is described on his website thus: 'On the edge of civilisation, the edge of madness, the edge of extinction – the most extreme sport of all … Paris is excited.' How can we not be inspired – and Phillip Gross is a hugely wonderful writer.

Elizabeth Laird's brave and serious political book, *A Little Piece of Ground*, takes Karim, a Palestinian boy, into the world of conflict and football; Stephenie Meyer's Twilight series of four vampire-themed fantasy romance novels takes Bella Swan and her beau, Edward Cullen, through the paths of forbidden love through to vicarious sexuality. Inherent in stories like these, with their vibrant and relevant ideas, is the notion of vicarious experience, where readers can indeed seek the privacy of self-reflection, psychological insight, thrill of the mysterious and seductive power of narrative that stimulates their inner exploration of life and learning. But this research tells us something quite huge, does it not?

You must read and read and read what your readers read to get to know what they know and know not, and to get to know them better. Melvin Burgess has already said that ' … we live in a multi-cultural, multi-faith, multi-value society in an age where television, radio, the press and the internet have rendered the secrets adults may wish to keep from children impossible to hide.'[9] But what we can do is tell them stories so they may see the connections.

Of course, this is a loaded issue and I come back time and time and time again to the issue I highlighted in Part 1. The entire writing for children exercise is one of shared experience, where the writer and the reader can meet to explore the narratives of their lives. For the author, it is important to acknowledge that they have to ensure their cultural prejudices and social ideologies are in a constant state of critical vigilance. It is all about getting life and feelings and emotions and ideas and knowledge into a context that is ever shifting and changing.

# Chapter 10

# Social realism, narrative non-fiction and *The Tiger Who Came to Tea*

As I said and at great length in Part 1 of this book, the idea of 'making the connections' isn't a new one I have just thought about, and it can be summed up quite simply in the example I gave. My reading of it goes back as far as Socrates, 469–399 BCE, as far as we know, but as far as we don't know it has been going on forever. While we are thinking about social realism and non-fiction we can still 'imagine' facts to be correct or worthy of speculation. When I think about the idea of 'making the connections' I came up with early man, bees, hives, stings, honey; someone made all these connections once and don't we just wonder how we got to our present stage of knowledge without ideas, knowledge and experience being passed down through the centuries? And nowhere is this more relevant than when we are dealing with ideas and the idea of facts being incorporated into a narrative. Socrates in the instance I was thinking about earlier was attempting to explain a complicated mathematical theory to an uneducated slave. He did so simply by prompting the slave, step by step, with things he already knew. But this idea of slippage in the dialectical master/servant binary is very much what I have been saying. It's not so much explaining or showing but helping others to connect to what they already know from other parts of life and then asking them to take the ideas forward into something they may or may not have thought about but are ready to explore. The children will then take what you have offered and incorporate it with their own thinking to take possession of the knowledge it imparts.

And is this not a true Socratic journey? Socrates never claimed to be wise, only to understand the path a lover of wisdom must take in pursuing it – and making the connections is implicit in this, surely. It is such a simple idea, and as I discussed in the first part of this book, I cannot understand why this is such a problem with the adult/children, connection. It is not a question of binaries, them and us, me and you, adults and children but a mutual stroll down a Socratic path, making connections as we go. I have discussed how fiction can be used to impart such connections in the body of a story, where the story carries the wider ideas and knowledge a child can explore as they gain experience. But as I have intimated before, this is not a child to adult journey but an ongoing journey down the path of experience. I became an adult legally when I was 18 but the years since haven't been that much different in my learning process because each day brings something new. There is always something new to see, to learn, to be, because as I grow older so too do my children and their challenges, and so too does the world change. What I aim to do with this section is show how there are three different ways to present factual material as a fictional narrative.

*Social realism* is just a phrase that doesn't really hold much rigour at all. I like to think of it as a type of fiction rather than a genre because so many things can fit into the category. Soap operas are the most obvious source and indeed the whole manufactured, popular televisual programming from *Pop Idol* to *Scrubs* is unregulated (apart from the nine o'clock watershed ruling) and available for child consumption. But in children's fiction and some television it has an element of the cautionary that makes it so appealing. So in taking the social realism to one side, let's talk about sex, because in exploring this side of it we can reveal how everything else follows – i.e. for sex read everything else.

I mentioned Judy Waite's *Game Girls* before. It is described on her website[1] as 'A gripping story of teenage girls who use sex to make money … ' Goodness me, you might say, but this description does come with the caveat and the complete description is 'A gripping story of teenage girls who use sex to make money – and then find that money is not, after all, going to resolve all ills.' The social realism of the narrative, girls and prostitution in this case, underpins a deeper and more thoughtful set of ideas. It's a tale with a warning story but one that addresses teenage sexuality with a responsible eye, because clearly the general idea of the subject of teenage sexuality is simply not yet being addressed honestly in a lot of fiction. As Waite has said to me, it does address teen sexuality but, more importantly, it addresses dangers that teens may find themselves facing, the dangers of peer pressure, the manipulation of more powerful characters and the lure (and moral outcome) of going for 'easy money' and the potential for exploitation. Also the fact that it is set in a middle-class suburban area (rather than somewhere downtown and dingy) makes what the girls get into even more shocking and relevant for debate. And this kind of fiction is extremely important for ideas on social realism. The book isn't a junior 'chick-lit' but sits at a cutting edge in 'young adult fiction'.

One other person who does address sexuality honestly is Meliyn Burgess, for example in his book *Doing It* (2008), but what a furore that caused. In an article in *The Guardian* newspaper, Anne Fine[2] said that *Doing It* is a 'grubby book', which demeaned both boys and girls and was a form of sexual bullying. She considered Burgess to be misogynistic and writing pornography, and that no girl or young woman should have to read this sort of thing. Well the truth is no one did have to read it. But what Fine was doing was closeting the whole debate by claiming that it did not reflect a reality. A charge Burgess rejected while saying Fine's argument had no intellectual support and was based on attitude rather than fact because 'it is about revolting boys'.[3] But crucial to this debate is the idea of normalisation, which I have written of before.

> The coupling of children's literature with controversial subjects such as sex and drugs should perhaps be considered as a cultural oxymoron, a combination that immediately signals an end of innocence and thereby an end to childhood itself. However, there is another side to the argument which suggests that when addressing such topics, children's literature is exactly where they should be located.
>
> (Melrose and Harbour 2007: 176–90)

Charles Sarland (Hunt 1999: 50) has suggested: ' … research evidence uncovers a complex picture of the young seeking ways to take control over their own lives, and using the fiction that they enjoy as one element in the negotiation of cultural meaning and value.' But in looking at realism, this negotiation cannot avoid the pitfalls of the really real, and sex, drugs and alcohol, for example, are a part of that real. In fact it becomes so real that social realism begins to address the normalisation of the real issues that present themselves. Children do not live solely in the leafy suburban, safe zones that are reflected in a lot of fiction. They mostly live in the cities, with the rest of the population, and so the urban and the cosmopolitan and the multicultural is part of their normal discourse and normalised within that are the inherent problems. For example, Manning says: 'recreational drug use is now so familiar to those aged below 35 years that it should be regarded as "normal" rather than an activity confined to minor subcultures'(Manning 2007: 49). What Manning is pointing to is the broad idea that fiction should be able to reflect what is 'real', and doing so openly and fully aware that it is really 'real' it can be addressed sensibly, as Waite and Burgess do! Consider again what I said in Part 1, thinking about it historically, we could return to Foucault's notion of sexuality in the Victorian period *when we didn't speak of it* and in doing so *it became pretty much all we spoke about*. I feel this way about the silent realism of difficult subject matters in children's fiction. We should be talking about them because not doing so only presents a skewed representation of the real and that the difficult, the awkward and even the illegal is more normal than the text is presenting responsibly.

What I am trying to say here is that in my view the best way to present the 'real' in a story is to 'not' avoid it. Of course reading age and experience dictates what is and is not suitable for different readers. The subject of teen fiction will not transfer easily to the lower age range but every age range has its own 'real' to tackle and incorporating it into a story as 'normal' removes the stigma while allowing the writer to address its underlying problems. What makes the bad worse is not talking about it.

Kimberley Reynolds highlights a problem when she writes:

> By far the largest and most fashionable groups in British bookshops today are those books that depict and address teenagers as superficial, hedonistic, and narcissistic. Books such as Louise Rennison's highly popular 'confessions of Georgia Nicholson' (beginning with *Angus, thongs and full frontal snogging*, 1999) ignore the established wisdom that teenagers want realistic books about social issues ... They disseminate an image of young people as dependent, parasitical, and powerless, a group transfixed by their own narcissistic natures.
>
> (Reynolds 2007: 79–80)

This is true up to a point but readers can see this is not real life too, and is in fact a cartoon representation, which is often replicated in the entertainment television they watch. It is a diet of chocolate and fizzy drinks and the idea that readers are fooled by this isn't really defensible. But this is all the more reason for making issues accessible. And indeed, as Judy Waite revealed in *Game Girls*, there are strategic ways of encroaching into this junior, chick-lit territory by subverting the genre in a subtle and convincing way. Publishers may look to chuck out pulp fiction but there is a lot of responsible material getting published too, and it's a question of balance.

Incorporating the real into the text allows for such great character development across a wide range of topics (it's not all sex, drugs and alcohol). Imagine what would be the best way to address the Palestinian conflict for a child reader – through the eyes of an Israeli soldier or a Palestinian boy, as Elizabeth Laird does. *A Little Piece of Ground* is a book about oppression but that comes through the story of Karim Aboudi and his friends who just want to play football (on a little piece of ground). *The Kite Runner* by Khaled Hosseini (2003) takes us to Kabul and the world of a young Amir; *Two Weeks With The Queen* by Morris Gleitzman (2003) tackles the tricky issue of sibling jealousy and cancer and yet the novel is about a proactive boy named Colin; this kind of list can go on and on, the authors writing on societal issues through a realistic story are doing so with a narrative dexterity that makes this kind of novel hugely interesting and entertaining, while still able to address some pretty huge issues. There is always going to be a battle for the hearts and minds of readers, glossy fame magazines and celebrity culture continue to vie with more serious work on the literary shelf but storytelling cannot rely on market forces when there are important things to be addressed and we can only keep fighting the fight, to give in is to give in to market forces, and I do not believe anyone finds this desirable – especially child readers.

From my research and experience, I feel the best way to approach this is to 'normalise' the problems into the story. The problem is 'not' the story, it is only part of it, it snakes its way through it, like a shadow following the main character, present but subtly so. But it is important to remember this; nothing is unacceptable. What needs to be considered is this: is your imagined reader ready to receive it? And the answer to that comes from research coupled with common sense and the responsibility of the writer.

Narrative non-fiction is another way to deal with non-fictional issues and ideas, to write the non-fiction as a story. I really don't like biographies. It often feels like I am reading more about the author than the subject. And in truth I would rather see a Rothko than read about him; listen to Steve Earle than read about him; watch a Coen than read about them and sometimes the poets I read tell me much more about themselves in their poetical narratives than any biographer ever could.

Sigmund Freud once wrote: 'Anyone who writes a biography is committed to lies, concealments, hypocrisy, flattery and even hiding his own lack of understanding, for biographical truth does not exist' (Freud 1968), and it is an interesting thesis. But there are exceptions to every rule and when non-fiction is written as a narrative I find myself absorbed in the story. It is hard not to like Michael Foreman's autobiographical *War Boy: A Country Childhood* (1990), which combines photographs and adverts with watercolours and pen-and-ink drawings or indeed the adult book from Blake Morrison, *When Did You Last See Your Father?* (2008), which writers for children would do well to read because it deals extensively with the exploration of a father/son relationship. Indeed a similar book to this is *Fever Pitch* by Nick Hornby (1992). But narrative non-fiction is more than this. If we consider it carefully the dividing line between fiction and non-fiction is very slim. As Margaret Meek says:

> The simplified formulation of this division is in the labels 'fiction' and 'non-fiction'. The latter are thought of as books offering readers representations of the 'actual' world from which that world can be learned about. The former is the category of stories, novels, which are for pleasure, recreational reading and informal learning.
>
> (Meek 1991: 8)

But the fact is both of these 'labels' can be bridged in a creative way. Scholastic do a series of children's books called *My Story*, which are historical stories wrapped in a fictional narrative, but the classic version of such stories would be the James Cameron movie *Titanic* (1997), which is the true story of the ship's disaster told through the fictional viewpoint of Jack Dawson and Rose DeWitt Bukater. It is not difficult to see how this kind of narrative works to great effect (well my daughter enjoyed it and it was targeted at her). Crucial to writing such material is to get the research right. If the ship had left from

London rather than Southampton the whole credibility of the story would be lost. But it's not just about facts, it's all about storytelling and historicity. Historicity is about historical authenticity, it's about narrative voices, clothing, habits, etc., not a museum but about capturing the historical period in narrative form. *Apollo Thirteen* (directed by Ron Howard 1995) is another such example of narrative non-fiction where the factual near disaster is fictionalised for the cinema and where the border between fact and fiction is not easily defined.

Eleanor von Schweinitz has said that the writer of non-fiction is allowed to personally engage with the text:

> Some of the most lively writing can be found in books on controversial topics where publishers have been willing to tackle subjects that give rise to strong emotions and differences of view. The insistence in some quarters that an issue should be considered from all viewpoints and in a dispassionate manner is hardly a prescription for lively writing. And the dutiful drawing up of a balance sheet is unlikely to provoke interest, let alone thought, on the part of the reader.
>
> (von Schweinitz, cited in Powling 1994: 126)

I agree, and the engagement of the writer as storyteller is equally important because crucially, too, non-fiction is simply more interesting when it is about the people. What is interesting, the pyramids or the people who commissioned them and the people who built them? Their narrative is so much more interesting to the child reader – while and at the same time the historicity can incorporate the history and geography. As Hayden White once wrote:

> Only a chaste historical consciousness can truly challenge the world anew every second, for only history mediates between what is and what men think ought to be within humanising effect. But history can serve to humanise experience only if it remains sensitive to the more general world of thought *and* action from which it proceeds and to which it returns.
>
> (White 1978: 50)

But the crucial element in all of this is it has to be a story and a story has to have that 'wow' factor, the element of surprise as a page turner.

## The Tiger Who Came to Tea

I have named this section after the wonderful Judith Kerr book of the same name (1968). This is an interesting approach that relies more on historicism and cultural materialist critical ideas than anything else. But I would like to suggest that a lot of non-fiction is often actually incorporated into a text, which then goes on to become (perhaps unwittingly) a historical document. Stories by their very nature 'are culturally marked: they are informed by the language that the writers employed, their respective cultures and the socio-historical context in which the narrative was created' (Zipes 2006: 41). History and culture is embedded in writing and it is one of those wonderful exploring moments that a reader faces. However, it has been acknowledged that ' ... the full meaning of experience is not simply given in the reflexive immediacy of the lived moment but emerges from explicit retrospection where meaning is recovered and re-enacted ... '[4]

Thus, it is difficult to tell how effective the subtlety of a text such as *The Tiger Who Came To Tea* is. Let me explain this by first giving a short plot outline.

A little girl named Sophie is having tea with her mother in their kitchen. Soon they are joined by a hungry tiger who drinks all the tea, eats all the food in the house and drinks everything, including Daddy's beer and all the water in the tap so that Sophie cannot have a bath. Then he leaves. Sophie's father comes home and being made aware of the problem he suggests that they all go out and have a lovely meal in a café. The following day Sophie and her mother go out to buy some more food, including a big tin of tiger food. But the tiger never returns. When I read the book now what I see is a book that very much reflects a time when I grew up. A historical documentation of 1960s domesticity that I recognise all too well, and what the story really says to me is this:

A stay at home mother is in the house with her daughter and Daddy is out working.
It is the end of the week and there are no groceries left in the house.
There is nothing for them to eat until Dad comes home with his weekly pay packet.

This was the story of much of my childhood where we lived week to week, the housekeeping money was handed over in the pay packet that was brought home from the coal mine my father worked in, and taking into account the bills to be paid, rent, gas, electricity, etc., it only stretched so far. So pay day was the day when replenishing the household was dependent on him coming home – to chase the tiger away. I am not sure I would have discussed this critical analysis of the story with my three-year-old child in this way. But it is a book I remember reading to my younger sister when I was 14(ish) and then years later, when I thought about it, I realised what it was actually saying. Therefore, the imbedded history and culture may take some time to filter into our experience, but that does not mean to say that it is not there when written, and of course we never stop learning.

Milan Kundera writes: 'I have long seen youth as the lyrical age, that is, the age when the individual, focused almost exclusively on himself, is unable to see, to comprehend, to judge clearly the world around him'(Kundera 2007: 88). But this does mean that when we reflect on the reading that informed our youth we can see the effect it had on our experience. Most don't reflect that much, I have taken a critic's view of *The Tiger Who Came To Tea* but my reflection only investigates my own subconscious thoughts and I can begin to track the experiential value of reading. For the most part we are unconsciously aware but that doesn't mean we are immune to the influence of the experience.

## Fantastic fiction for children

The writing that comes under this heading has been discussed at some length but it is essentially fantasy, sci-fi, historical, gothic and its particular spin offs, for example vampires are very current as I write. What is curiously fascinating about them from both a writing and reading perspective is that while the stories essentially carry the same messages, they are delivered in worlds that are imagined and 'other' and strange and uncanny. As Brian Stableford writes:

Because sf [science fiction] writing involves changing the world, the actual change which is made becomes the 'focal point' of such a story. Mundane fiction [so called – and his term] tends to take the world in which its stories are set for granted, and the focal point of such a story tends to be a particular character or a specific incident.

(Stableford 1989: 11)

This is a wee bit reductive but it does highlight different ways of approaching fiction, especially the enormous opportunity for the intertextual story. But the complexity of the stories being offered is tangible and the opportunity for the writer to address really big topics and ideas is huge. Karen Coates has said: 'Ideologically speaking, the monsters of fantasy encode our current views about what it means to be human and how we should respond to those whom we consider other' (Coates, cited in Rudd 2010: 84) and this is extremely important. Because what fantastic fiction does is highlight the human juxtaposed with its other the 'inhuman', but also the uncanny and the strange. She goes on to say:

> This kind of ideological work is where Jack Zipes locates his version of the uses of enchantment; unlike Bettelheim, who sees the work of fairy tales in terms of a developing inner world, Zipes values fairy tales for helping children see and contest the often unexamined ideologies concerning such things as gender, entitlement and consumerism that are operative in their life worlds … for instance it would be important for an ideological analysis to note that vampires are no longer the sexually rapacious, immoral demons they once were.

(Ibid.)

What is increasingly obvious is that it's 'ideas' that attract most readers to fantastic fiction and therefore the opportunity to explore these is often the perfect site for the 'making the connections' idea of vicarious experience. Stableford says:

> To rush headlong through a vast series of changed worlds can be wonderfully stimulating to the imagination; the real world is moved into a new context, where it ceases to be the be-all and end-all of experience, but takes up instead a specific location in a grand scheme of pasts and presents that might have been and futures possibly to come. This enriches our mental life by making us sensitive to what might be as well as what is.

(Stableford 1989: 11)

The idea of 'making us sensitive to what might be as well as what is' is certainly an appealing prospect and a fecund place of exploration. And Coates agrees when she adds: 'without the dynamism of fantasy, readers would be far less able to meet and conquer their dragons [demons?], name and enact their own desires, and change their world' (Coates, cited in Rudd 2010: 85). And this idea of being able to imagine change is surely an appealing one. If we cannot imagine it how can we ever hope to help address its necessity? And in some sense we can see that the real hero of fantastic fiction is not necessarily the characters but the ideas.

However, and this is a big however, the story still needs a strong character to drive the ideas. Take Pullman's Lyra, once again, she is the litmus test, the benchmark of a character embodying an idea and an idea made human through the representation of it as a character. Story can do that and as a writer you can see how vital it can be.

Another however in this is the idea of credibility. The fantastic writer needs to be inventive but what they write has to make sense too. A plot concerning a boy who goes back in time to kill his own grandfather isn't really doing his own sense of survival any favours. But just because we haven't encountered wizards and witches or people with daemons it doesn't mean they don't have anything to say to us.

*Historical fiction* is also worth mentioning in this fantastic fiction section. I touched on it above and essentially it has been covered, but how it relates to SF and fantasy is quite obvious in the idea that we are still essentially imagining the world that came before. In some ways it is an easy genre to research, the library is full of history books. But all too importantly, the story and the characters have to be both believable and energetic enough to carry us through the historical information. And once again, normalising the historical elements while the characters perform their page-turning exercises is desirable. The big difference though is the factual part of the fiction has to be credible and not made up, as in SF and fantasy. You will have some creative licence but research the period you are writing, this is very important indeed.

The most important idea in historical fiction is the idea of 'historicity', which is the authentic story and for the writer this can be carried through the characters and setting and the clues that can be dropped into the writing. The other day I was thinking about the 1960s and it is a bit of cliché to try and reveal the period through images of Carnaby Street, Lambrettas, The Who singing 'My Generation' to the mods in their desert boots, sharp mohair suits and skinny ties as they organise a trip to my adopted home town, Brighton. But to a child, sometimes a cliché comes like a breath of fresh air. Okay, a cliché can be defined as a dead metaphor but I think about it in the way I think about Picasso, he learned the art of exquisite pencil drawing before he moved onto his more abstract work. A child is no different. When they are trying to assemble a picture of a period they know existed but know little about the odd smattering of cliché can help them to define the image. We cannot honestly think Derek Jarman came to the collages in his Caravaggio (1986) film without an eye on pastiche, parody and a little cliché for support?

What is most important is the story but there is little point in setting it historically if it has nothing to offer in the way of ideas, except that it is situated in a time that is other and strange. The characters are essentially the same, they have the same thoughts, desires and problems as you or I, the only difference is their story is embedded in a cultural moment that has its own historicity, mores and morals. Walter Benjamin reminds us that the storyteller provides counsel for his or her reader and to some extent this is true of historicity;[5] however, the historical novelist is also aware of the fact that their stories cannot help being ' … culturally marked … [and] informed by the language that the writers employed, their respective cultures and the socio–historical context in which the narrative was created … ' (2006: 41). Thus, every adjustment to maintain the historical authenticity is desirable. Don't be frightened of the odd cliché in this process – hoots, as they say in my cliché.

Remember, what you are trying to do is define the culture from whence the cliché arrived. Mods and rockers, The Who, mohair suits and skinny ties were becoming a cliché when I was 12 or 13 years old, but my goodness did we envy those boys on their Lambrettas. It took me a lot longer to realise it was imported and adapted Milanese fashion – by the way, I still have a classic three-button fastening, single-breasted, thin lapels and side-vented suit that I wear with a Fred Perry, twin-tipped Polo shirt, 'Talkin' 'bout my generation'.[6] But when we are writing about a historical period we look to the high points that stand out, so that we can attach a story to them. For example, with 1960s pop culture having once been dismissed as ephemeral and transient, by its very emphasis on the ephemeral and transient, it has become a cultural lightning rod for storytellers. Attracted to its conductive spaces are the questions and debates about what it means to be human in the twenty-first century, where those of us who can remember when 'pop' and 'rock' first started are its historians who still enjoy it – I remembered to forget to die before I got old. But I also remember that this ephemeral glossing over of the 1960s is not the whole story, it has its 'other' side, its dark side, its unheimlich moments, as Freud would say, and the story is a path negotiated through the highs and lows. This is what I would write about the 'Sixties'.

As I said before, Melvin Burgess proposed that

> ... we live in a multi-cultural, multi-faith, multi-value society in an age where television, radio, the press and the internet have rendered the secrets adults may wish to keep from children impossible to hide.[7]

The lesson for historical writers is your reader can check out your facts so be authentic in your historical writing – it matters, even in representation. As Webb states: 'What we see is not what is there, but what our social and cultural traditions and their contexts gave us' (Webb 2009: 2), as ' ... we constantly, if subconsciously, produce meanings out of the material world.' It is important to understand that the world you are recreating is still about making the connections through ideas, and not about laminating a Kipling-esque style of nostalgia for an age that never existed in the first place. Furthermore, it almost seems insulting to say this but I was thinking about Kipling and ideas around colonialism, post-colonialism and imperialism, and a twenty-first-century historical novel must reflect the multicultural state the world has reached. To repeat something I said above, writing is an art form and as such its engagement with words, culture and communication allows it to try and negotiate other cultural practices and normative ideas with a critical and creative vigilance – and it is in this sense that I consider writing for children to be a critically creative and creatively critical process that comes with a huge burden of responsibility. Repeating Primo Levi when he says: 'I always thought that [building] bridges is the best job there is ... because roads go over bridges, and without roads we'd still be savages. In short, bridges are the opposite of borders, and borders are where wars start' (Levi 1986). History is always a rewriting and a rerepresentation but there is much we can do to recover the authentic in the story we propose.

*Series fiction* too is something to consider because publishers love it – they love to be able to hook a reader again and again with a character that children take to. Victor Watson in the introduction to his book, *Reading Series Fiction*, quotes a wonderful little anecdote from an unknown schoolchild who said: ' ... starting a new novel was like going into a room full of strangers, but starting a book in a familiar series was like going into a room full of friends.' Cute as the quotation is, though, there is also something quite important being implied. I am sure we all feel this when we finish a good novel that we wish could just go on and on. Once I begin a really good novel I hate its ending – most recently (and I am not really sure I know why) Jonathan Franzen's *Freedom* (2010) encouraged me to spend hours and hours reading when I should have been writing and sleeping, and I was still disappointed about putting the book down. Indeed even in adulthood we cling to series fiction, look at the recent (as I write) success of Stieg Larsson's books. Mikael Blomkvist and Lisbeth Salander captured the imagination of millions worldwide.

Series fiction has its highs and lows but there are some very important rules to be considered when writing series fiction. As someone who has written 13 novels in a series, as a television tie-in, I will give you some idea of what you need to pay attention to.

Character continuity is very important. It is for this reason that you might find it wise to create a series 'bible'. In the bible you can write down the name of each major character (i.e., each character who will have a repeating part throughout the series – this is not required for occasional bit-part players). In *Dilly the Dinosaur*, for example, Dilly, Dorla, Mother and Father are defined through specific personality traits, use of dialogue, viewpoint, etc., and this has to be maintained through each story (not as easy as it looks, I can assure you). Imagine it in a televisual sense, with Homer Simpson talking in a new voice and becoming something he is not, like English, unless it was part of the plot for an episode. I mean how would that look if it just stuck, without explanation? For a larger series, though, the bible helps you to define your characters, giving them an age, family (or not), definable traits, like scary, sporty, posh, etc. In the series of novels I wrote there were so many characters, ranging from Emperor Nero and his sidekick, Snivilus Grovelus, to Ben the Baker and a collection of fictional children. But the bible had already been done for the animation films and I found it extremely useful when developing the personalities of the children into the novels. A recent documentary on J. K. Rowling revealed that she even had drawings of her characters – and how could she have sustained the Snape's 'red herring'; Dumbledore's fatal flaw; Voldemort's weakness; Harry's genealogy for seven books if she didn't really 'know' her characters, how they would develop, from their family trees downwards?

But in truth I find a bible useful for most novel writing and you should consider this too. It does not mean your characters cannot develop. They can and do and must, but writing series fiction you must be careful to make their development relevant. If your reader does not read the stories in sequence, for example, development can get confusing. Acquiring a new baby brother in book six when it did not exist in book two, for example, is the kind of change that could be problematic. As Victor Watson reveals, 'Antonia Forest once admitted in an author's note to *The Thuggery Affair* that her characters had aged only eighteen months in a historical period of seventeen years – and that was only the sixth novel in a series of ten' (Watson 2000: 8). Also, you have to be aware of the difference between a series and something like a trilogy or Rowling's septology (as I called it[8]) where the characters do grow and age.

But here is an imaginary bible for our old friend Icarus (thought I had forgotten about him, didn't you?):

| | |
|---|---|
| **Name** | Icarus |
| **Age** | 12 |
| **Height** | 1.2 m |
| **Weight** | 48 kg |
| **Father** | Daedalus |
| **Mother** | Naucrate (missing) |
| **Siblings** | None |
| **Cousins** | Thalus |

| | |
|---|---|
| **Nationality** | Cretan |
| **Hair** | Black and curly |
| **Eyes** | Aegean Sea blue |
| **Sexuality** | Undetermined |
| **Likes** | Sugar almonds |
| **Dislikes** | Marzipan (just like me). |

You get the idea, what you are doing is keeping the things that are important for continuity but once you begin this you can add to it as your character develops and as they interact with others. I wonder if Rowling ever thought Harry would have become a fan of the narcotic, Felix Felicis, which seems to have a slightly more magical quality than jellies.[9]

# Chapter 11

# Poetry for children

The children's poet Roger Stevens recently reported that 'research by Roehampton University (*Teachers as Readers: Phase 1, Research Report for UKLA Web* – www.ukla.org/downloads/TARwebreport.doc.www) revealed that the number of primary school teachers who read poetry for their own pleasure was 0.01%.' What a depressing statistic that is when we consider that these teachers 'are the people responsible for teaching poetry as literature to their pupils/our children'.[1] And I wonder why this is? I firmly believe that if you want to write good poetry you do need to know what it reads like. I try to read a poem every single day of my life. It isn't hard, it needn't take long, but I am lucky I can just reach out to the shelf in front of the desk I am writing at right now, where I can grab books by, let's see, Jen Webb, Jeri Kroll, Phillip Gross, Nigel McLoughlin, Wallace Stevens, Susan Hampton, Ovid, Dante, Paul Muldoon, Philip Larkin and Robert Hull (as you can see my filing system is a delightful chaos). And when I pull their books off the shelves I realise that there is little difference between writing poetry for children and adults. Perhaps the erudite ideas of a T.S Eliot's *Four Quartets* are beyond your average child (and schoolteacher by the look of it) but the similarities are tangible and real.

Indeed it seems fair to say that early exposure to poetry is a wonderful way of exposing children to the world of ideas through rhythm and rhyme, wordplay and creative freedom because the truth is they can write poetry, as can you. In fact everyone can write a poem – like most things it's just a case of getting the right words in the right order. But surely that is half the fun – choosing the words, getting the images right. And such fun can be had with this; the colour yellow is custard, bananas, the sun, sherbet lemons, my girlfriend's pants, my auntie's teeth; and ideas are easy, Elvis works in a chip shop; Icarus is a boy who can fly; can you swallow a swallow; cabbage is yum; Brussels sprouted; the sea is green with envy (a small cliché ok, but if it fits it fits in fits and starts which rhymes with something much more scatological – and I blame the cabbage).

> There was an Old Man in a tree,
> Who was horribly bored by a Bee;
> When they said, 'Does it buzz?'
> He replied, 'Yes, it does!'
> 'It's a regular brute of a Bee!'

(Edward Lear 1861)[2]

Poems for children come in many guises, as Robert Hull states in his extremely useful book, *Poetry – From Reading to Writing* (2010) where he encourages children to read and write from the following list:

- Rhyming and non-rhyming poems
- Riddles
- Short poems
- Haiku, tanga, renga
- Poems from stories
- Free verse
- Narrative poems
- Poems drawing on history and the world in general.

And we can see how little is left out of the scope of the poem. But what is really important is the child-centred-ness of the poem. As Stevens says:

> You need to engage your young readers. Unless you've done something very clever with your subject, it is likely that a child will enjoy a poem about school more than, say, a poem set in an office. As well as place, you also need to consider the behaviour depicted in your poem. Is it real to a modern child? Before submitting your work ask yourself – Will a child of today find something they can relate to in this poem? In fact, don't just ask yourself, ask a child!
>
> (Stevens 2010: 58)

Crucially he does not omit the opportunity for doing something clever. But it doesn't have to be anything as long as it can be understood as a poem, even in the nonsensical of Edward Lear. I often feel we get too hung up on the wordy-rapping-hooded-ness of poetry when we should be reading it out loud and encouraging children to write more and more of it. Because it is an ideal time for them to begin to understand the intricacies of form, verse, rhythm and rhyme, discipline, literal and lyrical control and those all important tools – words.

There is a point we should consider whether poetry for children is morphing into crazy verse for kids. And while we are at it we might also consider just how much whimsical versifying the world can accept. That is not to say a little doggerel or whimsy can't be addressed but it is all about getting balance. When the American poet John Ashbery was asked why his poems were so difficult he said that 'he noticed that if you go on talking to people they eventually lose interest, but when you start talking to yourself they want to listen in' (Phillips 2000: 323). I find this very persuasive. Listening in to the inner thoughts, feelings and emotions of the poet seems to me to be the closest way of engaging with the writer's very creativity. But then in understanding this, consider what can be said in the poem that can act as a catalyst for thought and exploration. If the reading child is exposed to ideas in poetry and understands what is being written, it means the poet is 'articulating' what the child already knows, while, and at the same time, helping the child to understand something it doesn't know by allowing the child to explore the radical, comfortably predictable and the unsettlingly unexpected special social space that is childhood. In this sense, the poem returns us to Peter Hunt's idea that the poem for children can be that 'eccentric blend of the comfortably predictable and the unsettlingly unexpected', which becomes a talisman in describing child and adult literacy, knowledge, culture and ongoing experience in poetic form.

It was Eliot who wrote that 'No poet, no artist of any art, has his complete meaning alone' (Eliot 1951: 14).[3] Making the connections in poetic form, thinking out loud, is surely a desirable way to encourage serious thought, symbolic, emblematic, figurative and representative of what Seamus Heaney called 'a working model of inclusive consciousness' (Heaney 1995: 1–9)[4] as acute observation of life and living.

## In other words

I opened this book with, 'I am not being coy,' wrote Jack Zipes, 'children's literature does not exist' (Zipes 2002: 40) and I am closing it with the same quotation because I feel it bookends many of the ideas I have tried to incorporate into it. First, I do think it does exist as an adult-given, child-centred discourse. But as Kimberley Reynolds reveals (2007: 180–83) we are about to see a major cultural change. This book essentially talks about print-based children's writing but the kindle kids are just around the corner. The web-based 'fan novel' is already online, written by children and truly children's fiction, but this new revolution opens up a huge and new 'round of narrative innovation'; it is the future that we will all have to address now, absolutely now, and I can report I have already held discussion on the publishing potential. But I concur with Reynolds when she writes, these new child writers 'may change the meaning of children's literature for the future generations, they like generations of writers before them, their understanding of narrative, culture and self will continue to be indebted to the fictions they encountered in childhood' (2007). Write for children, by all mean, but write well for them, it is no more than they deserve.

Without storytelling, without the ongoing accumulation of knowledge, that which we connect in stories, we would all be chasing chimeras. Storytelling is the Rosetta Stone of modernity. As I have written elsewhere, it's the key that opens the door to life's connections, helping us make sense of the world, from faith to fortune and everything in-between, as we grow in experience from children into adults, embracing spiritual, physical, irrational and intellectual uncertainty – it is the key to the future for the world's children and their children's children. It shouldn't matter what television, the internet, 24/7 media etc. throws at children if we can keep them in the story loop, which is so huge in their education, so we can teach them to think about the stories that will make up the connections in their lives; stories that define their existence; the rich intertextuality of their lives; the narrative that sustains their continuing sense of being in the communities in which we all of us co-exist, so that they may keep questioning the issues that threaten them: poverty, inequality, poor ethics, maltreatment and so on. If we give up challenging the story, intervening in the narrative, we allow the dictators, tyrants and despots the last word – the world's children deserve better. That is what writing for children is all about! I have tried to relate this by taking you through a small tour of some connecting, critical fragments that make up a trace of my own mind map, because in my own personal quest there are far-reaching questions – it has been a bit random but in doing so I hope I have made a connection.

But let me say one final thing, every children's story should end with the promise of a new beginning: I end so you can begin for as wise Harold Rosen once wrote, 'Sentences end with full stops. Stories do not!' (Rosen 1985). The end is just the beginning.

# Notes

## Introduction

1 Professor Severus Snape, with apologies to J.K. Rowling.
2 See Maria Nikolajeva, *Power, Voice and Subjectivity in Literature for Young Readers* (2010: 1).
3 Those who are interested in the intricacies of these ideas should read Sonia Livingstone's *Children and the Internet*, Cambridge: Polity Press, 2009.

## 1 Here comes the bogeyman ...

1 Harold Rosen, *Stories and Meaning*, Sheffield: NATE Papers in Education, 1985.
2 In 1985, Chris Powling and I ran the first MA: Writing for Children in the world at the University of Winchester, UK.
3 See Nodelman; Rudd; Hunt; Rose; Steedman; Kincaid; Lesnik-Oberstein; Nikolajeva; Zipes.
4 See Rudd, as well as Melrose (2002: 62–64).
5 Roderick McGillis, 'Learning to Read', *Children's Literature Association Quarterly,* 1997, Vol. 22 No. 3, 126–33.
6 Perry Nodelman wrote about the 'hidden adult' in child-centred culture – but I think the hidden child is a more relevant idea for the writer to pursue.
7 Nikolajeva's extremely interesting idea of *aetonormativity* is addressed at length, if a little abstractly.

## 2 A cultural, critical and creative context

1 *Braveheart* (1995). Directed by Mel Gibson, although of course that film was about William Wallace – up to a point – and something else, altogether.
2 www.unicef.org/protection/index_childlabour.html (accessed 23 January 2011).
3 www.guardian.co.uk/books/2010/may/12/best-childrens-books-eight-twelve-years (accessed 12 January 2011). On 16 April 2011, after writing this, *The Guardian* announced their 'new improved' website, www.guardian.co.uk/childrens-books-site, designed and curated with the help of an editorial panel of 100 children and teens around the world and it is really worth looking at. It is an ambitious project; though it cannot claim to be a children's website it is child-centred and aimed at children who read.
4 www.guardian.co.uk/books/2010/may/12/best-childrens-books-twelve-years-over (accessed 12 January 2011).
5 www.guardian.co.uk/books/2009/nov/28/lucy-mangan-building-childrens-library (accessed 12 January 2011).
6 As I write, there is a national debate underway in the UK regarding the closure of libraries, due to financial necessity. Goodness only knows what closing libraries will do to national literacy where access to books will become even harder. Furthermore, the UK government is thinking of publishing its own list of desirable authors whose work can be taught in school – what this is dependent on is, as yet, unclear.

7 www.guardian.co.uk/books/2010/may/12/best-childrens-books-ever?intcmp=239 (accessed 12 January 2011).

8 I am not opposed to censorship – it's the censors that worry me, especially those with ill-informed, political or religious (so called) motivations that are more parochially agenda laden and subversive than is healthy in our multicultural world where issues on race, gender, sexuality, religious and secular ideas should be freely aired without prejudice, force or violence. On censor sites, see, for example, PABBIS, http://www.pabbis.com/.

9 I still love family trips to bookshops but in my home town of Brighton, UK, we have seen the demise of two out of the three major book chains slide into bankruptcy in the past 12 months – leaving the available choice up to the (considerable) buying power of one major chain, which owns both remaining major bookshops in the city centre. It will be an interesting thesis that tracks the 'shopping online' Amazon/Kindle © debate on this issue in the coming months.

10 See above.

11 George Orwell, *1984,* London: Martin Secker and Warburg Ltd., 1949.

12 www.guardian.co.uk/books/2000/oct/28/booksforchildrenandteenagers.philippullman (accessed 30 November 2010), though I often wondered what Pullman thought of being called a heretic.

13 Adam Smith, in *The Theory of Moral Sentiments* (1759) Sect. II: Of Justice and Beneficence, Ch. 2.

14 Daniel Altman, *Managing Globalization,* in: *Q & Answers* with Joseph E. Stiglitz, Columbia University and *The International Herald Tribune,* www.guardian.co.uk/books/2000/oct/28/books forchildrenandteenagers.philippullman (accessed 11 October 2006). See, too, Joseph E. Stiglitz, *Making Globalization Work: The Next Steps to Global Justice,* London: Allen Lane, 2006.

15 Beginning with Terry Eagleton's measured reply to Fredric Jameson on postmodernism is as good a place to begin as anywhere but I do not have the space to go into it here.

16 See A. James and A. Prout, eds, *Constructing and Reconstructing Childhood: Contemporary Issues in the Construction of Childhood,* London: Falmer Press, 1997; Karen Lesnik-Oberstein, *Children's Literature: Criticism and The Fictional Child,* Oxford: Clarendon Press, 1994 and the 'Essentials: what is Children's Literature? What is Childhood?' in *Understanding Children's Literature,* ed. Peter Hunt, London: Routledge, 1999, 15–29; Rex and Wendy Stainton Rogers, *Stories of Childhood: Shifting Agendas of Child Concern,* London: Harvester Wheatsheaf, 1992.

17 www.philip-pullman.com/about.asp (accessed 12 January 2011).

18 'Wovon man nicht sprechen kann, darüber muss man schweigen.' Trans. 'Whereof one cannot speak, thereof one must be silent.' Ludwig Wittgenstein, *Tractatus Logico-Philosophicus,* 1922: Tractatus 7.

19 Richard Ellmann, *James Joyce,* Oxford: Oxford University Press, 1983.

20 Rose also mentions the 'magic' of reading on page 135.

21 See Michel Foucault, *Power/Knowledge* in his books: *The Will of Knowledge, The History of Sexuality: 1,* trans. R. Hurley, London: Penguin Books, 1976; *Discipline and Punish: The Birth of the Prison,* trans. A. Sheridan, London: Penguin, 1977.

22 I appreciate and acknowledge the helpful conversation I had with Prof. Jen Webb, University of Canberra, on this issue.

23 Sigmund Freud, 'The "Uncanny"', *Art and Literature,* Albert Dickson ed., trans. James Strachey, London: Penguin, 1953.

24 Septology, probably not a word but I guessed it up, from septenary, meaning of or in relation to the prime number seven. But what is the point of being a writer if you can't bring in new words? J.K. Rowling gave us plenty of them, after all.

25 I have tried to source the original quotation link to a website at the University of Birmingham, UK, without success.

26 I cannot rehearse the idea of child, language and literacy here for it would take a whole book to do so but there are others who have already approached this.

27 M. M., Bakhtin, 'Discourses in the Novel', *The Dialogic Imagination: Four Essays,* ed. M. Holquist, trans. C, Emerson, Austin: University of Texas Press, 1981 – for an explanation see Rudd 2010: 165.

28 Walter Benjamin, 'The Storyteller', *Illuminations,* trans. Harry Zorn, London: Jonathan Cape, 1970.

29 Fanon wrote, 'The negro is not. Any more than the white man' in the book *Black Skin, White Masks,* London: Pluto, 1986: 231.

## 3 Bridging the gap between child reader and adult author

1 I will explain ideas on the 'other' as I proceed but, of course, that does not mean that 'adult' is the only 'other' as far as the child (like the adult) is concerned; issues such as race, gender, sexuality, etc., are all in the mix too.
2 Kimberley Reynolds, 'Transformative Energies' in Janet Maybin and Nicola Watson, eds, *Children's Literature Approaches and Territories*, Basingtoke: Palgrave Macmillan, 2009: 99.
3 'Normative': implying, creating or prescribing a norm or standard.
4 I am indebted to Jen Webb for our conversations that allowed me to talk through these ideas.
5 See Reynolds, op. cit.
6 I am taken by Homi Bhabha's explanation of this in his essay, 'Postcolonial Authority and Postmodern Guilt', in Lawrence Grossberg, Cary Nelson and Paula Treichler, eds, *Cultural Studies*, London: Routledge, 1992: 56–68.
7 As Rudd and I have shown previously (Melrose 2002) and (Rudd in Hunt 2004: 39).
8 Jacqueline Rose, 'The Imaginary' in Colin MacCabe, ed., *The Talking Cure*, London: Macmillan, 1981.
9 Pixie Lott, *Cry Me Out*, Mercury, 2009.

## 4 The (im)possibility of writing for children …

1 W. Benjamin, 'Child Reading' in *One-Way Street*, trans. J.A. Underwood, London: Verso Classics, 2006 (1979).
2 Mikhail Bakhtin, *Rabelais and his World,* trans. H. Iswolsky, Bloomington: Indiana University Press, 1984.
3 Ibid.: 263.
4 Google (accessed 27 February 2011).
5 Coleridge coined the phrase in his *Biographia Literaria*, published in 1817 when talking about the *Lyrical Ballads*. The notion of such an action by an audience was however recognised well before this, especially with the concerns of Horace, in his *Arts Poetica*.
6 That language can be as obscure as it likes. My daughter Abbi is an international tennis player and she recently played a doubles tournament with a Mexican partner against a Kenyan and a Panamanian; their only shared words were 15, 30, 40, deuce, advantage, love and ¡*vamos*!
7 Jalāl ad-Dīn Muammad Rūmī (Persian: جلالالدین محمد رومی).
8 Jacques Derrida 1978: 95.
9 Roland Barthes, *Image, Music, Text*, trans. R. Howard, 'Death of the Author', 1977, http://evans-experientialism.freewebspace.com/barthes06.htm (accessed 13 July 2011).
10 Jacqueline Rose, 'The Imaginary' in Colin MacCabe, ed., *The Talking Cure,* London: Macmillan, 1981.
11 www.guardian.co.uk/uk/2006/jan/24/books.politics (accessed 16 March 2011).
12 R. Burch, 'Phenomenology, Lived Experience: Taking a Measure of the Topic', *Phenomenology & Pedagogy*, Vol. 8: 130–60, www.phenomenologyonline.com/articles/burch2.html (accessed 10 March 2011).

## 5 Elements of storytelling for children

1 M. Burgess, 'What is Teenage Fiction?' undated, http://web.onetel.com/~melvinburgess/ARTICLES. htm#teenage%20fiction (accessed 1 October 2007). For an informed and coherent reading of this I suggest Sonia Livingstone's highly informative book, *Children and The Internet* (Cambridge: Polity Press, 2009).
2 Christopher Booker, *The Seven Basic Plots: Why We Tell Stories*, London: Continuum, 2004.
3 www.philip-pullman.com/ (accessed 20 April 2011).
4 The answer to the riddle is a mirror.
5 Here is one of the many reviews on Amazon (presumably written by a child) which appealed to me: 'Angus Solomon is the main character in this brilliant story by Morris Gleitzman, he is 12 years old and has 2 younger children 2 look after, (WARNING: DO NOT read this book if you are strong on whats fair and whats not, because this book is VERY unfair) it is a bit rude *and don't read it if you are 8 and under because it might offend ur parents.* Angus meets Rindi one day after school, and he

thought HE had problems … Read this book if u like books on family problems and everyday life' (sic to all of the spelling but it is reproduced as it was written, except the italics which are mine), www.amazon. co.uk/product-reviews/0141303557/ref=cm_cr_dp_synop?ie=UTF8&showViewpoints=0&sortBy= bySubmissionDateDescending#R1W1P5XPOQKLVG (accessed 1 March 2011).

6 www.dubitresearch.com/ (accessed 13 July 2011).

7 I found the essays in the book *Modernism and Theory: a critical debate*, ed. Stephen Ross, New York: Routledge, 2009, very useful in helping me to understand this.

8 'Bertolt Brecht Against György Lukács', *Aesthetics and Politics Debates Between Bloch, Lukács, Brecht, Benjamin and Adorno*, trans. Ronald Taylor, London: Verso, 1977.

9 www.ox.ac.uk/media/news_stories/2011/110804.html (accessed 13 April 2011).

10 Eleanor Farjeon, 'Writing "for" Children' from *The Writer's Desk Book: A Comprehensive Guide to the Various Aspects of the Writer's Craft*, London: A & C Black, 1935.

11 Andrew Melrose, Snr., in private conversation, circa 1971.

12 'I am black/ my skin is white/so I am white and my blood is black/ … I love that because it is a difference that's beautiful … ', 'some of us are beautiful some are not/some are black some are white/all that difference was on purpose … for us to compete each other/let everyone get his love and dignity/the world will be beautiful'. *La Différence*, Salif Keita, 2009, Emarcy/Umgd, ASIN: B002SBV0QW.

13 Ovid, *Metamorphoses*, Book VIII, trans. A.D. Melville, Oxford: Oxford University Press, 1986.

14 Geoff Danaher, Tony Schriato and Jen Webb, *Understanding Foucault*, London: Sage, 2000.

15 Interview, the *Canberra Times*, 22 June 2010.

16 Philip Pullman, quoted by Nigel Reynolds, 'Writers are losing the plot, says prize-winner', *The Daily Telegraph*, 18 July 1996.

# 6 Engaging with Icarus

1 *Thoughts for the Times on War and Death*, Sigmund Freud, 1915, which can be read here: http://www.panarchy.org/freud/war.1915.html (accessed 19 July 2011).

2 Ovid, *Metamorphoses*, Book VIII, trans. A. D. Melville, Oxford: Oxford University Press, 1986: 171–78.

3 Ibid.

4 Michel Foucault, 'The life of infamous men' in Meaghan Morris and Paul Patton, eds, *Michel Foucault: Power, Truth, Strategy*, trans. Paul Foss and Meaghan Morris, Sydney: Feral Publications, 1979 (1977): 76–91.

5 Francis Fukuyama, *The End of History and the Last Man*, London: Penguin, 1992.

6 Slavoj Žižek, *Welcome to the Desert of the Real*, London: Verso, 2002.

7 'Dialectics at a standstill – this is the quintessence of the method', Walter Benjamin, *The Arcades Project*, Walter Benjamin, Rolf Tiedemann, ed., trans. Howard Eiland and Kevin McLaughlin, Cambridge, MA: Belknap/Harvard University Press, 1999: 865. But 'dialectics at a standstill' is more than a footnote – and refers to a lot of Walter Benjamin's ideas in the *Passengen Werk* or *Arcades Project* – the term, incidentally, Walter Benjamin may have found, without really knowing that Kierkegaard's melancholy had long since conjured it up (Notes 2: 228). It would be worth looking at, *The Dialectics of Seeing Walter Benjamin and the Arcades Project*, Susan Buck-Morss, The MIT Press; Reprint edition (July 1, 1991). Walter Benjamin's magnum opus was a book he did not live to write. In *The Dialectics of Seeing,* Susan Buck-Morss offers an inventive reconstruction of the *Passagen Werk,* or *Arcades Project*, as it might have taken form. Although much can be made of Theodor Adorno and the whole Frankfurt School ideas in relation to this idea. But, as The *Arcades Project* editor, Rolf Tiedemann, maintains, there is a noteworthy drift away from the traditional Marxian conception of historical materialism and dialectic in this work. After many years of organising the various snippets of dialogue, image and discourse that constitute the *Passagen-Werk*, Tiedemann arrived at the conclusion that the whole project involves what Benjamin himself referred to as a state of 'dialectics at a standstill'. What is meant by this phrase is that historical time becomes encapsulated in images forming what Tiedemann calls a 'historical constellation'.

8 John Richard Thackrah, *Dictionary of Terrorism*, 2nd ed., London: Routledge, 2004.

9 'Thoughts for the Times on War and Death', Sigmund Freud, 1915, which can be read here: www.panarchy.org/freud/war.1915.html (accessed 19 July 2011).

10 *Beo*, Karine Polwart, Bay Songs Ltd., 2006, and it is on the very excellent album/cd/iTunes download etc. entitled *This Earthly Spell* (2008) – the full text can be seen on her website, which is: http://www.karinepolwart.com/.

11 In private correspondence dated 25 August 2010.

12 Ovid, op. cit.

13 *Problems of Knowledge and Freedom* (Chomsky, 1971: 110).

14 M. M., Bakhtin, 'Discourses in the Novel', *The Dialogic Imagination: Four Essays*, M. Holquist, ed., trans. C, Emerson, Austin: University of Texas Press, 1981.

15 'Musée des Beaux Artes', W. H. Auden, © 1976 by Edward Mendelson, William Meredith and Monroe K. Spears, Executors of the Estate of W. H. Auden.

16 I found Gabriel Josipovici's book, *The World and the Book*, London: Macmillan, 1979 useful on this idea, particularly the chapter, 'Surface and Structure', pp. 266–85.

# 7 Considering the bogeyman …

1 www.randomhouse.com/features/pullman/author/carnegie.html (accessed 3 April 2011).

2 See www.kidsatrandomhouse.co.uk/ (accessed 3 April 2011).

# 8 Story structure

1 See Angela Carter, *The Bloody Chamber*, London: Vintage Classics, 2011 (1979).

2 For some reason my footballers always called me 'And'. It is not a nickname I encountered from anyone else in my lifetime. I don't know why this is relevant except to say it seemed to be a way they found to express their social interaction with an adult (me) who wasn't a parent or a teacher but an 'other' as a football coach to them, whose identity was defined by its own set of social rules, some of which were governed by the Football Association and some through plain old common sense. My job was to explore and develop their football skills, team skills and the way they behaved on the pitch, with referees and opponents etc. – which had a knock on effect in their social skills too. I found you couldn't tell them what to do, how to behave and how to be but even the most problematic child integrated into the unusual normativity of a team dynamic through a process of cooperation.

3 Philip Pullman, *'The Subtle Knife', Partial Typescript,* Seven Stories: The Centre for Children's Books, Philip Pullman MSS, PP/13/02, 1996.

   Seven Stories said, 'We have an early, incomplete draft of 'The Subtle Knife' [reference number PP/13/02] in the collection here, which implies that Will is 16. This isn't stated explicitly as fact, but on page 21 of the typescript one of the policemen investigating the murders at Will's home is asked how old Will is and he replies: "Sixteen … I don''t know.' His age isn't referred to again, but he is later described as "a big strong lad" (p. 23) and "big, not as formed as a grown man, but on his way to being powerful" (p. 36), and he is strong enough to beat a grown man to death (in this version of the story, Will murders the pastor of the church that his mother has become involved with, after his mother has killed herself, and that is the reason he flees home). His being several years older than Lyra is also evident from Lyra's response to him when they first meet. Most notably in the following text from the typescript:

   > 'Lyra stood over him for some moments, frankly staring. She had never been this close to an older boy. She realised forcefully the greatest disadvantage of this new world, for all the convenience of its canned drinks, for in her own world, you could tell easily when someone was grown up, because the form of their daemon was fixed. Children like her and Roger had daemons whose form could change at will, but at the time known as puberty that power faded, and the daemon became fixed in one form for life. Was this boy full-grown or not? He was powerful and heavily built, but something made her feel he was not yet adult.' (p. 44)

4 Mary Ann Evans wrote under the name George Eliot.

5 T. Pateman, 'Empty Word and the Full Word: the Emergence of Truth in Writing', in *The Self on the Page: Theory and Practice of Creative Writing in Personal Development*, ed. C. Hunt and F. Sampson

(London: Jessica Kingsley, 1998): 159, www.selectedworks.co.uk/creativewritingemptywordfull word.html (accessed 14 July 2011).

6 Andrew Melrose, *Kyoto* (*a big story about a boy and a little bear – and a little story about global warming*), Illustrations Karenanne Knight (Falmouth: Polar Bear Press, 2010).

7 Abbi Melrose, age four and a half, cf. Melrose 2001: 20.

## 9 Early readers, middle years and pre-teens

1 I found the essays in the book *Modernism and Theory: a critical debate*, ed. Stephen Ross, Abingdon: Routledge, 2009 very useful in helping me to understand this.

2 Martin Waddell, *A Kitten Called Moonlight*, illustrations by Christian, Birmingham: Walker Books, 2000.

3 www.guardian.co.uk/books/2000/oct/28/booksforchildrenandteenagers.philippullman (accessed 30 November 2010).

4 C. Lee, D. Conroy, C. Hii, 'The Internet: A consumer socialization agent for teenagers', *ANZMAC 2003 Conference* Adelaide, 1–3 December 2003.

5 I am grateful to Vanessa Harbour for sharing this research from her as yet unpublished PhD thesis entitled: 'Problems of Representation/Representing Sex, Drugs and Alcohol in British Contemporary Young Adult Fiction', 2011.

6 *Red Riding Hood* was originally a French folk tale that was adapted by Perrault to include this warning.

7 W. Benjamin, 'The Storyteller', in *Illuminations*, trans. H. Zorn, London: Pimlico, 1999 (1955).

8 'Bertolt Brecht Against György Lukács', *Aesthetics and Politics Debates Between Bloch, Lukács, Brecht, Benjamin and Adorno*, trans. Ronald Taylor, London: Verso, 1977.

9 M. Burgess, 'What is Teenage Fiction?', http://web.onetel.com/~melvinburgess/ARTICLES. htm#teenage%20fiction (accessed 10 October 2007).

## 10 Social realism, narrative non-fiction and *The Tiger Who Came to Tea*

1 Judy Waite, www.judywaite.com/gamegirls.html (accessed 10 April 2011).

2 Anne Fine, 'Filth, whichever way you look at it', *The Guardian,* 29 March 2003, www.guardian.co. uk/books.2003/mar/29/featuresreviews.guardianreview24 (accessed 10 April 2011).

3 M. Burgess, 'Sympathy for the Devil', www.web.onetel.net.uk/~melvinburgess/ARTICLES.htm (accessed 15 November 2008).

4 R. Burch, 'Phenomenology, Lived Experience: Taking a Measure of the Topic', *Phenomenology & Pedagogy*, vol. 8: 130–60, www.phenomenologyonline.com/articles/burch2.html (accessed 10 April 2008).

5 W. Benjamin, 'The Storyteller', in *Illuminations*, trans. H. Zorn, London: Pimlico, 1999 (1955).

6 *My Generation* was written by Pete Townsend, 1965.

7 M. Burgess 'What is Teenage Fiction?', http://web.onetel.com/~melvinburgess/ARTICLES. htm#teenage%20fiction, (accessed 23 October 2007).

8 Septology, probably not a word but I guessed it up, from septenary, meaning of or relating to the prime number seven. But what is the point of being a writer if you can't bring in new words? J.K. Rowling gave us plenty of them, after all – see Chapter 3.

9 Street terms for temazepam include jellies.

## 11 Poetry for children

1 Roger Stevens, *Writing in Education*, Issue Number 52, Winter 2010.

2 www.nonsenselit.org/Lear/BoN/index.html (accessed 3 April 2011).

3 T. S. Eliot, *Selected Essays*, London: Faber and Faber, 1951.

4 Seamus Heaney, *The Redress of Poetry*, New York: Straus and Giroux, 1995.

# Bibliography

Abbs, Peter (1996) *The Polemics of Imagination*, London: Skoob Books.

Adorno, Theodor (1991) *The Culture Industry*, London: Routledge.

Appleyard, J.A. (1994) *Becoming a Reader: The Experience of Fiction from Childhood to Adulthood*, Cambridge: Cambridge University Press.

Arendt, Hannah (1958) *The Human Condition*, Chicago: University of Chicago Press.

Armstrong, Karen (2005) *A Short History of Myth*, Edinburgh: Canongate Books Ltd.

Auden, W. H. (1963) *The Dyer's Hand, and other essays*, London: Faber and Faber.

Auerbach, Erich (1998) *Mimesis: The Representation of Reality in Western Literature*, trans. Willard Trask, Cambridge: MA: Harvard University Press.

Bakhtin, Mikhail (1984) *Rabelais and His World*, trans. H. Iswolsky, Bloomington: Indiana University Press.

——(1990) *Art and Answerability: Early Philosophical Essays*, ed. by M. Holquist and V. Liapunov, trans. V. Liapunov, Austin: University of Texas Press.

——(2008 [1981]) 'Discourses in the Novel', *The Dialogic Imagination: Four Essays*, ed. by M. Holquist, trans. C. Emerson and M. Holquist, Austin: University of Texas Press.

——(2010 [1986])*Speech Genres & Other Late Essays*, ed. by C. Emerson, C. and M. Holquist, trans. V. McGee, Austin: University of Texas Press.

Bal, Mieke (1997) *Narratology: Introduction to the Theory of Narrative*, second edition, Toronto: University of Toronto Press.

Barthes, Roland (1972) *Mythologies*, London: Jonathan Cape.

——(1975) *The Pleasure of the Text*, trans. Richard Miller, London: Hill and Wang.

——(1977) 'Death of the Author', *Image, Music, Text*, trans. R. Howard, http://evans–experientialism. freewebspace.com/barthes06.htm (accessed 15 July 2011).

Batchelor, S.A., Kitzinger, J., Burtney, E. (2004) 'Representing young people's sexuality in the "youth" media', *Health Education Research*, 19 (6), pp. 295–313.

Baudrillard, Jean (1990) *The Transparency of Evil: Essays on Extreme Phenomena*, trans. J. Benedict, London Verso.

Bawden, Nina (1974) 'A Dead Pig and My Father', *Children's Literature in Education*, 3–13.

Benjamin,Walter (1973) *Illuminiations*, ed. by Hannah Arendt, trans. Harry Zohn, London: Fontana.

——(1999) *The Arcades Project*, ed. by Rolf Tiedemann, trans. Howard Eiland and Kevin McLaughlin, Cambridge, MA: Belknap/Harvard University Press.

——(2006 [1979]) *One-Way Street*, trans. J.A. Underwood, London: Verso Classics.

Bennett, T. (1983) 'Text Readers, Reading Formation', *The Bulletin of the Midwest Modern Language Association,* 16 (1), Spring 1983, pp. 13–17, www.jstor.org/stable/1314830 (accessed 15 July 2011).

Bettelheim, Bruno (1976) *The Uses of Enchantment: The Meaning and Importance of Fairy Tales*, New York: Knopf.

Bhabha, Homi K. (2004 [1994]) *The Location of Culture*, London: Routledge Classics.

Bourdieu, Pierre (1993) *The Field of Cultural Production*, Cambridge: Polity Press.

Blake, Andrew (2000) 'Of More than Academic Interest: C.S. Lewis and the Golden Age', *Behind the Veil of Familiarity: C.S. Lewis (1898–1998)*, ed. by M. Carretero-Gonzalez and E. Hidalgo Tenorio, Oxford: Peter Lang.

Booth, Wayne (1983) *The Rhetoric of Fiction*, Chicago: University of Chicago Press (Penguin reprint – 1991).

Boulter, Amanda (2007) *Writing Fiction: Creative and Critical Approaches*, Basingstoke: Palgrave Macmillan.

——(2004 [1993]) *The Field of Popular Culture*, ed. by R. Johnson, Cambridge: Polity.

Brande, Dorothea (1934) *Becoming a Writer*, London: Macmillan.

Brecht, Bertolt (1977) 'Bertolt Brecht Against György Lukács', *Aesthetics and Politics Debates Between Bloch, Lukács, Brecht, Benjamin and Adorno*, trans. Ronald Taylor, London: Verso.

Butler, R.J. and Green, D. (2007) *The Child Within: Taking the Young Person's Perspective by Applying Personal Construct Psychology*, second edition, Chichester: Wiley.

Butt, M. (ed.) (2007) *Story: The Heart of the Matter*, London: Greenwich Exchange.

Calvino, Italo (1982) *The Uses of Literature*, trans. P. Creagh, London: A Harvest Book.

——(1996 [1988]) *Six Memos for the Next Millennium*, trans. Creogh, New York: Vintage.

Carpenter, Humphrey (1985) *Secret Gardens: The Golden Age of Children's Literature*, London; Allen and Unwin.

Carter, James (ed.) (1999) *Talking Books*, London: Routledge.

Carter, R.A. (1997) *Investigating English Discourse: Language, Literacy and Literature*, London: Routledge.

Chambers, Aiden (1993) *Tell Me: Children, Reading and Talk*, Stroud: Thimble Press.

Chambers, Nancy (ed.) (1980) *The Signal Approach to Children's Books*, Stroud: Thimble Press.

Chomsky, Noam (1971) *Problems of Knowledge and Freedom*, New York: Vintage.

Crook, Charles (2008) *Theories of Formal and Informal Learning in the World of Web 2.0*, www.education.ox.ac.uk/esrcseries/uploaded/08_0314%20ESRC%20report_web.pdf (accessed 23 March 2011).

Danahaer, G., Schirato, T. and Webb, J. (2000) *Understanding Foucault*, London: Sage.

De Bono, Edward (1972) *Children Solve Problems*, London: Allen Lane.

De Certeau, M. (2010 [1986]) *Heterologies: Discourse on the Other*, trans. B. Massumi, Minneapolis: Minnesota University Press.

Deleuze, G. Guattari and F. (2004 [1980]) *A Thousand Plateaus*, London: Continuum.

de Man, Paul (1986) *The Resistance to Theory*, Manchester: Manchester University Press.

Derrida, Jacques (1978) *Writing and Difference*, trans. Alan Bass, London: Routledge.

——(1982) *Margins of Philosophy*, Chicago: The University of Chicago Press.

——(2002) 'The Law of Genre', in *Acts of Literature*, ed. by Derek Attridge, New York: Routledge, pp. 221–52.

Eaton, Anthony (2010) 'Growing Older – Young Adult Fiction Coming of Age', *Writing in Education*, Issue 52, November 2010, pp. 50–53.

Eliot, T. S. (1951) *Poetry and Drama*, Cambridge, MA Harvard University Press and London: Faber.

Fanon, Franz (1986) *Black Skin, White Masks*, London, Pluto.

Farjeon, Eleanor (1935) 'Writing "for" Children', *The Writer's Desk Book*, London: A&C Black.

Fiske, John (1989) *Understanding Popular Culture*, London: Unwin Hyman.

Foster, Hal (ed.) (1985) *Postmodern Culture*, London: Pluto Press.

Foucault, Michel (1979 [1977]) 'The life of infamous men', *Michel Foucault: Power, Truth, Strategy*, ed. by Meaghan Morris and Paul Patton, trans. Paul Foss and Meaghan Morris, Sydney by Feral Publications.

——(1984) *The Foucault Reader*, ed. by Paul Rabinow, London: Penguin.

——(1991) *Discipline and Punish: The Birth of the Prison*, trans. A. Sheridan, London: Penguin.

——(1998 [1976]) *The Will to Knowledge: The History of Sexuality: 1*, London: Penguin.

——(2002 [1994]) *Power: Essential Works of Foucault 1954–84 Vol 3*, ed. by J. Faubion, London: Penguin.

——(2008) *The Birth of Biopolitics: Lectures at the Collège de France 1978–1979*, ed. by M. Senellart, F. Ewald, A. Fontana and A.I. Davidson, trans. G. Burchell Basingstoke: Palgrave Macmillan.

Freud, Sigmund (1915) 'Thoughts for the times on war and death', trans. James Strachey, in collaboration with Anna Freud, assisted by Alix Strachey and Alan Tyson, *The Standard Edition of the Complete Psychological Works of Sigmund* Freud, London: Hogarth Press, pp. 273–300.

——(1968 [1927–39]) *The Letters of Sigmund Freud and Arnold Zweig*, ed. by Ernst L. Freud, trans. W. D. Robson-Scott, London: Hogarth Press.

——(1995) *The Freud Reader*, ed. by P. Gray, London: Vintage Originals.

——(1990) *Art and Literature*, London, Penguin.

Frey, James (1987) *How to Write a Damn Good Novel*, New York: St Martin's.

Friel, J. (2000) 'Reading as a Writer', ed. by J. Newman J. *et al.*, *The Writer's Workbook*, London: Arnold.

Fukuyama, Francis (1992) *The End of History and the Last Man*, New York: The Free Press.

Gardener, J. (1991)*The Art of Fiction*, New York: Vintage Books.

Gilligan, Carol (1982) *In a Different Voice*, Cambridge, MA: Harvard University Press.

Gleitzman, Morris (1998) *Bumface*, London: Puffin.

Goldthwaite, J. (1996) *The Natural History of Make Believe: A Guide to the Principal Works of Britain, Europe and America*, New York: Oxford Univesity Press.

Gordon, J. (1975) *The Thorny Paradise: Writers on Writing for Children*, ed. by E. Blishen, Harmondsworth: Kestral.

Grenby, M.O. (2008) *Children's Literature*, Edinburgh: Edinburgh University Press.

Grenby, M.O. and Immel, A. (eds) (2009) *The Cambridge Companion to Children's Literature*, Cambridge: Cambridge University Press.

Griffiths, M. (1995) *Feminisms and the Self: The Web of Identity*, London: Routledge.

Hall, Stuart (ed.) (1980) *Culture, Media, Language*, London: Hutchinson.

Hardy, G.H. (1940) *A Mathematician's Apology*, Cambridge: Cambridge University Press.

Heaney, S. (1979) *Preoccupations: selected prose 1968–78*, London: Faber & Faber.

——(1995) *The Redress of Poetry*, London: Faber.

Heath, Shirley Brice (2011) 'Foreword', in *Literacy Myths, Legacies, & Lessons*, by H.J. Graff, New York: Transaction Publishers.

Hollindale, P. (1988) *Ideology and the Children's Book*, Stroud: Thimble Press.

——(1997) *Signs of Childness in Children's Books*, Stroud: Thimble Press.

hooks, bel (2000) 'Remembered Rapture: Dancing with Words', *Journal of Advanced Composition*, 20, 1 (Winter): 1–8.

Hourihan, Marjorie (1997) *Deconstructing the Hero*, London: Routledge.

Hughes, T. (1968) *Poetry in the Making*, London: Faber and Faber.

Hull, R. (2001) 'What Hope For Children's Poetry': *Books for Keeps*, 126.

Hunt, Peter (1991) *Criticism, Theory, & Children's Literature*, Oxford: Basil Blackwell.

——(1994) *An Introduction to Children's Literature*, Oxford: Oxford University Press.

——(1999) *Understanding Children's Literature*, Abingdon: Routledge.

——(2001) *Children's Literature*, Oxford: Blackwell.

——(ed.) (2004) *International Companion Encyclopaedia of Children's Literature*, London: Routledge Falmer.

——(2010 [2005]) *Understanding Children's Literature*, second edition, London: Routledge.

Inglis, Fred (1981) *The Promise of Happiness, Value and Meaning in Children's Fiction*, Cambridge: Cambridge University Press.

Irigaray, Luce (1985) *This Sex Which is Not One*, trans. C. Porter, New York: Cornell University Press.

——(2008a) *Sharing the World*, London: Continuum.

——(2008b)*Teaching*, ed. by M. Green, London: Continuum.

James, A., Jenks, C. and Prout, A. (1998) *Theorizing Childhood*, Cambridge: Polity Press.

James, A. and Prout A. (eds.) (2000 [1997]) *Constructing and Deconstructing Childhood: Contemporary Issues in the Sociological Study of Childhood*, London: Routledge.

James, K. (2009) *Death, Gender and Sexuality in Contemporary Adolescent Literature*, London: Routledge.

Jameson, Fredric (1981) *The Political Unconscious: Narrative as a Socially Symbolic Act*, Ithaca, NY: Cornell University Press.

Jenkins, H. (ed.) (1998) *The Children's Culture Reader*, New York: New York University Press.

Kaplan, E. Ann (ed.) (1988) *Postmodernism and its Discontents, Theories and Practices*, London: Verso.

Krauth, Nigel (2006) 'The Domains of the Writing Process', in *Creative Writing Theory Beyond Practice,* eds. T. Brady, N. Krauth, Tenerife Post Pressed.

Kundera, Milan (1984) *The Unbearable Lightness of Being,* London: HarperCollins.

——(2000 [1968]) *The Art of the Novel,* trans. L. Asher, London: Faber and Faber.

——(2007) *The Curtain: An Essay in Seven Parts,* trans. L. Asher, London: Faber and Faber.

Leeson, Robert (1985) *Reading and Righting,* London: Collins.

Lesnik-Oberstein, Karin (1994) *Children's Literature: Criticism and the Fictional Child,* Oxford: Clarendon Press.

——(ed.) (2004) *Children's Literature: New Approaches,* Basingstoke: Palgrave Macmillan.

Lévi, Primo (1986) *Bridges of Knowledge (New Directions in European Writing),* London: Berg.

Lévi-Strauss, Claude (1966) *From Honey to Ashes,* London: Octagon.

Lewis, C. S. (1966) *Of Other Worlds: Essays and Short Stories,* Oxford: Bles.

McCaw, N. (2011) 'Close Reading, Writing and Culture', *New Writing: The International Journal for the Practice and Theory of Creative Writing,* 8 (1): 25–34.

McGillis, R. (1997) 'Learning to Read, Reading to Learn; or Engaging in Critical Pedagogy', *Children's Literature Association Quarterly,* 22 (3) (fall): 126–32.

McKee, Robert (1999) *Story,* London: Methuen.

Manning, Paul (ed.) (2007) *Drugs and Popular Culture: Drugs, Media and Identity in Contemporary Society,* Cullompton: Willan Publishing.

Mason, Zachary (2010) *The Lost Book of the Odyssey,* London: Jonathan Cape.

Maybin, Janet and Watson, Nicola, J. (eds) (2009) *Children's Literature: Approaches and Territories,* Basingstoke: Palgrave Macmillan and Milton Keynes: Open University.

Meek, Margaret (1988) *How Texts Teach What Readers Learn,* Stroud: Thimble Press.

Melrose, Andrew (2001) *Storykeeping: the story, the child and the word,* Carlisle: Paternoster.

——(2002) *Write for Children,* London: Routledge.

——(2007) 'Reading and Righting: Carrying on the "Creative Writing Theory" Debate', *New Writing: The International Journal for the Practice and Theory of Creative Writing,* 4 (2): 109–17.

——(2010) 'Jesus, Judas, Jimi and John: Culture, communication, media and art in delightful chaos', *TEXT,* 14 (1).

——(2011) 'Icarus in ellipses … some thoughts on textual intervention' http://aawp.org.au/files/Icarus%201%20Melrose.pdf (accessed 15 July 2011).

Melrose, Andrew and Harbour, Vanessa (2007) 'Junk, Skunk and Northern Lights – representation of drugs in children's literature', in *Drugs and Popular Culture: Drugs, Media and Identity in Contemporary Society,* ed. by Paul Manning, Cullompton: Willan Publishing.

Melrose, Andrew and Webb, Jen (2011) 'Intimacy and the Icarus Effect', Canberra, Axon, Creative Explorations: University of Canberra.

Melrose, Andrew, Webb, J., Kroll, J. and May, S. (2010) *Icarus Extended,* Brighton: Lulu.

Nabokov, Vladimir (1936) *Laughter in the Dark,* London: Vintage.

Natov, Roni (2006) *The Poetics of Childhood,* Abingdon: Routledge.

Nikolajeva, Maria (2002) *Children's Literature Comes of Age: Towards a New Aesthetic,* New York: Garland.

——(2005) *Aesthetic Approaches to Children's Literature: An Introduction,* Oxford: The Scarecrow Press.

——(2010) *Power, Voice and Subjectivity in Literature for Young Readers,* London: Routledge.

Nikolajeva, Maria and Scott, Carole (2006) *How Picture Books Work,* New York: Routledge.

Nodelmen, Perry (1988) *Words and Pictures: The Narrative Art of Picture Books,* Athens: University of Georgia Press.

——(2008) *The Hidden Adult: Defining Children's Literature,* Baltimore: Johns Hopkins University Press.

Ovid (1986) *Metamorphosés,* transt. A. D. Melville, Oxford: Oxford University Press.

Phillips, Adam (1995) *Terrors and Experts,* London: Faber and Faber.

——(2000) *Promises Promises,* London: Faber.

Powling, Chris (ed.) (1994) *The Best of Books for Keeps,* London: Bodley Head.

Pullman, Philip (1996) 'Carnegie Medal Acceptance Speech', www.randomhouse.com/features/pullman/author/carnegie (accessed 19 July 2011).

——(1997) *The Subtle Knife*, Oxford: Scholastic.

——(1998) *Northern Lights*, Oxford: Scholastic.

Reynolds, Kimberley (2007) *Radical Children's Literature: Future Visions and Aesthetic Transformations in Juvenile Fiction*, Basingstoke: Palgrave Macmillan.

Richards, I. A. (1954) *How to Read a Page: a Course in Effective Reading with an Introduction to a Hundred Great Words*, London: Routledge & Kegan Paul.

Richardson, L. (1991) *Writing Strategies: Reaching Diverse Audiences*, London: Sage.

Ricoeur, Paul (1965) *History and Truth*, trans. Charles A. Kelbley, Evanston, IL: Northwestern University Press.

Rorty, Richard (1989) *Contingency, Irony and Solidarity*, Cambridge: Cambridge University Press.

Rose, Jacqueline (1984) *The Case of Peter Pan or The Impossibility of Children's Fiction*, London: Macmillan.

Rosen, Harold (1985) *Stories and Meanings*, Sheffield: NATE Papers in Education.

Rosen, Harold (1985) *Stories and Meanings*, Stroud: Thimble Press.

Rowling, J. K. (1997) *Harry Potter and the Philosopher's Stone,* London: Bloomsbury.

Rudd, David (1996) 'Beatrix Potter and Jacques Derrida – Problematic Bedfellows in the Teaching of Children's Litarature?' *English in Education* 30 (1): 8–17.

——(ed.) (2010) *The Routledge Companion to Children's Literature*, London: Routledge.

Sarland, Charles (1996) 'Revenge of the Teenage Horrors', in *Voices Off Contexts and Readers*, ed. by Morag Styles, Eve Byrne and Victor Watson, London: Cassell.

Spivak, Gayatri (1988) 'Can the Subaltern Speak?', in *Marxism and the Interpretation of Culture,* ed. by Cary Nelson and Lawrence Grossberg, Evanston, IL: University of Illinois Press.

Stableford, Brian (1989) *The Way to Write Science Fiction*, London: Elm Tree Books.

Steedman, Carolyn (1995) *Strange Dislocations: Childhood and the Idea of Human Interiority*, Cambridge, MA: Harvard University Press.

Steig, M. (1993) 'Never Going Home: Reflections on Reading, Adulthood, and the Possibility of Children's Literature', *Children's Literature Association Quarterly*, 18 (1) (spring): 36–39.

Stevens, Roger (2010) *Writing in Education*, 52, autumn.

Stevens, Wallace (1953) *Selected Poems*, London: Faber.

Taylor, Ronald (ed.) (1977) *Aesthetics and Politics: Debates Between Bloch, Lukács, Brecht, Benjamin and Adorno*, London: Verso.

Townsend, John Rowe (1971) *A Sense of Story*, London: Longman.

Tucker, Nicholas (1981)*The Child and the Book: A Psychological and Literary Exploration*, Cambridge: Cambridge University Press.

Umberto, Eco (2006 [2002]) *On Literature*, trans. M. McLaughline, London: Vintage.

Watson, Victor (2000) *Reading Series Fiction*, London: Routledge.

Webb, Jen (2009) *Understanding Representation*, London: Sage.

——(2010) 'Critical and creative tendencies: about Naucrate', *Strange Bedfellows: Refereed Conference Papers of the 15th Annual AAWP Conference,* http://aawp.org.au/files/Icarus%202%20Webb.pdf (accessed 20 July 2011).

Webb, J. and Melrose, A. (2011) 'Intimacy and the Icarus effect', http.//www.axonjournal.com.au/issue-1/intinacy-and-occurs-effect.

Webb, J., Schirato, T. and Danaher, G. (2002) *Understanding Bourdieu*, Crows Nest: Allen & Unwin.

Weir, Peter (1998) *The Truman Show*, Paramount Pictures.

White, Hayden (1978) *Topics of Discourse*, Baltimore, MD: Johns Hopkins University Press.

——(1987) *The Content of the Form*, Baltimore, MD: Johns Hopkins University Press.

Williams, A. and Methen, M. (2008) 'A review of Online Social Networking Profiles by Adolescents: Implications for Future Research and Intervention (Report)', *Adolescence*, 43 (170), Summer, www.find.galegroup.com/ips/printdoc?contentSet=IAC-Documents+docType/1A (accessed 10 July 2008).

Zipes, Jack (1993 [1983]) *The Trials and Tribulations of Red Riding Hood*, second edition, London: Routledge.

——(1997) *Happily Ever After – Fairy Tales, Children and the Culture Industry*, London: Routledge.

——(2002a) *Sticks and Stones: The Troublesome Success of Children's Literature from Slovenly Peter to Harry Potter*, Abingdon: Routledge.

——(2002b [1988]) *The Brothers Grimm: From Enchanted Forests to the Modern World*, second edition, New York: Palgrave.

——(2006) *Why Fairy Tales Stick*, London: Routledge.

——(ed.) (2007) *The Oxford Encyclopaedia of Children's Literature*, www.oxfordreference.com/views/ Entry.html?entry=t204.e3482& sm (accessed 23 August 2007).

——(2009) *Relentless Progress: The Reconfiguration of Children's Literature, Fairy Tales, and Storytelling*, Abingdon: Routledge.

Žižek, Slavoj (2002) *Welcome to the Desert of the Real*, London: Verso.

Zornado, J. (2006) *Inventing the Child: Culture, Ideology and the Story of Childhood*, New York: Garland Publishing.

## Some useful websites

http://www.wordpool.co.uk/wfc/wfc.htm
http://www.booktrustchildrensbooks.org.uk/Features-Interviews
www.write4children.org
www.cwteaching.com
http://britishscbwi.jimdo.com/
http://www.irscl.com/
www.cool-reads.co.uk
www.achuka.co.uk
www.literacytrust.org.uk

# Index

*A la Recherche du temps perdu*, 46
Act of Union, 8
adult, child-centred discourse, 11, 16, 21
*aetonormativity*, 10, 123 (notes 1.7)
Arendt, Hannah, 47, 129
Aristophanes, 63
Armstrong, Karen, 117, 129
Armstrong, Neil, 57
Ashley, Bernard, 106
Auden, W. H., 60, 65, 127 (note 6.15), 129

Bakhtin, Mikhael, 4, 35, 92, 94, 124
    (notes 2.27), 125 (notes 4.2), 127
    (notes 6.14), 129
Barthes, Roland, 10, 40–41, 47–48, 61, 125
    (notes 4.9), 129
Baudrillard, Jean, 4, 15–16, 31–37, 129
Bawden, Nina, 24, 44, 129
becoming not being, 28, 30
Benjamin, Walter, 4, 26, 34, 36–38, 42–43, 46,
    50, 54, 56–59, 63, 98, 108, 116, 124 (notes
    4.1), 125 (notes 5.8), 126 (notes 6.7), 128
    (notes 9.7, 9.8, 10.5), 129
*Beo*, 60–61, 127
Bettleheim, Bruno, 41, 115
Bhabha, Homi, 4, 29–30, 38, 46, 129
biological essentialism, 19
Blackman, Malorie, 52
Blake, Andrew, 13, 130
Blyton, Enid, 10, 14, 74, 88
Bonnie Prince Charlie, 8
Booker, Christopher, 43, 125
    (notes 5.2)
Boulter, Amanda, 24, 84, 92, 94, 130
Bourdieu, Pierre, 4, 11, 50, 130, 133
Boys and girls come out to play … 8–9
Bradman, Tony, 90, 98
Brady, T., 54, 131
Brandt, Dorothea, 38
Brecht, Bertolt, 47, 108, 16, 126 (notes 5.8), 128
    (notes 9.8), 130, 133
bridging the gap, 5, 26

Burgess, Melvyn, 42, 108, 110–11, 117, 125
    (notes 5.1), 128 (notes 9.9, 10.3, 10.7)
Butt, Maggie, 40–41, 43, 74, 130

Calvino, Italo, 4, 37, 53, 130
Carter, Angela, 75, 127 (notes 8.1)
Chesterton, G. K., 48
Child, children, childhood and children's
    -referred to throughout
child-centred, vii–iii, 11–12, 16–21, 28–29,
    31–32, 34–35, 37, 45, 48, 62, 80, 121–23
child labour, 8
childhood innocence, 21–22, 25, 39, 46, 53, 55,
    83, 99, 104, 110
childism, 19
childist, 32
Chomsky, Noam, 62, 127 (notes 6.13), 130
Class, 19, 24, 106, 110
Coates, Karen, 115
cognitive development, viii, 24, 81, 96–99
comfortably predictable, 24–25, 30, 32–33, 56,
    91, 121
constructed child, viii, 19, 23, 25, 33
constructive child iii, 23
Corder, Zizou, 98
creatively critical, viii, 4–5, 11, 16, 32, 37, 40,
    52–53, 104, 117
Crete, 9, 55, 61, 78–79, 81–82
critical theories, vii
critically creative, viii, 4–5, 11, 16, 32, 37, 40,
    52–53, 104, 117
Crook, Charles, viii, 130
cult and culture of child and childhood, vii–iii,
    8, 6–8, 19, 22–23, 26, 69
cult of the child, viii, 7, 15
cultural commodity, 14
cultural determinism, 19
culture, communication and media, 16
curiosity, 39, 104

Daedalus, 49–51, 54–60, 77–81, 86–87, 89–94, 118
Danaher, Schirato and Webb, 9, 130, 133

Davis, Tom, 24
Delillo, Don, 31, 53
Derrida, Jacques, 4, 18, 23, 37, 88, 125 (notes 4.8), 130, 133
*dialectic im stillstand*, 57, 64
dialectics at a standstill, 57, 64, 126 (notes 6.7)
Dickens, Charles, 17, 46, 87
*différence*, 23, 29
Disney, 15
*Duino Elegies*, 72

Earle, Steve, 99
eccentric blend, 24, 30, 32, 56, 121
ellipses, 11, 17, 25, 35, 44, 51, 53, 60–68, 65, 91, 97, 132
*Erfahrung*, 38, 42–43, 50, 56, 96
Escape from the Island, 70
essential child, 19, 2q
exploring, viii, 30, 38, 41–42, 44, 47, 49–50, 58–62, 76, 81–89, 92, 100, 106, 110, 113

Fanon, Franz, 29–30, 124 (notes 2.29), 130
Farjeon, Eleanor, 48, 126 (notes 5.10), 130
Felix Felicis, 103, 119
Feminism, 19, 21, 28, 32, 76
Fine, Anne, 110, 128 (notes 10.2)
flag of childhood, 31, 35
Foster, Hal, 15, 130
Foucault, Michel, 4, 9, 15, 23, 26, 30, 52, 56, 63, 124 (notes 2.21), 126 (notes 6.4), 130
Free-market, 15
Freud, Sigmund, 4, 39–41, 54, 59, 112, 117, 124 (notes 2.23), 126 (notes 6.1), 130–31
Fukuyama, Francis, 43, 56, 126 (notes 6.5), 131

Gagarin, Yuri, 57
*Game Girls*, 109, 110–11
Gender, viii, 19, 38, 102, 105–6, 115, 124–25, 131
Genre, 16–18, 35, 106, 109, 111, 116, 130
Gleitzman, Maurice, 44, 125 (notes 5.5), 131
Goldthwaite, J., 13, 131
Gordon, John, 33, 131
Greek Mythology, 49, 70
Gross, Phillip, 108, 120

Hardy, G.H., 5, 131
Harper, Graeme, 41
Harry Potter, 24, 30, 62, 64, 73–74, 79, 81, 90, 100–103, 133
Heaney, Seamus, 104, 127 (notes 11.4)
Heath, Shirley Brice, 106, 131
*Heteroglossia*, 35
hidden adult, 34, 123 (notes 1.6), 132
hidden child, 34, 37, 123 (notes 1.6)
*His Dark Materials Triligy*, 47, 101, 108

hooks, bel, 53
Hosseini, Khaled, 111
Hull, Robert, 120–21, 131
Hunt, Peter, 4, 6–7, 16–17, 19, 21–22, 24, 32–33, 39, 56, 110, 124 (notes 2.16), 125 (notes 3.7), 131
hypothetical postulate, 26, 91

Icarus, 49–65, 70, 77–83, 86–91, 93–94, 118–20, 132–33
identity under erasure, 28
(im)possibility, v, viii, 33–41, 97
inbetween space, 29, 44
Inglis, Fred, 102, 131
inter-illumination, 53
invisible hand, 14

Jameson, Fredrich, 15, 25, 124 (notes 2.15), 131
Joyce, James, 19–20, 70, 94, 124 (notes 2.19)
Jung, Karl, 24

Kaplan, E. Ann, 15, 131
Keita, Salif, 51, 126 (notes 5.12)
Kerr, Judith, 113
King Minos, 49, 77–78, 81–82, 87
knowing child, 46, 104, 106
Krauth, Nigel, 54, 131
Kroll, Jeri, 120, 132
Kundera, Milan, 4, 36, 3, 62, 65, 79, 114, 132
*Kyoto*, 86, 88

Laird, Elizabeth, 111
Lesnik-Oberstein, Karin, 4, 19, 21, 123 (notes 1.3), 124 (notes 2.16), 132
Levi, Primo, 33, 117, 132
Lewis, C. S., 12–14, 28, 130, 132
limitless trust, 33
Little Red Riding Hood, 71, 75, 107
Lott, Pixie, 16, 32, 125 (notes 3.9)

Mahy, Margaret, 52, 106
making connections, 5, 16, 36–37, 53, 109
Mandela, Nelson, 62
Mangan, Lucy, 10, 123 (notes 2.5)
Mason, Zachary, 72, 132
McCaw, Neil, 5, 43, 132
McGillis, Roderick, 4, 18, 22, 123 (notes 1.5), 132
McKee, Robert, 71, 132
Meek, Margaret, 112, 132
Melrose, Andrew, 3–4, 17, 36, 39, 42, 70, 77, 79, 6, 95, 123 (notes 1.4), 125 (notes 3.7), 128 (notes 8.6, 8.7)
Melrose and Harbour, 110
Melrose and McCaw, 43
Melrose and Webb, 51, 55, 58, 60

*Monsters Under the Bed: Critically Investigating Early Years Writing*, 70, 96
Morphology, 25, 28
Murakami, Haruki, 37, 53
must reads, 18
mute child, 19, 50, 80
Mythologies, 40, 129

Nabokov, Vladimir, 77, 132
naïve trust, 39
Natov, Roni, 25, 46, 69, 99–100, 132
Naucrate, 55, 61, 78, 118, 133
Nikolajeva, Maria, 4, 6, 10, 12, 16–17, 23–24, 28, 95, 123 (notes I.2, 1.3), 132
Nickolajeva, Maria and Scott, Carole, 95, 132
9/11, 56, 58, 60
Nix, Garth, 106
Nodelman, Perry, 4, 11, 16–18, 34–35, 123 (notes 1.3, 1.6), 132
normative, 28–29, 31–32, 35, 48–50, 52, 55, 57–59, 63, 79–80, 84, 93, 117

Odysseus, 45
'oh', 63–65
Orientialism, 23
other and otherness, 14, 19–38, 44, 78, 106–7
Ovid, 49–50, 55, 60, 64, 77, 81, 86, 120, 126 (notes 5.13, 6.2), 127 (notes 6.12), 132

Pasiphae, 87, 94
Pelé, 64
Penelope, 45–47, 52, 58–59, 61, 96
Perera, Anna, 1–8
Peter Pan, 20, 26, 28, 62, 88, 133
Phillips, Adam, 3–4, 36, 39–42, 48, 4, 69, 96, 121, 132
Polwart, Karine, 60, 127
Polymorphous, 92
possessive apostrophe, 20–21
post-colonial theory, 28–32, 117
post-feminism, 19, 28
Proust, Marcel, 46–47
Pullman, Philip, 12–14, 16, 28, 43, 47, 52–53, 64, 69, 71–72, 78, 82–83, 85, 101–3, 108, 115, 124 (notes 2.12, 2.17), 125 (notes 5.3), 126 (notes 5.16), 127 (notes 7.1, 8.3), 128 (notes 9.3) 132–33

Race, 19, 35, 106
Rees, Celia, 101
Reynolds, Kimberley, 32, 6, 48, 111, 125 (notes 3.2, 3.5), 133
Richards, I. A., 61, 133
Riddler, 71
Rilke, Rainer Maria, 64

Rose, Jacqueline, 3–4, 19–23, 25–28, 30–31, 36, 38, 81, 87, 112, 123 (notes 1.3), 124 (notes 2.20), 133
Rosen, Harold, 122, 123 (notes 1.1), 133
Rowe, Dorothy, 52
Rowling, J. K., 14, 52, 64, 74, 85, 100, 102, 106, 118–19, 123 (notes I.1), 124 (notes 2.24), 128 (notes 10.8), 133
Rudd, David, 4, 8, 16, 18–19, 21–22, 33–34, 115, 123 (notes 1.4), 124 (notes 2.2.7), 125 (notes 3.7), 133
Rumi, 37
Russell, Bertrand, 5

Said, Edward, 22
Schweinitz, Eleanor von, 113
Sexuality, 19, 35, 57, 62, 105–6, 108, 110–11, 124–25, 129
Smith, Adam, 14, 124 (notes 2.24)
Snape, 99, 123(notes I.1)
social contract, 27
social hierarchies, 22
Socrates, 53, 109
Socratic, 53, 109
soul mining, 51
Spivak, Gayatri, 32, 133
Stableford, Brian, 114–15, 133
Steedman, Carolyn, 4, 46, 99–100, 123 (notes 1.3), 133
Steig, Michael, 2, 16, 20, 133
Stevens, Roger, 63, 120, 133
Stevens, Wallace, 63, 120, 133
Stiglitz, Joseph E., 14, 124 (notes 2.14)
story and storyteller-referred to throughout
subaltern, 32
symbolic framework, 29, 80

Talus, 45, 57, 94
Taylor, Mark, 39
Telemachus, 45, 61, 65, 70
*Textum*, 51
The child is not, 26, 29, 31, 33, 36
The Declination of Wills, 32
The Guardian, 10, 12, 110, 123 (notes 2.3, 2.4, 2.5), 124 (notes 2.7, 2.12, 2.14), 125 (notes 4.11), 128 (notes 9.3, 10.2)
*The Interpretation of Dreams*, 39, 59
*The Odyssey*, 45, 72
The Storyteller, 6, 124 (notes 2.28), 128 (notes 9.7, 10.5)
*The Tiger Who Came to Tea*, 119, 113
*The Wealth of Nations*, 14
*Theory of Moral Sentiment*, 14
theory of writing for children, 6
third way, 29–30, 52, 63, 80
Tiedemann, Rolf, 57, 126 (notes 6.7), 129

Tolkien, J. R. R., 13
top reads, 10
Townsend, John Rowe, 12, 4, 20, 27, 133
Toys, 10, 12, 34, 40–41, 47–48
Tucker, Nicholas, 13, 107, 133

UNICEF, 9
unsettlingly unexpected, 24–25, 30, 32, 56, 91,
  121–22

vicarious experience, 37, 54–55, 72, 104,
  107–8, 115

Waite, Judy, 101, 110–11, 128 (notes 10.1)
Watson, Victor, 32, 5, 117, 133

Webb, Jen, 9, 5, 51, 55, 57–58, 60–61, 64, 117,
  120, 124 (notes 2.22), 125 (notes 3.4) 126
  (notes 5.14), 130, 132–33
White, Hayden, 113, 133
Williams, Imogen Russell, 10
Wilson, Jacqueline, 108
Wittgenstein, Ludwig 124 (notes 2.18)

Yeats, W. B., 20

Zipes, Jack, vii–viii, 3–4, 7, 12–15, 9–20, 43, 50,
  36–37, 59, 76, 83–84, 107, 113, 115, 122,
  123 (notes 1.3), 133–34
Žižek, Slavoj, 4, 67, 59, 126 (notes 6.6), 134
Zornado, Joseph, 16, 58–59, 62, 134

# Monsters Under the Bed

Critically investigating early years writing

## By Andrew Melrose

This user-friendly textbook for students of creative writing explores the issue of picture books, literacy and writing for children in their early years. Andrew Melrose encourages students to examine the critical questions in child literacy through an exploration of the fusion of text and images. Accessibly written and lively in its approach, this textbook includes:

- a critical and creative investigation of early years writing and reading creative writing craftwork ideas which could be used as seminar topics or as individual reflections
- a road map to developing critical awareness of children's literature, allowing students to develop their critical and writing skills
- tasks for use in group or individual learning contexts
- end of chapter 'checkpoints', through which undergraduates are encouraged to reflect on their own creative and critical development so far
- a fully up-to-date exploration of critical approaches to children's writing, including theories of creativity and creative writing.

This book will be particularly relevant to education students and students on Creative Writing and English BA and MA programmes and teacher training students who are interested in writing for children.

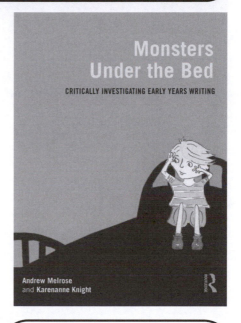

**November 2011 | 160pp**
**Paperback: 978-0-415-61750-5**
**Hardback: 978-0-415-61749-9**

## Contents

Introduction:
What and How and Who
1. Not little stories but big stories told short
2. Text and Image
3. Phonics and Fusion
4. The Big Read
5. Keep Them Reading
6. Critical checkpoint
7. Story and Narrative Conclusion

**To order a copy please visit ...**

## www.routledge.com/education